MODERN
PROSE STYLE

Oxford University Press, Amen House, London E.C.4

GLASGOW NEW YORK TORONTO MELBOURNE WELLINGTON
BOMBAY CALCUTTA MADRAS KARACHI LAHORE DACCA
CAPE TOWN SALISBURY NAIROBI IBADAN ACCRA
KUALA LUMPUR HONG KONG

MODERN
PROSE STYLE

•••

BONAMY DOBRÉE

SECOND EDITION

OXFORD
AT THE CLARENDON PRESS

... they wholly mistake the nature of criticism who think its business is principally to find fault. Criticism ... was meant a standard of judging well; the chiefest part of which is, to observe those excellencies which should delight a reasonable reader.

JOHN DRYDEN

© Oxford University Press 1964

FIRST EDITION 1934
REPRINTED FEBRUARY 1935; 1939
1944, 1946, 1950, 1956
SECOND EDITION 1964
REPRINTED LITHOGRAPHICALLY
BY D. R. HILLMAN & SONS LTD., FROME
1964

PRINTED IN GREAT BRITAIN

PREFACE TO SECOND EDITION

WHEN, nearly thirty years ago, this book was first published, that admirable man of letters G. M. Young asked in a review whether there was, in fact, such a thing as 'modern prose', a voice distinguishably that of our own day. 'For in the end,' he said, 'the Voices are reducible to two, that in which we "debate and assert" and the other in which we "whisper conclusions to one another".' That is true 'in the end', but what, I suppose, I was concerned with, and still find of interest, is the variation within the two voices; for

There are, it may be, so many kinds of voices in the world, and none of them is without signification.

Therefore, if I know not the meaning of the voice, I shall be unto him that speaketh a barbarian, and he that speaketh shall be a barbarian unto me.

(1 Corinthians xiv. 10, 11.)

There is no need to embroider the theme.

Yet there are periods, of rather short duration, when one kind of voice seems more acceptable than another, more in tune with the ethos of the day. It may be a reaction against an accepted mode, as in the thirties, where an attempt was made to expel 'the literary' from literature, as though 'the literary' implied a falsity, a veneer to cover falsity, or a sound to fill an emptiness. (The recent 'anti' movement would appear to have to do with politics rather than with writing.) But that impulse seems to have passed; at least I have found that the most striking passages, those in which the voices of the writers have individual meaning, come from those authors who are open to the influence of words, to their aura, who have come to know—as, according to Bagehot, all good writers do—that 'words are good to eat'. They do not think, as it was something of a fashion to do, that prose can make its impact solely as a kind of goods-train to convey facts or even ideas from one place to another, though if enough ideas are conveyed this kind of prose can be very effective. At all events we have passed, it may be hoped, through the phase in which 'literary' was an abusive term.

Also we have apparently overgone the period of *radical* experimentation, as embarked on by, pre-eminently, James Joyce. This is probably all to the good, since, to quote G. M. Young once more, though such things 'could not create a tradition [they] might easily destroy one, and prose is the one art to which, in the nature of things, tradition is essential'. All to the good, for more than a tradition in prose alone is involved, since a whole civilization may be affected by the quality of its prose. When in Orwell's *Nineteen Eighty-Four* a traditional civilization was being re-placed, Syme, the dictionary-maker, could exclaim: 'It's a beautiful thing, the destruction of words. Of course the great wastage of words is in the verbs and adjectives, but there are hundreds of nouns that can be got rid of as well.' This is not to say that no experiments are being made, for all original writing is in a sense experimental, the outcome on every separate occasion of the constant struggle to make words do what you want them to do.

In choosing examples to bring the matter of this essay once more to conform with its title, I have for the most part added extracts from younger writers, but included a few from those who were about to emerge as of note some thirty years ago. Except for the passage from Miss Ivy Compton-Burnett, all my fresh examples have been chosen from those in the full developing flow of their writing, and likely to affirm their style. This is not to say that much admirable prose along the lines illustrated in the first edition of this book is not being written under all sections—criticism, history, biography, and so forth (to select a few names would be to make invidious distinctions)—and there are, naturally and properly, differences between the voices. Such differences are less marked in law and science, realms in which prose seems to have remained static. The greatest departure is in fiction, where the individual is more likely to give rein to his idiosyncrasies; yet even there we meet no great departure in general tone between the good prose of a dozen or more deservedly reputed novelists and that of the bulk of their predecessors. Nevertheless it is among novelists in the main that the reaction against the austere, the abandonment of the anti-literary, is most apparent, and where new manners of writing are being attempted. Selection is unavoidably individual, just as it must be to some extent a matter of chance, the field being so enormous, and all I can hope is that the passages quoted will delight 'the reasonable reader'.

Just as Mr. Kenneth Sisam helped and encouraged me in the first edition of this book, so did Mr. D. M.

Davin in preparing this one; and I should like to thank him for suggesting this more 'up-to-date' edition, and for his advice and help throughout.

B. D.

Blackheath, 1963

PREFACE TO FIRST EDITION

THIS book is not intended for writers in general, nor for critics, though I naturally hope that some of them will find it entertaining if they read it. It is meant for anybody who takes lay interest in writing, who might perhaps be helped to understand why he likes some authors better than others; it is in fact meant for those who have never thought much about writing, but like it for its own sake, as well as for what it conveys. Authors and critics will either find what I have to say commonplace and obvious, or will be irritated into disagreement. And when I say that this book is 'meant' for such and such people, I do not mean that it was written for their instruction: it was written for my own, because it gave me pleasure to think in this way about the craft that I follow.

I ought to add that I have chosen my examples because they illustrate my ideas, and have not tried to work in every good writer. I have no doubt that there are many admirable writers, especially in America, whose books I have never seen: but I have omitted even some which I have read since they were not to my purpose. I think, however, that anyone reading my extracts will have a very fair notion of how prose is being written today, and I have taken my selections from as many fields as I could.

I would like to offer my grateful thanks to Mr. Kenneth Sisam, whose interest in this book, and whose encouragement and advice, have helped me a great deal in the writing of it.

B. D.

Mendham, June 1934

CONTENTS

ACKNOWLEDGEMENTS

For permission to include copyright passages in this volume, thanks are due to the following:

Messrs. Macmillan and Co. for extract from *Foundations of Empirical Knowledge* by Professor A. J. Ayer; George Weidenfeld and Nicholson Ltd. and the Vanguard Press Inc. for extract from *Dangling Man* by Mr. Saul Bellow; Victor Gollancz Ltd. and Alfred A. Knopf Inc. for extract from *Darkness and Day* by Miss Ivy Compton-Burnett; Rupert Hart-Davis Ltd. and the Viking Press Inc., New York, for extract from *The Drunken Forest* by Mr. Gerald Durrell; Messrs. Faber and Faber Ltd. and E. P. Dutton and Co. Inc. for extract from Mr. Lawrence Durrell's *Mountolive*, © 1958 by Lawrence Durrell; The Caxton Press for extract from *The Lagoon* by Miss Janet Frame; Messrs. Faber and Faber Ltd. and Messrs. Harcourt, Brace and World Inc. for extract from *The Two Deaths of Christopher Martin* by Mr. William Golding, © 1956 by William Golding; Messrs. Collins and World Publishing Co. for extract from *The Homeward Journey* by Mr. Gerald Hanley, © 1961 by Gerald Hanley; Messrs. John Murray and E. P. Dutton & Co. Inc. for extract from *Chinoiserie* by Mr. Hugh Honour, © 1961 by Hugh Honour; John Murray and Harper and Row for extract from *Violins of Saint Jacques* by Mr. Patrick Leigh Fermor; Messrs. William Heinemann Ltd. and Little Brown and Co. for extract from *A Buyer's Market* by Mr. Anthony Powell; Messrs. Macmillan and Co. and Messrs. Charles Scribner's Sons for extract from *The Masters* by Sir Charles Snow; Alan Swallow for extract from *Collected Essays* by Professor Allen Tate; Messrs. Martin Secker and Warburg Ltd. and the Viking Press Inc., New York, for extract from *The Liberal Imagination* by Professor Lionel

xiv ACKNOWLEDGEMENTS

Trilling; Joyce Weiner Associates and the Macmillan Company for extract from *The King's Peace* by Dr. C. V. Wedgwood; Messrs. Eyre and Spottiswoode Ltd. and the Viking Press Inc., New York, for extract from *Riders in the Chariot* by Mr. Patrick White.

INTRODUCTION

WE read for pleasure, but then we do not read for only one sort of pleasure, and we get different enjoyments from different kinds of writing. We do not, for instance, read a novel of Hardy's for the same reason that we devour detective fiction. Yet perhaps even those such different forms have something in common to make us read them both—they both take us away from the immediacies of our lives. As we read them we are, as it were, shut up in a box with this other world; we forget the things which we have to do, while the things which fret us are miraculously dissolved. A novel by Hardy, however, tells us something about life, it reveals our own emotions to us in revealing the emotions of other people: in reading it we actually live another life, gain fresh experience; we are enriched. That is part of the pleasure that belongs to it. We read, then, from a variety of motives, perhaps to learn, as we do, say, Sir James Jeans' *The Universe Around Us*; we read to feel, we read to forget. Nor are these emotions separated, for we may take up a book from many impulses, all urging us at the same time.

But there is one thing which we do every time we read, whether we are aware of it or not: we come into contact with the personality of the writer. We enlarge our acquaintance, and by so doing we enter farther into life, and however little we may mean to, we enlarge our own personality, at least if the writer whose book we are reading himself possesses a personality of any

value at all. Any book of which we say to ourselves
when we have done with it, 'That is a good book', we
find to be so by virtue of the personality which we have
been in contact with: we say so, possibly, because we
find that our own self has been affected, even though
only for a while. That is an appeal to experience; yet
the statement is at any rate to some extent borne out
for us when we notice that any serious book about
a man's writings comes to deal, to a greater or less
extent, with the man himself. Criticism almost invariably reaches that point, even when written by so
abstract a critic as Dryden, who was more concerned
with structure in literature than with any other aspect.
Even he did not discuss one of the greatest philosophical poems of the world without saying of its
author, 'If I am not mistaken, the distinguishing
character of Lucretius (I mean of his soul and genius)
is a certain kind of noble pride, and positive assertion
of his opinions. He is everywhere confident of his
own reason.'

It is not, we see, by a man's thoughts alone that we
become acquainted with him in his books any more
than we do in actual life; and it is not for a writer's
thoughts alone that we read a book, though some
books we plunge into mainly for the sake of the
thought, as we do, shall we say, into A. N. Whitehead's *Science and the Modern World*. Some books we
read in spite of the thought: we can, for instance, dis-
agree almost wholly with what Macaulay says, not care
a fig for his opinions, yet enjoy his *History* enormously.
The mind is only a part of the personality, and we can
arrive at the latter in a man's work without his ever

actually expressing a thought. Thinking, naturally, has gone to the making of any book from which we get a deep or lasting pleasure, because though the mind is not the personality, it enters largely into it. Of course 'there are some', as Don Quixote said, 'who write and fling books broadcast upon the world as if they were fritters'; but the books of those persons are hardly worth considering, because not much of a man's self can go into the concoction of a fritter. Only those books into which much of the writer's self has entered make that peculiar appeal to us which we feel when we say, 'This is a good book'. How good we think it to be depends upon the personality of the man who wrote it, and upon how much of it went into the making of the book.

This is not to say that a writer is concerned with his personality: the greater artist he is, the less he will think about it, the more he will be intent on the thing he is doing. Only lesser writers scribble to display their personality. How then, it will be asked, do we come into contact with the man? The answer seems to be 'By the sound of his voice'. For whenever we read a book, although we do not read it aloud, or even consciously form the words in our minds, we are aware of a voice. It is as though someone had been speaking to us, telling us something, or working upon our feelings. It is this voice which we roughly call style, and however much a writer may ignore his personality, even seek to conceal it, he cannot disguise his voice, his style, unless he is deliberately writing a parody. It is here that the truth will out: *Le style, c'est l'homme même*; and if we know a writer of any note, it is extraordinary how we seem to hear the inflexions of his living voice as we read what he has written.[1] Moreover it is ultimately by his style that a writer is great, and remains great, for only books that are well written survive, though that is not to say that all well-written books do: it is by his style that we recognize a writer.

Yet one cannot deny that there is an impersonal style:

The official announcements regarding the repayment of credits and the withdrawal of exchange regulations did not come early enough to have an important effect on Lombard Street. Nevertheless discount steadily declined under the pressure of demand from home and foreign buyers with increased reluctance of sellers.[2]

Anybody might have written that: the voice is the voice of a tape-machine. But the man who wrote it was not eager to tell his news, it was a matter of mechanical routine. He was not explaining anything, nor trying to arouse the emotions of his readers. He was not interested, so fell into the anonymous tone, which is the result of a long tradition. But the moment a man is really interested he speaks with his own voice; you are at once aware of a personality. Take the first sentence of Henry James' *The Death of the Lion*[3]:

[1] This is not a new view, but it seems to have been neglected for the last few centuries. William Puttenham (1530–90) wrote: 'Style is a constant and continual phrase or tenour of speaking and writing, extending to the whole tale or process of the poem or history, and not properly to any piece or member of a tale; but is of words, speeches, and sentences together, a certain contrived form and quality ... such as he ... will not, or peradventure cannot, easily alter into any other.'—*The Arte of English Poesie.*   [2] *Daily Telegraph*, 3 March 1932.   [3] Martin Secker.

I had simply, I suppose, a change of heart, and it must have begun when I received my manuscript back from Mr. Pinhorn.

At once we hear someone speaking, and recognize that we are listening to the speech of a man different from other men.

And since this contact, the essential contact without which we cannot enjoy reading, is a matter of voice, we naturally turn for pleasure to writers of our own day rather than to those of the past, because the voices of one age are, mysteriously, not those of another. Most of us feel the pleasure of reading more easily when we read the works of men or women of our own day. Old writers seem to speak in a slightly different language, and thus a barrier proportionate with the difference is interposed between us and the writer's personality. Let us take a few lines from the works of two men, both of great distinction, writing upon the same subject, the human mind.

To these tortures of fear and sorrow, may well be annexed uriosity, that irksome, that tyrannizing care, *nimia solicitudo*, superfluous industry about unprofitable things, and their qualities, as Thomas defines it: an itching humour or a kind of longing to see that which is not to be seen, to do that which ought not to be done: to know that secret which should not be known, to eat of the forbidden fruit.

That is Robert Burton, in his *The Anatomy of Melancholy*,[1] written early in the seventeenth century: and now we turn to Lord Russell's *The Analysis of Mind*[2] —the very titles of the books have a different flavour.

[1] Part I, Sect. 2, Memb. 4, Subs. 7.
[2] By Bertrand Russell, George Allen and Unwin, 1921.

Images also differ from sensations as regards their effects. Sensations, as a rule, have both physical and mental effects. As you watch the train you meant to catch leaving the station, there are both the successive positions of the train (physical effects) and the successive waves of fury and disappointment (mental effects). Images, on the contrary, though they *may* produce bodily movements, do so according to mnemic laws, not according to the laws of physics. All their effects, of whatever nature, follow mnemic laws. But this difference is less suitable for definition than the difference as to causes.

It is not only that Burton quotes Latin, which Lord Russell does not; that he uses strong adjectives, while Lord Russell uses none at all; that he refers to forbidden fruit, whereas Lord Russell reminds us of the train we once missed, but that the whole rhythm and inflexion are different; the *tempo* has changed.[1] Burton's is a voice of long ago, Lord Russell's one of today. We feel that besides any differences in personality, or of what they are trying to get at, there is one of the centuries: it will be harder to get into contact with Burton than with Lord Russell. The latter's voice is one of those we hear about us every day; we have to leap centuries in imagination to gather what Burton's is really like: we may have to spend hours, days even, not only in his company, but in that of his contemporaries, to arrive at the man. This is clearly a barrier.

The great writer, of course, breaks down this barrier—the proof is that we read his works. The lesser men of a past period, whom those living in their time could read as cheerfully as the now classic ones, we

[1] But see Part IV, § 1.

of today find unreadable: their voices do not come through to us. Or if they do, they all seem to sound much the same, or at any rate to have much in common; and it is only after familiarizing ourselves with the writings of their period that we can distinguish one from another. We can fairly easily guess at what period a man wrote on having a passage read to us, and after listening to scraps of Swift, Addison, and Defoe, we should most of us at once be able to say 'Early eighteenth century': but we should have to know the authors and the period well to be able to declare with certainty, 'Swift', or 'Addison', or 'Defoe'. That is why, excellence being equal, we get more pleasure from reading the work of people alive today than that of people long since dead, and indeed very often when the excellence is by no means equal. Our contemporaries speak with voices that we recognize, and between which we can easily distinguish. Nobody, for example, would mistake a paragraph by Shaw for one by Dean Inge or one, say, by Sir Charles Snow for one by Mr. Lawrence Durrell: we therefore find it comparatively easy to get into contact with the writers of our own day, and thus one of the objects of reading is more easily attained, one of the pleasures more readily gratified.

But, of course, men do not always speak with the same voice: a sergeant-major when courting will not make the same sounds as he does on parade, or if he did, he would fail miserably in one or other of his objects. Thus we may expect a man's style to vary when the object in writing is different. But here we must slightly change our angle. Men write for all sorts of reasons, sometimes for more than one at a time. They may write because they are excited, or because they are bored; because they are happy, or because they are wretched; because they want to express themselves, or because they want something done—or simply for the mysterious reason that they want to create something. But if we take their works at their face declarations, men write on the whole with three various purposes, or so we may infer from the effect upon ourselves. They want to tell us something, to describe an action (to tell us what happened), to describe a thing (something they have seen), or to describe a person (someone they know, or whom they have invented). This type of prose is descriptive. Or they may want to explain something to you, to tell you why or how a thing happens (science) or to examine something (criticism), or to persuade you to think as they do. We may call this explanatory prose. Or, thirdly, they may simply want to arouse your emotions, to make you feel gay, mournful, angry—we need not complete the catalogue. This we may call emotive prose. Not that these types are kept apart in practice. A man may tell you a story so as to move you; he may wish to move you so as to make you think as he does; something of all three motives may have gone to his writing.[1] But still, the main types remain distinct.

[1] Thus in writing this book I am actuated by (1) a desire to talk about something which interests me: description. (2) A desire to make the reader think as I do: explanatory. (3) A desire to move him to the same enjoyment as I myself derive from this sort of inquiry: emotive. I am aware that some people dislike the word emotive: I shall be happy to adopt a better one if they will point it out to me.

By the time we have read any considerable number of books, a time which comes very soon in our lives if we read at all, we begin to ask ourselves, 'What is it that makes me decide "This is a good book"? What is it that gives me that peculiar satisfaction which causes me to say "This is well written"?' From that moment we are critics, and as such we are at once concerned with style, since in the end it is the style of a book which gives us pleasure, for even the best material can be spoiled by bad writing. We begin to listen more intently to the voice, so as to see how the effect is made on us, to distinguish between one kind of writing and another; we begin to derive a further pleasure from reading, an active one, quite distinct from the passive pleasure we may get from the images or thoughts presented to us. It is the pleasure of knowing about a thing. It is the difference between someone who does not understand chess watching a game, and someone who does. To the former this odd activity appears to be merely an aimless (and dreadfully slow) moving about of quaintly shaped objects on a chequered board; to the latter the pleasure of watching the moves may be intense. There is even a pleasure in seeing a bad play, and in the same way we may extract a joy from seeing why a piece of prose is bad. Then, because we cannot think at all without some sort of framework of order, we begin to make rules. Rules, where the arts are in question, fill some people with pious horror; but there is no harm in rules provided we use them in the right way, merely as summaries of facts we have observed, and not as dogmas to which we must rigidly adhere. We should always be ready to revise our judgements, to change our minds. To erect rules into dogmas or *ériger en dogmes ses préférences personnelles* is a dangerous temptation to the critic, but it is a form of laziness, a desire to have done once for all with the thing, so that he need not think any more, but proceed by rule of thumb. Such an attitude is likely to be fatal to the appreciation of anything original; the difficulty, however, is to keep the mind open while yet maintaining its standards; we must always be on the alert as much to reject what is meretricious and false in the new, as to welcome what is good.

And new there must be if language, if prose, is to be kept alive: only a changing language is a living one. Words, phrases, metaphors, means of approach, become worn out with use; they are like coins which gradually get rubbed so that we cannot see what is on them. They may still serve as a means of exchange, until they get too rubbed, but they no longer give us any distinct impression of a thing. A new sixpence, if it is a good one, is a pleasure to look at and handle; an old one, a mere disk of metal, may be fit to buy bootlaces with, but it does not give any pleasure in itself. So with words or metaphors. Take 'towel-horse' for instance: it just serves to describe a certain arrangement of sticks in the bathroom; but when the metaphor was first invented, what an amusing thing it must have been, how vivid it must have seemed! But now it strikes no spark in the mind, it is just a token; it has been used too much. The good writer, then, always keeps his coins new-minted. He cannot, it is true, invent many, or even any, new words. What he

does do is to place them differently, to combine them
in a new way, to choose with the freshness and exacti-
tude that comes from direct observation rather than
from idle repetition; he fights shy of the time-hallowed
expression or adjective which has ceased to convey
anything—'black as Erebus' (who or what is Erebus? most people will ask); 'white as driven snow'
(why 'driven'? and was the object, usually some luck-
less person's face, really of that whiteness?); 'happy
as the day is long'; 'flat as a pancake'; or such horrible
affectations as 'gives furiously to think'. These things
are so common that it is difficult not to fall into them
without noticing, especially as much language is metaphorical, unnoticeably (did anybody notice that my
saying 'it is difficult not to fall into them' was a metaphor?); one could *multiply them by the score*. It is easy
enough to recognize the originality of a writer by the
words he uses.[1]

The question of words, however, is largely a matter
of the mind; and the mind, we know, is only a part
of the personality. But what seems to be outside the
control of the writer, or rather what he forges deliberately without knowing why he does so, or should we
say for the simple reason that it pleases him better that
way, is the phrasing, the rhythm, the general harmony
of sounds. It is by these things that we recognize the
voice, and with some writers it is quite unmistakable.
I suggested earlier that you could not confuse Shaw's

---

[1] Remy de Gourmont has pointed out that *most* of what one writes
must be commonplace; otherwise it would be too great an effort to read,
would indeed not be understood. It is a question of knowing what to
make vivid, and when.

prose with Inge's. Why? Is it the words they use? or
the things they discuss? Let us see.

When the subman gets his innings, though he has a short
life and a merry one, he may do irreparable damage, especially
in a highly organised state. Russia has been almost literally
decapitated, by the extermination of all its intelligent citizens;
the materials for recovery in that unhappy country no longer
exist. And the ruin in a more advanced community would be
even more complete.

That is Inge.[1] Let us now take Shaw.

Now for England's share of warning. Let her look to her
Empire; for unless she makes it such a Federation for civil
strength and defence, that all her peoples will cling to it
voluntarily, it will inevitably become a tyranny to prevent
them from abandoning it; and such a tyranny will drain the
English taxpayer of his money more effectually than its worst
cruelties can ever drain its victims of their liberty. A political
scheme that cannot be carried out except by soldiers will not
be a permanent one. The soldier is an anachronism of which
we must get rid.[2]

These writers, it will be observed, were dealing with
the same subject, what they belived to be political
truths, which they were expressing in the hope that
their readers would agree with them: yet their prose
is markedly different. You would, of course, expect
different prose if one of them was telling a funny
story about a sailor, as W. W. Jacobs did, and the
other was describing a death-bed scene. But both
these writers were talking about the same thing, and

[1] *Lay Thoughts of a Dean*, Putnam's, 1927.
[2] Preface to *John Bull's Other Island*, Constable, 1907.

neither used words to which we are not accustomed.
Inge, however, brought out the cant phrase every
time: 'a short life and a merry one'; 'irreparable
damage' (no damage produced by a revolution has
been irreparable); 'almost literally' (when you cannot 'literally' decapitate a country); 'that unhappy
country'. Shaw never fell into this ready-made language; he even surprises, and where we should expect
the victims of cruelty to be drained of their blood, it
is of their liberty that Shaw's victims are to be
drained; he had made a new metaphor. Yet, quite
outside such considerations, how wide apart the voices
are! Inge, with the suspicion of a pulpit drone, spoke
with a level flow, on the slow side (he was a little
fatigued, we feel), giving a slight air of portentous
solemnity by ending the clause or the sentence on
a long syllable—damage, state, exist, complete; he
liked the 'dying fall'. Shaw, on the other hand,
spoke with a lively voice; there is no fatigue there;
it is all vigour. The prose is swift; you naturally raise
and drop your voice as you read it; there is no sense
of solemnity, though it is serious enough, and Shaw
preferred to end the clause or sentence sharply, like
a hammer-tap, or rattle—it, liberty, rid. The style
of the two men, we say, is radically different.

Criticism, a pleasurable activity, is the discussion
of a thing you are interested in. Farmers debating the
merits of pigs of one breed rather than another,
mechanics expatiating upon the performances of
different makes of engines, are critics. People who
discuss literature are literary critics. But just as the

farmer or the mechanic must know what it is he is talking about—you do not compare pigs for the tunefulness of their voice, nor motor-cars for the complexity of their registration number—so the literary critic must know what aspect he is discussing when he talks about prose. Even to say this much is to limit the realm, for you can discuss prose literature without mentioning prose; you can swim deliciously, if inconclusively, in its metaphysics. But I suggest that what we should do is to examine modern prose to see what there is in it to give us pleasure, limiting our inquiry to a few specific points. Firstly, how far the various writers use prose as a fitting instrument to operate on us with (that is, here we shall deal with writing only as a means of communication, leaving the aspect of self-expression to look after itself); what different methods are used to make us see, think, or feel. We shall, because we cannot avoid it, come with prejudices, certain theories which we hold tentatively as a result of reading earlier work, or the works of these very writers; perhaps we shall arrive at a few conclusions. Finally, all the while, we shall listen for the voice which betrays individuality, the personality which no writer who goes to work honestly can keep out of anything he writes, whether it be presentation, argument, or appeal.

PART I

DESCRIPTIVE PROSE

§ 1

Description of Action
(Narrative; Story-telling)

IT is probable that there is no such thing as 'pure' narrative, something told merely for the telling. If you tell a policeman how your pocket was picked, it is in the hope that he will take some action: if you relate your wittiest story, it is to make people laugh: if you inform Mr. and Mrs. Smith how the Joneses behave, it is because—well, there may be a dozen motives, but you certainly do not take the trouble to hold forth with the idea that what you say will make no impression whatever on the Smiths. Of course, beyond any ulterior motive there may be the desire to release your emotions, or to live them over again, or the queer impulse to create, but with these things we have nothing to do: we are concerned with the *effect* of prose. Possibly the only pieces of narrative which, as narrative, produce no effect whatever, are such pieces as Dr. Johnson's famous parody:

> I put my hat upon my head
> > And walked into the Strand;
> And there I met another man
> > With his hat in his hand:

otherwise all narrative is meant to move or to instruct. Perhaps the purest narrative is that of the historian who wants to interest you, but a little aloofly, so that you may be able to deduce some general principle from the things he sets before you: he is telling you not merely that things happened, but how they did. History we shall come to later; it is a very mixed art, and paradoxically, while we may find the purest narrative in it, it is the most impure of all prose forms. Here we are concerned with story-telling.

And though story-telling is due to various impulses, we all know that there is such a thing as good narrative style; at least we talk as if there were. We usually associate the word 'plain' with it. But then prose can only be plain when it deals with plain things, as normally with Defoe; if, for instance, the story to be told has to do with very complicated emotional and intellectual states, the prose is bound to be complicated: the classic instance might be Marcel Proust's great work, so brilliantly translated by Scott-Moncrieff. The fact is that the great stories carry within them such an abundance of implication, they mean so much, that the less they are adorned the better. We do not want our attention distracted from what is happening, never mind how pleasing or exciting in itself the irrelevance may be. The best stories in the world are some of those in the Bible: there is so much in them that any addition to them would spoil them. Take the story of Jephthah's vow, or of Naaman the Syrian. Nothing that you can do can deepen their effect, for by the greatest good luck for English literature, they were translated at the richest period of English prose, so that the words are beautifully apt, vigorous, coloured. In reading them we hardly notice the voice of a previous century, but that may be because even now we are familiar with them.

At all events it is safe to say that it is only the greatest stories that can be told in simple prose; it is only where the stuff itself does the work that prose had better do as little as possible, though that little it must do effectively. If prose has to do more, and after all some lesser stories are well worth telling, it should do only so much more as is necessary; for in prose, as well as in poetry, the passage should contain in itself, as Coleridge said, the reason why it is so and not otherwise, if it is to please permanently. Now in a story we want to know only what is essential, though different kinds of story, as already suggested, call for different kinds of treatment. The qualities, for instance, of a good story of adventure are, as Sir Herbert Read has said, speed, suspense, visibility, with the incidental details standing out significantly:[1] and he himself has given an example:

I've forgotten that walk: it was only about two miles, but our utter dejection induced a kind of unconsciousness in us. It would be between ten and eleven o'clock when we got to Roye. I reported to a staff officer, who sent me off to the town major to get billets. The town major I found distracted, unable to say where I should find a billet. Apparently the town was packed with stragglers. We peered into two great gloomy marquees, floored densely with recumbent men. Meanwhile two other officers joined me with their men, and together we went off to search on our own. We found a

[1] *The Sense of Glory*, Cambridge University Press.

magnificent house, quite empty, and here we lodged the men.
Some kind of rations had been found. They soon had blazing
wood fires going, and seemed happy in a way.

The town major had indicated a hut, where we officers
might get rest, and perhaps some food. We went round,
tired and aching though we were; we lifted the latch and
found ourselves in a glowing room. A stove roared in one
corner—and my teeth were chattering with cold, my clothes
still being sodden—and a lamp hung from the roof. A large
pan of coffee simmered on the stove, and the table was laden
with bread, tinned-foods, butter; food, food, food. I hadn't
had a bite since early morning, and then not much.

I forget, if I ever knew, who or what the two occupants
were, but they were not stragglers. Roye had been their
station for some time. One of them was fat, very fat, with a
tight, glossy skin. I don't remember the other. We explained
that we would like a billet for the night; anything would do
so long as it was warmth. They were sorry: they had no
room. Could they spare us some rations? They were sorry:
this was all they had got till to-morrow noon. We stood very
dejected, sick at our reception. 'Come away!' I said. 'Before
I go away', cried one of my companions, 'I would just like
to tell these blighters what I think of them.' He cursed them,
and then we walked away, back to the men's billet. I looked
in at my fellows; most of them were naked, drying their
clothes at the fire. Some slept on the floor.

We went upstairs into an empty room. Two of us had
agreed to make up a fire, while the other, the one who had
given vent to his feelings, volunteered to go off in search of
food. We split up wood we found in the house, and lit a fire.
I took off my clothes to dry them, and sat on a bench in my
shirt. If I had been asked then what I most desired, besides
sleep, I think I would have said: French bread, butter, honey,
and hot milky coffee.

The forager soon turned up. God only knows where he got

that food from: we did not ask him. But it was French bread, butter, honey, and hot milky coffee in a champagne bottle. We cried out with wonder: we almost wept. We shared the precious stuff out, eating and drinking with inexpressible zest.[1]

Here, at once, we run against the difficulty of giving the flavour of prose by extracts, for any good prose book is cumulative in its effect: it imposes its own atmosphere. But even in this trivial episode, hungry and tired men seeking food and rest, we get something of the sense of the whole. Sir Herbert was writing of the epic retreat of the 5th Army in March 1918, and by its simplicity the style allows the epic quality to come through in all its force. The facts alone are enough to provide all the emotion needed. And though this is a personal record, yet, and this is masterly, the person never intrudes. The 'I' throughout might be a third person. Sir Herbert, that is, was concerned to tell what had happened; as far as he enters into the story, he is a mere unit: even when he talks about himself he never draws attention to himself: he is one of a million others, and the unit gets merged in the mass. That is not to say the prose is impersonal; we hear a very distinct voice, the voice of a man who is profoundly moved, yet in control of his emotion. It is not only the fact that we get, but his sense of the fact. There is nothing obviously literary about the passage, except perhaps the phrase 'floored densely with recumbent men', yet the careful choice of words, the balance of every sentence, creates and reinforces the emotion. Except for 'floored with

[1] *In Retreat*, by Captain Herbert Read, D.S.O., M.C., Faber and Faber; originally Hogarth Press, 1925.

men' there is not a metaphor in the whole passage.
Johnson said of Swift, 'The dog never hazards a
metaphor' (a shocking misstatement); but suppose
that he did not need them for his purposes? If we
have speed, suspense, visibility, with the significant
details standing out vividly, that is all we ask for.
Subtlety here would be out of place. Yet the undertones of feeling are there, and they reach us through
the inflexions of the voice, the alternations of fatigue,
bitterness, courage, hope, never stated, always implied.

Simplicity is not necessarily an ideal; it depends on
what you are trying to do. If you rely entirely on your
story, the plain manner is probably the best to aim at.
Mr. David Garnett is fastidiously simple:

When Francis and Tulip came in sight of the inn they saw
that the door was wide open, with a hurdle lying across the
threshold, and William's coat beside it on the ground, then as
they drew nearer the loud rumour of many voices came to their
ears. There was no one in either of the bars, but looking
further they found the kitchen and the scullery full of men,
whilst in the orchard beyond, groups of labourers were standing under the apple trees. A silence fell when Tulip entered
the kitchen, and in that moment she could hear the sound of
heavy boots in the bedroom. She stood still then, threw up
her hands, and without waiting to be told fled upstairs, and
Sambo ran after her.

'The Governor's been fighting and has got hurt,' said one
of the men to Francis. 'They have taken him upstairs,' and
suddenly Francis saw that in the scullery two men were holding a limp figure in a chair from which he would have slid,
and that this figure was spitting blood. The boy went forward
to see better; there was a basin of blood, a bucket of water,

and several bloodstained cloths. 'That is the fellow who did it.' 'He'll swing for it if the Governor dies.' 'Coo, how his ear does bleed,' said the onlookers grinning foolishly. It was Jack Sait of Portsmouth, occasionally he made noises, asking for something, but no words could be distinguished. Francis turned back and found Tom Madgwick coming down the stairs. 'How did this happen?' he asked.

'I was in the cellar,' answered Tom. 'I don't know how it started, I was bottling sherry. When I came up I saw Freddy Leake come in at the door. He asked me for a bucket of water and said the Captain was out in the orchard giving a fearful hiding to a fellow that had come along with Mr. Molten and his carter from Tarrant, and that they had fought two rounds already.

'We filled the bucket, and then went out into the orchard, and for the first minute we couldn't see anyone there because of the little dip in the ground. When we had got close up to him we saw Captain Targett lying as if he were dead, and that chap there sitting under a tree all over blood. There has been foul play somewhere.' Then Tom turned to the men in the kitchen and shouted angrily: 'Now then you get out of here,' and pointed to the door. 'A lot of dirty cowards,' he cried as they moved out of the room leaving only the old blacksmith Burden and his mate Freddy Leake, who were holding up the drooping figure of the boxer. 'There has been foul play, and not one of them will own to seeing anything, but I saw them poking their heads over the hedge. There will be some questions for them to answer.' Then Tom turned to the smith. 'That chap must be taken to the police,' he said.

'That's all right mate,' answered Fred; 'we won't let him go.'

Just at that moment there was the sound of a woman's skirts rustling, and Tulip appeared in the doorway. Her eyeballs rolled; the flashing whites were the only movement in her black and stolid face; her hands were folded in front of her.

'Have you sent for the doctor?' she asked, and almost as

soon as she had spoken, without waiting for an answer, she
went out of the room.

At her words all the men started guiltily; no one had
thought of the doctor.

'I'll ride over and fetch him,' said Francis, who wanted to
do something. 'Where does he live?' And while the blacksmith began to give directions Tom ran to saddle the pony.[1]

Now where, precisely, is the difference between
the two passages? They are both as plain and straightforward as they can be, yet the voices are not the same.
We know without thinking about it that different
people are speaking. If we read the passages again,
one immediately after the other, we see that the difference has something to do with the rhythm: it is
through our sense of rhythm that Mr. Garnett is,
partly, affecting us. Sir Herbert continually breaks his
pace; he gives us image after image, or idea after idea,
starkly, without connexion. 'We went upstairs into an
empty room': that is enough; each sentence makes its
separate impact. The lack of continuous rhythm, of
course, is just as important, just as craftily achieved, as
Mr. Garnett's flow. Mr. Garnett aims at continuity,
at keeping the up and down of the voice (the imaginary
voice we hear when reading to ourselves), at never
losing the link. Take his first sentence. It begins with
'When . . .' which is significant. Suppose we rewrite
the sentence:

Francis and Tulip came in sight of the inn, and saw that
the door was wide open. A hurdle was lying across the
threshold, and William's coat was beside it on the ground.
As they drew nearer . . ., &c.

[1] *The Sailor's Return*, Chatto and Windus, 1925.

But that was not what Mr. Garnett meant. To write it like that would not convey the undertone of feeling he was all the time implying, perhaps not consciously, but certainly within himself, as he was writing. In not leaving the images or the ideas isolated, but making each merge into the next, he is gradually drawing you into the sort of sense-atmosphere he wishes you to be in to appreciate what he has to say. You move with the events as they take place. His sentences are carefully balanced, you cannot help being influenced by the cadence, and what he is doing becomes noticeable (if you stop to notice it, which he is far too skilful to allow you to do unless you are examining for the sake of finding out) when his ear makes him invert a clause. 'Said one of the men to Francis'. The natural way would be, 'One of the men said to Francis'. We can perhaps best see what is happening if we mark a few words with long and short signs (– or ∪), the long sign conveying also stress, as we might poetry:

∪ – – ∪ – ∪ ∪ – ∪ – ∪
has got hurt,' said one of the men to Francis.

∪ – – – ∪ ∪ – ∪ ∪ – ∪
has got hurt,' one of the men said to Francis.

In writing it as he did, he avoided the three heavy stresses

– – –
got hurt, one

and also the repetition of ∪ ∪ –;

∪ ∪ – ∪ ∪ –
of the men said to Fran

He has made it smoother, more uniform. He is as guiltless of metaphor as Sir Herbert, but he occasionally uses the literary word, such as 'rumour'. But then 'loud sound' would have grated, especially as 'ground' comes a little earlier, and 'found' a little later. Sir Herbert Read is just as careful, as we can see if we compare the later version of his story with the earlier one; but he is aiming at something different, and, since he is himself and not Mr. Garnett, speaking in a voice unlike Mr. Garnett's. We might, exaggerating, say that Sir Herbert is shaking his reader into attention, Mr. Garnett lulling him into receptivity: but how far either was aware of what he was doing is another thing.

We already realize that to say, as is often said, that narrative in prose should be plain, direct stuff, does not much help us to clarify our ideas. Let us see if first-rate narrative prose is really as simple as it looks by examining a piece by Kipling, a piece which is pure narrative, neither expressing any of Kipling's firmly held philosophy, nor dealing with any of his special subjects.

As he spoke, the fog was blown into shreds, and we saw the sea, gray with mud, rolling on every side of us, empty of all life. Then in one spot it bubbled, and became like the pot of ointment that the Bible speaks of. From that wide-ringed trouble a Thing came up—a gray and red Thing with a neck—a Thing that bellowed and writhed in pain. Frithiof drew in his breath and held it till the red letters of the ship's name, woven across his jersey, straggled and opened out as though they had been type badly set. Then he said with a little cluck in his throat, 'Ah me! It is blind. *Hur illa!* That thing is blind,' and a murmur of pity went through us all, for we could see that the thing on the water was blind and in pain. Something had cut and gashed the great sides cruelly and the blood was spurting out. The gray ooze of the undermost sea lay in the monstrous wrinkles of the back, and poured away in sluices. The blind white head flung back and battered the wounds, and the body in its torment rose clear of the red and gray waves till we saw a pair of quivering shoulders streaked with weed and rough with shells, but as white in the clear spaces as the hairless, maneless, blind, toothless head. Afterwards, came a dot on the horizon and the sound of a shrill scream, and it was as though a shuttle shot all across the sea in one breath, and a second head and neck tore through the levels, driving a whispering wall of water to right and left. The two Things met—the one untouched and the other in its death-throe—male and female, we said, the female coming to the male. She circled round him bellowing, and laid her neck across the curve of his great turtle-back, and he disappeared under water for an instant, but flung up again, grunting in agony while the blood ran. Once the entire head and neck shot clear of the water and stiffened, and I heard Keller saying, as though he was watching a street accident, 'Give him air. For God's sake give him air.' Then the death-struggle began, with crampings and twistings and jerkings of the white bulk to and fro, till our little steamer rolled again, and each gray wave coated her plates with the gray slime. The sun was clear, there was no wind, and we watched, the whole crew, stokers and all, in wonder and pity, but chiefly pity. The Thing was so helpless, and, save for his mate, so alone. No human eye should have beheld him; it was monstrous and indecent to exhibit him there in trade waters between atlas degrees of latitude. He had been spewed up, mangled and dying, from his rest on the sea-floor, where he might have lived till the Judgement Day, and we saw the tides of his life go from him as an angry tide goes out across rocks

in the teeth of a landward gale. His mate lay rocking on the
water a little distance off, bellowing continually, and the smell
of musk came down upon the ship making us cough.

At last the battle for life ended in a batter of coloured seas.
We saw the writhing neck fall like a flail, the carcase turn
sideways, showing the glint of a white belly and the inset of
a gigantic hind leg or flipper. Then all sank, and sea boiled
over it, while the mate swam round and round, darting her
head in every direction. Though we might have feared that
she would attack the steamer, no power on earth could have
drawn any one of us from our places that hour. We watched,
holding our breaths. The mate paused in her search; we could
hear the wash beating along her sides; reared her neck as high
as she could reach, blind and lonely in all that loneliness of the
sea, and sent one desperate bellow booming across the swells
as an oyster-shell skips across a pond. Then she made off to
the westward, the sun shining on the white head and the
wake behind it, till nothing was left to see but a little pin
point of silver on the horizon. We stood on our course again;
and the *Rathmines*, coated with the sea-sediment from bow to
stern, looked like a ship made gray with terror.[1]

Kipling, as everybody knows, was rigorous in the
use of words, but it is not that aspect we will consider here, though there are examples enough. First
we notice two things. While he is as sustained in his
rhythm as Mr. Garnett, the impact of his sentences is
as clear as Sir Herbert Read's. The voice is keen, that
of a man who is noticing everything; he catches us
up in the excitement of the moment. Then we notice
something else.

We see that the passage can be divided up into three
parts, the speed of each being different. The first half

[1] 'A Matter of Fact', from *Many Inventions*, Macmillan, 1893.

of the first paragraph is intensely swift; things are moving rapidly; there is no time for emotion—anything may happen at any moment. Then the movement ceases, the eye is fixed on one point, where the giant fish, or whatever it is, is dying; and emotion, fleetingly mentioned in the first part, begins to take hold in the form of pity. Then all is over, the tension relaxes, the nerves are released, the emotion is frittered. Now how is this done? Let us look at the end of Kipling's sentences, always the first thing to look at, because it is the most revealing thing in speech. When a man stops talking, it is what he has last said that lingers in the ear, that makes the final impression. Now in the first part of the passage Kipling ended his sentences hard, sharp, not quite so sharp to begin with, but arriving at a maximum. Let us put down the end words in the three parts, all of them, without cheating.

I	II	III
life (long and soft)	male (long and soft)	seas (long, rather harsh)
speaks of (indeterminate)	ran (liquid)	
pain (long and hard)	air (long and soft)	flipper (disjuncted)
set (hard)	air (long and soft)	direction (disjuncted)
blind (long and hard)	slime (long and soft)	hour (long and soft)
pain (long and hard)	pity (long: soft by association)	breaths (long and rather harsh)
out (hard)		
sluices (rasping)	alone (long and soft)	pond (long: final)
head (hard)	latitude (long and softish)	horizon (disjuncted)
left (hard)	gale (long and soft)	terror (disjuncted)[1]
	cough (harsh)	

These words, of course, are reinforced by others in the sentences, and by the balance of the sentences.

[1] These terms are purely 'subjective'; I have made no attempt to conform to the accepted phonetic descriptions.

Kipling's rhythms are far more accentuated than Mr. Garnett's, both in the sentence and in the paragraph. He placed the accents just where they would be most effective, using every art to make them do so, alliteration in 'We saw the writhing neck fáll like a fláil', the vowel sound or the natural stress in 'looked like a ship made gráy with térror'. He avoided the stress where he wanted none: 'till nothing was left to see but a pin point of silver on the horizon', no heavy vowel sound like 'pond' or 'gale', but the *i* or *ee* sounds—see, pin, silver—the thing is dwindling, the force of the prose dwindles with it. We are not concerned with how far Kipling was deliberately doing all this, only with its effect upon ourselves.

The only virtue which we can judge these three passages to have in common, is that the writers all had their eye on the object; nothing extraneous is for a moment allowed to enter. Pure narrative, story-telling, is objective; it describes things happening. It is rare, and becoming increasingly so, even in the novel-form, where we should most expect to find it. Nowadays, indeed, we should not tolerate a novel written in the manner of Defoe;[1] even Mr. Garnett, who is perhaps the most pure, the most objective, of our story-tellers, does not go as far as that. In the short story it is still fairly common. Narrative, however, goes on being written, but it is of a different kind; it is the story of a mind that we are being told, and the events are related chiefly because they affect the mind of the person we are being told about. We may take as an example a piece of narrative by Miss Kay Boyle.

[1] I am not so sure now, in 1963.

It is narrative in the sense that it consists only of fact, though not wholly of fact that can be observed:

On the other side sat Ayton, eating peanuts and laughing aloud, and Leonie looked away from him and shook her head. Munday saw her face, soft and close beside him, with her eyes chiding the hilarity in the tent, and her lashes turned up, thick, to her brows. The bold glances of the actors were on her as they played, but she had no thought for them or for their loving eyes. Instead she must turn to Munday in appeal now that all she had been taught by other women to believe special and pure was being defiled.

He sat in the half-darkness of the tent and looked at her face lifted to him for unction as the face of a postulant might have been. He thought: *This is the symbol of all temptation offered me.* There was no temptation in the flesh, for his flesh was given in love; but in this woman beside him there was the corruption of her pliancy that wooed him like desire. He could take her gentle grievous chiding and exalt it with holy fervour, he could make her condemnation fruitful by the wild breath of the Scriptures. Whether he believed the words now, or whether he had passed from the Church's belief forever, still he could speak to her in the untamed unforgiving speech of the Prophets.

'Do you go to confession now?' he said to her, feeling his two-sided tongue in his mouth.

'Confession?' said Leonie, and then her hand fled up to her face. 'Oh, no, never now, never any more,' she said. 'What will become of me, Munday?'

'Nothing will become of you,' said Munday. 'Nothing harmful. Perhaps you will want to go to confession one day.'

But she looked at him, suddenly unalterable and stern.

'I'll never go to the Church again,' she said, whispering. 'It never showed me how to be patient and forbear. All my life I saw myself,' she said, 'sitting still, in a big chair, maybe, with my good husband on one side of me, and my child on my lap. But it was never given to me. Everything else was given to me, whether I asked for it or not, but that thing was never given me.'

'Maybe it will be given you,' said Munday, speaking softly in the darkness. 'You are young, and things come slowly in life, as if you grew slowly up to them. The Virgin,' he said, 'was not as young as you.'

"*Y a des loups, Muguette*," sang the women, kicking across the stage, "*y a des loups!*"

'But the Virgin was never a lost woman,' said Leonie, whispering to him in the dark. 'I am a lost woman,' she said, 'I can't be saved.'

She had come so close to him that her soft shoulder and breast were lying heavy and warm against his arm.

'How are you lost?' he said.

'I don't want to be saved,' she whispered to him. 'Not from the thoughts I have all day in my head, and for the things I want, dresses, and pretty shoes. I want them to be real. I don't want to be any more without them.'[1]

It is narrative because the facts themselves are allowed to make their effect; there is no directly emotional appeal. There are, in fact, two narratives, the story of what is going on in the people's minds being set within that of what is going on in the circus. The emotive effect of the woman's words is obtained through the tension set up in the previous paragraphs, by the way the sentences are sustained, and by the imaginative impulses set up by such terms as 'the wild breath', the 'untamed unforgiving speech of the Prophets'. The

[1] From *Gentlemen, I Address You Privately*, by Kay Boyle, Faber and Faber, 1934.

sentences are never slack; they are nervous and clean. The whole thing is simple in statement because Miss Boyle is dealing with broad issues, the power of spiritual temptation and the manner of life. It is scrupulously plain once we get to the conversation: there is no emotion expressed in connexion with all that must be involved in a frustrated life: there are no apostrophes, no attempts to deepen the effect of the fact by discussing it, as was Thackeray's way. Where something less simple is involved the prose is necessarily more complex:

. . . Afterwards I sought thee along and across Palestine, till hearing of thee in Egypt I went thither and sought thee from synagogue to synagogue.

A man travels the world over in search of what he needs and returns home to find it, Jesus answered gently, and in a tenderer voice than his scrannel peacock throat would have led one to expect. And as if foreseeing an ardent disciple he began to speak to Joseph of God, his speech moving on with a gentle motion like that of clouds wreathing and unwreathing, finding new shapes for every period, and always beautiful shapes. He often stopped speaking and his eyes became fixed, as if he saw beyond the things we all see; and after an interval he would begin to speak again; and Joseph heard that he had met John among the hills and listened to him, and that if he accepted baptism from him it was because he wished to follow John: but John sought to establish the kingdom of God within the law, and so a dancing-girl asked for his head. It seemed as if Jesus were on the point of some tremendous avowal, but if so it passed away like a cloud, and he put his hand on Joseph's shoulder affectionately, and asked him to tell him about Egypt, a country which he said he had never heard of before. Whereupon Joseph raised his eyes and saw

in Jesus a travelling wonder-worker come down from a northern village—a peasant, without knowledge of the world and
of the great Roman Empire. At every step Jesus's ignorance
of the world surprised Joseph more and more. He seemed to
believe that all the nations were at war, and from further
discourse Joseph learnt that Jesus could not speak Greek, and
he marvelled at his ignorance, for Jesus knew only such
Hebrew as is picked up in the synagogues. He did not seek
to conceal his ignorance of this world from Joseph, and almost
made parade of it, as if he was aware that one must discard a
great deal to gain a little, as if he would impress this truth
upon Joseph, almost as if he would reprove him for having
spent so much time on learning Greek, for instance, and
Greek philosophy. He treated these things as negligible when
Joseph spoke of them, and evinced more interest in Joseph
himself, who admitted he had returned from philosophy to
the love of God.

And now sitting on his bed, kept awake by his memories,
Joseph relived in thought the hours he had spent with Jesus.
He seemed to understand the significance of every word much
better now than when he was with Jesus, and regretting his
obtuseness he recast all the answers given to Jesus, recalling
with sorrow how he tried to explain the teaching of the
Alexandrian philosophers regarding the Scriptures, and though
he saw he was paining Jesus he had continued for the sake of
the answer he knew would come at last. It did come: and
what a wonderful answer it was: that philosophies change in
different men, but the love of God is the same in all men.
A great truth, Joseph said to himself, for every school is in
opposition to another school. But how did Jesus come to know
this, being without philosophy? He had been tempted to ask
how he was able to get at the truth of things without the
Greek language and without education, but refrained lest a
question should break the harmony of the evening. The past
was not yet past, and sitting on his bed in the moonlight

Joseph could re-see the plain covered with beautiful grasses and flowers, with low flowering bushes waving over dusky headlands, for it was dark as they crossed the plain; and they had heard rather than seen the rushing stream, bubbling out of the earth, making music in the still night. He knew the stream from early childhood, but he had never really known it until he stood with Jesus under the stars by the narrow path cut in the shoulder of the hill, the way leading to Capernaum, for it was there that Jesus took his hands and said the words: Our Father which is in Heaven. At these words their eyes were raised to the skies, and Jesus said: Whoever admires the stars and flowers finds God in his heart and sees him in his neighbour's face. And as Joseph sat, his hands on his knees, he recalled the moment that Jesus turned from him abruptly and passed into the shadow of the hillside that fell across the flowering mead. He heard his footsteps and had listened, repressing the passionate desire to follow him and to say: Having found thee, I can leave thee never again. It was fear of Jesus that prevented him from following Jesus, and he returned slowly the way he came, his eyes fixed on the stars, for the day was now well behind the hills and the night all over the valley, calm and still. The stars in their allotted places, he said: as they have always been and always will be. He stood watching them. Behind the stars that twinkled were stars that blazed; behind the stars that blazed were smaller stars, and behind them a sort of luminous dust. And all this immensity is God's dwelling-place, he said. The stars are God's eyes; we live under his eyes and he has given us a beautiful garden to live in. Are we worthy of it? he asked; and Jew though he was he forgot God for a moment in the sweetness of the breathing of earth, for there is no more lovely plain in the spring of the year than the Plain of Gennesaret.[1]

[1] *The Brook Kerith*, by George Moore, revised ed., Heinemann, 1927.

In that passage we are being told the story of what
went on in a man's mind, especially in his memory;
it is narrative in that nothing is allowed to intrude
beyond what was thought, or said, or done. But it is
not plain, downright prose, in any sense of the word.
The use of the verb, for instance, is very unusual.
So as to blend the past with the present, mind with
memory, Moore confused the times with great effect,
hardly ever using the pluperfect, indissolubly weaving
then and now. Moore speaks with an even voice; he
never raises it, never makes abrupt halts, nor jerks
the reader into attention. His prose may even be considered a little too lulling, but you will miss the richness of the texture if you allow yourself to be lulled.
He appeals largely to the eye, to the delicacies of
sense, and to the memory of sensations. Nor does he
refuse simile: 'his speech moving on with a gentle
motion like that of clouds wreathing and unwreathing, finding new shapes for every period, and always
beautiful shapes': it might describe Moore's own
prose.

Simile and metaphor are much the same thing; the
distinction is merely grammatical, and both really are
a development of the adjective. 'Scrannel peacock
throat' is really metaphor weakened until it has only
the force of an adjective. Metaphors can be used as
adjectives, for instance Wilde's 'shrill green'; but
when they die, as metaphors do (we remember towel-
horse), they receive no more attention than adjectives,
and 'shrill' has been used as such with 'green' by
Sir Osbert Sitwell. The point, however, of metaphor
or simile as opposed to the adjective is that they are

more arresting because they show likeness in dissimilar things. Things utterly unlike, in fact only alike at all by an effort of the imagination, are merged together, or one thing is translated on to another level: 'Life like a dome of many-coloured glass.' The plane of apprehension is raised. Sentences, for instance, cannot be like clouds, without mental gymnastic. Metaphors on the whole are more vivid in their effect than similes, make a sharper impact on the mind. 'Smith walked across the road like a broken-kneed horse' is not so strong as 'Smith, that broken-kneed horse, walked across the road'. Abolish 'like', and we get a more immediate sense of revelation. Put in the word, and we get a feeling of suspense; we stop to breathe, as when swimming in a rough sea we take breath at the top of a wave before plunging down into the next trough of tumult. The ability to create metaphor is, as Aristotle remarked, the surest sign of originality: but some modern writers seem to confine their originality to that alone, and George Eliot lamented that 'intelligence so rarely shows itself in speech without metaphor—that we can seldom declare what a thing is, except by saying that it is something else'.[1] Metaphor can be, and often is, used effectively as decoration, but when used too much it becomes irritation: a rock by the sea has to be like a hippopotamus emerging, a tuft of heather like somebody's beard, a footpath like a serpent, till we wish that things should sometimes be allowed to exist simply as themselves. Never to leave anything alone is to insult the readers' visual capacity. These remarks, however, do not apply to Moore. His

[1] *The Mill on the Floss,* Book, II. i.

use of the forms is admirable: they are not too insistent, nor too involved.[1] Without his similes or metaphors what he has to show us would not be so distinct; that is to say that they fulfil their function in narrative prose.

Narrative, as already suggested, is becoming more and more complicated. Let us look at one example in the hands of a very subtle modern novelist, to see how much it can be made to bear. If we read the following passage we shall see that what we might call the essay-content, the philosophic meaning, is so woven into the narrative that it is difficult, indeed impossible, to separate them without ruining both. The story is going on all the time, but its implications are widened to the utmost:

The Age of Property holds bitter moments even for a proprietor. When a move is imminent, furniture becomes ridiculous, and Margaret now lay awake at nights wondering where, where on earth they and all their belongings would be deposited in September next. Chairs, tables, pictures, books, that had rumbled down to them through the genera-tions, must rumble forward again like a slide of rubbish to which she longed to give a final push, and send toppling into the sea. But there were all their father's books—they never read them, but they were their father's, and must be kept. There was the marble-topped cheffonier—their mother had set store by it, they could not remember why. Round every knob and cushion in the house sentiment gathered, a sentiment that was at times personal, but more often a faint piety to the dead, a prolongation of rites that might have ended at the grave.

It was absurd, if you came to think of it; Helen and Tibby

---

[1] 'I am not fond of long-winded metaphors: I have often observed that they halt at the latter end of their progress', Cowper to Newton, 3 May 1780.

came to think of it: Margaret was too busy with the house-agents. The feudal ownership of land did bring dignity, whereas the modern ownership of movables is reducing us again to a nomadic horde. We are reverting to the civilization of luggage, and historians of the future will note how the middle classes accreted possessions without taking root in the earth, and may find in this the secret of their imaginative poverty. The Schlegels were certainly the poorer for the loss of Wickham Place. It had helped to balance their lives, and almost to counsel them. Nor is their ground-landlord spiritually the richer. He has built flats on its site, his motor-cars grow swifter, his exposures of socialism more trenchant. But he has spilt the precious distillation of the years, and no chemistry of his can give it back to society again.

Margaret grew depressed; she was anxious to settle on a house before they left town to pay their annual visit to Mrs. Munt. She enjoyed this visit, and wanted to have her mind at ease for it. Swanage, though dull, was stable, and this year she longed more than usual for its fresh air and for the magnificent downs that guard it on the north. But London thwarted her; in its atmosphere she could not concentrate. London only stimulates, it cannot sustain; and Margaret, hurrying over its surface for a house without knowing what sort of a house she wanted, was paying for many a thrilling sensation in the past. She could not even break loose from culture, and her time was wasted by concerts which it would be a sin to miss, and invitations which it would never do to refuse. At last she grew desperate; she resolved that she would go nowhere and be at home to no one until she found a house, and broke the resolution in half an hour.[1]

In some ways that passsage is a triumph of writing, a great deal being suggested in the simplest of phrases. The general ideas, it is true, are stated, quite shortly

[1] *Howard's End*, by E. M. Forster, Arnold, 1910.

as a rule; the suggestiveness lies in the hint that they have something to do with us. It is by his precision that Mr. Forster manages to keep his voice just aloof, but only just: to be further removed would make his statements too abstract. He maintains the familiar tone throughout, but again it is his precision that prevents it from being too familiar, precision in the words used, and, more important still, in the form of the phrases. But there is no flatness. Take the structure of the first paragraph; the attack of each sentence is skilfully varied, sometimes beginning arrestingly, sometimes without emphasis, as though to run you easily, unaware, into the matter of the sentence. Each sentence is beautifully balanced, as though the voice when it began it knew exactly what it was going to say, and how much breath would be needed to say it. And besides that, what we perceive is the complete absence of any pomposity, perhaps because Mr. Forster carefully avoids the sonorous, except when, deliberately, he brings in 'the downs that guard it on the north'. He is appealing to the intellect, and we feel his mind working all the time, the prose being responsive to the mind, which here seems completely merged in the personality, for all the while the former seems to play upon what it is that stirs the latter. The neat epigram, contrasted with the fact told, the sense of humour playing over it all, prevent any sentimentality creeping in. The writer's eye is still fixed on the object, but the object has become a very complex one, the human personality in its surroundings and in its ramifications. And this leads us naturally to descriptions of people.

Description of People

THE 'character' is a very old form of literature, and was extremely popular in England at the beginning of the seventeenth century. But it is no longer written now, singly, for in the eighteenth century it became integrated in the novel after passing through the form of Sir Roger de Coverley and his like. In the process the 'character' became clothed in flesh and blood; we are given the appearance of the man as well as his mental or idiosyncratic make-up; the 'humour' has become a human being. Moreover, today, analysis is much more acute, more inventive, thanks to psychology, or at least to the adoption of the jargon of the modern schools; it has a tendency towards a new sort of generalization. It is not merely the social aspect of the man that is considered, but his inner reactions, these again related perhaps to his physical being. We should not be surprised to read that 'Smith, being an introvert, was lanky', so prone are we becoming to this new coxcombry of scientific terms. But in the simple field of a straightforward memoir of a man we still sometimes get direct description; and since this is the most obvious approach of all, and by no means the least satisfactory (for after all, we like to handle a thing for ourselves, and not have all our thinking done for us), we may begin with an example which happens to be in the traditional manner, a portrait of Ingram Bywater:

My old friend was no walker. Yet the picture which

recollection chiefly invokes is of a spare figure, much swamped and muffled in greatcoats and a soft hat, stepping delicately down the High Street of Oxford, and pausing to regard the windows of booksellers and antiquarians with a chill glance of recognition and dispraise. There was an unconscious *fastidium* in that walk, and in the aquiline cast of his old face in repose, which expressed the innocent arrogance of his mind. A natural aristocracy spoke in his bearing, to the exclusion of any mark of occupation. He was no more like a great scholar than anybody else; but he might have been an ambassador, or the head of a great banking house. He might have been a duke of the premier line. . . .

Few even of his friends, I imagine, suspected the prodigious range of his attainments. He did not suspect it himself. He had no vulgar avidity of information or conceit of versatility, and of many branches of modern scientific knowledge was content to remain as ignorant as a gentleman need be. He acquired his knowledge with an easy deliberation, and kept it by mere tenacity and a sure instinct for selection. In conversation his native courtesy chose subjects with which he knew his interlocutor to be familiar; and the Renaissance scholar who knew that he lived on terms of close intimacy with Erasmus and the Scaligers might well remain in ignorance of his equal familiarity with Diogenes Laertius, or the Elizabethan dramatists, or the historians of the Peninsular War. Till he warmed to a subject his knowledge was always shy; he was not to be drawn; and it was felt that the attempt would be indecent. The loftiness of his own standard was more surely betrayed by the alarm he evinced at the rare discovery of a gap in his knowledge. At a meeting of a learned society over which he presided, a member, while reading a commentator's note, boggled at a word and applied to the president for its meaning. '*Sicilicus—sicilicus!*' There was a silence as he made his way to the dictionary. '*Sicilicus*. It means the forty-eighth part of an *as*, and, by metonymy, it means a comma.' Then, replacing the book and turning to his audience, in accents of unfeigned dismay—'I didn't *know that!*'[1]

What first strikes us about the passage is its artificiality (was not Lamb the model?); but it is a happy artificiality which seems itself to express a certain quality in Bywater which we recognize on being told, 'He was not to be drawn, and it was felt that the attempt would be indecent.' To know more of this scholarly figure than he presented would be to mis-know him: the very reticence of the passage makes the figure vivid. But if a writer is as scrupulous as this, he has to give the figure interest by means of the words themselves; he must keep the mind alert by a frequent change not only in the length but in the character of the sentences. This Chapman did. Contrast the simple 'My old friend was no walker' with the Johnsonian 'He had no vulgar avidity of information or conceit of versatility', giving a humorous twist to what might be a mere negative quality. Chapman, we feel, was not only re-creating his old friend, but creating an object; the voice is as impersonal as possible; the writer is detached, but affectionate.

Very different in purpose and in method is the extract which follows, from history this time; for after direct memoirs it is in history and biography that we are most likely to get isolated description of persons:

No biography of the Duke of Newcastle has yet been attempted; when written, it will have to be in terms of mental

[1] From *Portrait of a Scholar*, by R. W. Chapman, Oxford University Press, 1922.

pathology. His nature and mind were warped, twisted, and stunted, and his life must have been agony, though perhaps he himself did not clearly realise how much he suffered. He was haunted by fears; every small incident was the portent of terrible things to come; every molehill a volcano. With an abundant substratum of intelligence and common sense, he looked a fool, and with an inexhaustible fund of warm human kindness and sincere goodwill, he acquired a reputation for dishonesty. His thinking was sound, but it was paralysed by fears; unable to stand up to anyone or to refuse a pressing request, he could not keep honest, and the weak resentments of an exasperated coward, who felt constantly bullied and brow-beaten, were bound to create the appearances of treachery. There probably never was another man in a position out-wardly so great who felt so wretchedly poor in soul. If he was vain, this was merely a craving for some compensation for the insults and humiliations, real and imaginary, which he daily suffered and which cut him to the heart. He was not equal to greatness and success, and paid a heavy price for them. . . .

Like so many sufferers from obsessionist neurosis, great, middling, or insignificant, Newcastle wasted his life on trifles, pursuing them with an intensity which was to hide their inanity. *'Vive la bagatelle'*, wrote Swift; and Samuel Johnson remarked on one occasion that 'a man would never undertake great things, could he be amused with small. I once tried knotting . . . but I could not learn it'. Still, Johnson himself unconsciously achieved a compromise between the heavy strain of concentrated, creative work, and 'knotting', in his *Dictionary*, the sum total of thousands of small stitches, and in innumerable disconnected dicta. Similarly Newcastle made in politics disconnected detail his chosen province; patronage and the House of Commons, the doling out of financial advantages to importunate beggars and the engineering of elections, engrossed his thinking, which he seldom allowed to rise to the level of a political idea. Even into foreign politics

he managed to infuse his habits or obsessions; he insisted on
paying subsidies to petty German States, as useless to England
in a crisis as Newcastle's political retainers were to prove to
him; and between 1750 and 1753 made the election of the
son of the Empress Maria Theresa, the Archduke Joseph,
as King of the Romans, 'the great system, the great object'
of his labours in foreign affairs. Chesterfield, subtle and
ironic, seems to have perceived that this was merely another
expression of Newcastle's mania for electioneering. . . .[1]

Here, at any rate, the psychological method is justified; Newcastle, who baffled his own age, can perhaps best be explored in modern clinical terms. And
the prose is different from Chapman's because Namier
was intent, not to create an object, but to probe a
complicated human being. There is no attempt to
give an image of the man; reality has to be given to
the secret emotions. Instead of being presented with
the results of a writer's thoughts, we follow his mind
as it thinks. We might wish sometimes that some of
the searchings were suppressed: 'warped, twisted,
and stunted'—are all three words necessary?: 'great,
middling, or insignificant'—would not the sentence
be better without any of these adjectives? But just as
the figure is not built up for us (we have to put the
pieces together ourselves), so the prose remains un-
built into phrases which are in themselves objects.

The psychological method in the hands of a more
conscious artist is concealed, and Lord David Cecil
in *The Stricken Deer*, a study in pathology if ever there
was one, creates Cowper the object out of Cowper the

[1] From *England in the Age of the American Revolution*, by L. B.
Namier, Macmillan, 1930.

'case'. We do not feel that here is a man in a laboratory exploring a *corpus vile*, commenting on his dis-
coveries as he goes along, but a lecturer giving us his
results. The prose is more certain, it has its own graces;
but still even here the object is not altogether created;
there is a sound of argument in the voice betrayed
by the expletive 'did' at the end of the passage; the
prose, that is, is expository as much as descriptive:

. . . On the night of February 24th he had a dream. What
it precisely was no one knows; but in it, amid circumstances
of unspeakable horror, he heard from the lips of God Himself
the certain and irrevocable sentence of his damnation. The
next morning the last vestige of sanity had left him. He did
not know where he was or who was speaking to him. Cower-
ing back on his bed in that pleasant Vicarage room, he saw
only the distorted faces of the demons, heard only the roaring
of the flames of hell open to receive him.

Once again the powers of darkness had beaten him. Risen
in the storms of madness the short, strange day of his faith had
sunk to its setting. And it has been a commonplace of subsequent literary history that the madness was brought on by the
faith. A commonplace, but not a truth; Cowper's madness
finds its origin far deeper in the sufferings of childhood, it may
be in inherent physical defect. All his life it was hung over
him. And religion, so far from being the cause, was the most
considerable of the remedies by which he tried to get rid of it.
It failed. And once he realised that it had failed, it is true that
the emotional tension encouraged by Evangelicalism, and the
personal responsibility for its own state which it placed on
the individual soul, did increase Cowper's nervous agitation
and so accelerate the advent of his madness. But though it
accelerated it, it did not make that advent more sure.[1]

[1] From *The Stricken Deer*, by Lord David Cecil, Constable, 1929.

The second paragraph, except for the first sentence, is plain statement. Lord David is trying to get at the truth, and so arrive at his description of the person; the psychological knowledge of our day is there, but the terms are absent. Now let us take a passage from Lytton Strachey.

The old statesman was now entering upon the penultimate period of his enormous career. He who had once been the rising hope of the stern and unbending Tories, had at length emerged, after a life-time of transmutations, as the champion of militant democracy. He was at the apex of his power. His great rival was dead; he stood pre-eminent in the eye of the nation; he enjoyed the applause, the confidence, the admiration, the adoration, even, of multitudes. Yet—such was the peculiar character of the man, and such the intensity of the feelings which he called forth—at this very moment, at the height of his popularity, he was distrusted and loathed; already an unparalleled animosity was gathering its forces against him. For, indeed, there was something in his nature which invited—which demanded—the clashing reactions of passionate extremes. It was easy to worship Mr. Gladstone; to see in him the perfect model of the upright man—the man of virtue and of religion—the man whose whole life had been devoted to the application of high principles to affairs of State—the man, too, whose sense of right and justice was invigorated and ennobled by an enthusiastic heart. It was also easy to detest him as a hypocrite, to despise him as a demagogue, and to dread him as a crafty manipulator of men and things for the purposes of his own ambition. It might have been supposed that one or other of these conflicting judgments must have been palpably absurd, that nothing short of gross prejudice or wilful blindness, on one side or the other, could reconcile such contradictory conceptions of a single human being. But it was not so: 'the elements' were 'so mixed' in

Mr. Gladstone that his bitterest enemies (and his enemies were never mild) and his warmest friends (and his friends were never tepid) could justify, with equal plausibility, their denunciations or their praises. What, then, was the truth? In the physical universe there are no chimeras. But man is more various than nature; was Mr. Gladstone, perhaps, a chimera of the spirit? Did his very essence lie in the confusion of incompatibles? His very essence? It eludes the hand that seems to grasp it. One is baffled, as his political opponents were baffled fifty years ago. The soft serpent coils harden into quick strength that has vanished, leaving only emptiness and complexity behind. Speech was the fibre of his being; and, when he spoke, the ambiguity of ambiguity was revealed. The long, winding, intricate sentences, with their vast burden of subtle and complicated qualifications, befogged the mind like clouds, and like clouds, too, dropped thunderbolts. Could it not then at least be said of him with certainty that his was a complex character? But here also there was a contradiction. In spite of the involutions of his intellect and the contortions of his spirit, it is impossible not to perceive a strain of *naïveté* in Mr. Gladstone. He adhered to some of his principles—that of the value of representative institutions, for instance—with a faith which was singularly literal; his views upon religion were uncritical to crudeness; he had no sense of humour. Compared with Disraeli's, his attitude towards life strikes one as that of an ingenuous child. His very egoism was simple-minded: through all the labyrinth of his passions there ran a single thread. But the centre of the labyrinth? Ah! the thread might lead there, through those wandering mazes, at last. Only, with the last corner turned, the last step taken, the explorer might find that he was looking down into the gulf of a crater. The flame shot out on every side, scorching and brilliant, but in the midst there was a darkness.[1]

[1] From *Eminent Victorians*, by Lytton Strachey, Chatto and Windus, 1918.

What is the effect of that on us? Do we, after reading
the passage, feel that we know Mr. Gladstone any
more intimately? No; but we are delighted by a
work of art, the consummate fabrication of an object.
Strachey, in fact, had been writing a poem, and the
comparison that springs to the mind is precisely one
with a poem, namely *Absalom and Achitophel*.

> A fiery soul, which working out its way,
> Fretted the pigmy body to decay:
> And o'er informed the tenement of clay . . .

that is the sort of thing Strachey was doing; and as
he did it he ceased to think of Gladstone just as
Dryden forgot about Shaftesbury. His means, too,
were poetic: the complicated rhythm, the bringing
of the stress on the right word, the modulated vowel
sounds accumulating upon a finality of statement.
And, as prose, there is the variation of attack in each
sentence, the perfect transition from one sentence to
another (his transition from paragraph to paragraph
was also admirable), and the virtuoso construction of
the paragraph itself, its conception as a complete
whole. Strachey's style was not impeccable; he was
too much given to the dash, which is a sandy joint,
instead of the cement preferable in a sturdy structure;
in his later works he was too fond of a dying fall (this
is to consider only his prose style, not his wider bio-
graphical method where other instruments of criticism would have to be brought into service); always,
perhaps, the rhetorical question played too large a
part. It is possible, also, to take exception to his continual use of the cliché; a statement with him would

be *palpably* absurd, a prejudice would not fail to be
gross. But then, the question arises, would it have
served his purpose better to select fresher, more striking adjectives? Was it not part of his skill to subdue
the reader's mind, not by the impact of surprising
words, but by producing the strange effect out of commonplace materials, partly by the images presented,
partly by the rhythms? The adjective which strikes
the mind happily and sets it off on adventures of its
own might have been inimical to Strachey's purpose;
he wanted to bring your mind along on his own mind's
adventures. We may regret, indeed, that he did not
always examine his words more closely, that he should
have let pass '*unparalleled* animosity', for we are quite
sure that the animosity could easily be paralleled in
the history of many hated ministers, Castlereagh for
instance. But the total result is exhilarating: the polysyllables march along in bold confidence; Strachey's
voice is that of an eager anatomist, exhibiting, not a
mere dead object, but what he can make out of it: he
is all the while discovering new things to discover,
and because he is delighted, we are delighted too.

Discovery, in this sense, is creation; it is what we expect in the novel rather than in biography. But it is very
rarely that we get just Strachey's type of discovery,
which seeks for objects out of which the explorer himself can make something. We find it, however, in the
work of that very original writer Wyndham Lewis, but
his method is inherently different from Strachey's:

So emerging on the quay once more, and turning along the
front of the house, I again discovered myself in contact with
Bestre. He was facing towards me, and down the quay, im-

mobile as before, and the attitude so much a replica as to make it seem a plagiarism of his kitchen piece. Only now his head was on one side, a verminous grin had dispersed the equally unpleasant entity of his shut mouth. The new facial arrangement and angle for the head imposed on what seemed to be his stock pose for the body, must mean: 'Am I not rather smart? Not just a little bit smart? Don't you think? A little, you will concede? You did not expect that, did you? That was a nasty jar for you, was it not? . . .'

His very large eyeballs, the small saffron ocellation in their centre, the tiny spot through which light entered the obese wilderness of his body; his bronzed bovine arms, swollen handles for a variety of indolent little ingenuities; his inflated digestive case, lent their combined expressiveness to say these things; with every tart and biting condiment that eye-fluid, flaunting of fatness (the well-filled), the insult of the comic, implications of indecency, could provide. . . .

He is a large, tall man, corpulent and ox-like: you can see by his movements that the slow aggrandisement of his stomach has hardly been noticed by him. It is still compact with the rest of his body, and he is as nimble as a flea. It has been for him like the peculations of a minister, enriching himself under the nose of the caliph; Bestre's kingly indifference can be accounted for by the many delights and benefits procured through this subtle misappropriation of the general resources of the body. Sunburnt, with large yellow-white moustache, little eyes protruding with the curt strenuosity already noticed, when he meets anyone for the first time his mouth stops open, a cigarette end adhering to the lower lip. He will assume an expression of expectancy and repressed amusement, like a man accustomed to nonplussing: the expression the company wears in those games of divination when they have made the choice of an object, and he whose task it is to guess its nature is called in, and commences the cross-examination. Bestre is jocose; he will beset you with mocking thoughts as the blindfold man is danced round in a game of blind man's buff. He may have regarded my taps as a myopic clutch at his illusive person. He gazes at a new acquaintance as though this poor man, without guessing it, were entering a world of astonishing things! A would-be boarder arrives and asks him if he has a room with two beds. Bestre fixes him steadily for twenty seconds with an amused yellow eye. Without uttering a word, he then leads the way to a neighbouring door, lets the visitor pass into the room, stands watching him with the expression of a conjuror who has just drawn a curtain aside and revealed to the stupefied audience a horse and cart, or a life-size portrait of the Shah of Persia, where a moment ago there was nothing.[1]

It has been necessary to take pieces from here and there, for Lewis, like most modern novelists, abandoned the 'character' method, and his figure is built up piece by piece at different significant moments, catching a gesture here, a profile there, till the idea of the complete being, filtering little by little into the reader's mind, is finally put together. Naturally, in comparing this passage with Strachey's we must keep two things in mind, namely that Gladstone was a great figure and that Bestre is an innkeeper in a French sea-side village; and secondly that Lewis could invent any figure he liked. But still these great differences do not affect the question of style. Strachey got his effects from the image and the sentence, Lewis from the force of the word itself, and from suggestion. If the former derives from Dryden, the latter betrays descent from the romantic poets, whose purpose it

[1] From *The Wild Body*, by Wyndham Lewis, Chatto and Windus, 1927.

was to suggest rather than to state. What, precisely, is a *verminous* grin? We do not know; nor do we care, for the adjective arouses exactly the train of association needed to suggest Bestre and the quality of his grin. Again, Lewis exhibited an almost panic-stricken avoidance of the cliché: he was not going to let the images sink in as Strachey did; he challenges your mind to an equal agility with his in constructing the objects he sketched, and which he created as surely as Strachey did his own. He will tolerate no laziness in you. He goads you on by the use of the unusual word, an admirably chosen one, such as *ocellation*, 'an eye-shaped marking' (*O.E.D.*), not idly selected, for it conveys to a nicety what he meant. Though he had the acute observation of the painter, the sense of subtle differences, he insisted on presenting you, not with the visual aspects, but the intellectual ones. 'His inflated belly' would have produced a visual image for you, 'his inflated digestive case' arouses you with the surprises of a cross-section. The faculty in you upon which his prose works is not that of sight; the metaphors are not concrete, they imply action, a process. Though in a way traditional, starting from the outward aspect, his work was to build the object out of entirely new materials.

The contribution of our day to the character has, however, been the depicting it from inside, as James Joyce did in *Ulysses*, tracing every thought and impression of a man throughout the twenty-four hours of a day. At the end Mr. Bloom appears complete. The method has become almost universally employed now, in greater or smaller proportions, and in every novel, nearly, we are shown the workings of a mind, not logically, as in the old-fashioned novel from *Tom Jones* onward, but irrationally. Carried to extremes of realism the method can become deplorably dull; artistry is needed here as in any 'imitation of life', and the mental movements, while seeming natural and even wayward, must really be selected with the utmost rigour. This was achieved most perfectly by Virginia Woolf. *The Waves* is altogether a character novel; there is virtually no story, and the characters emerge and develop almost entirely by means of silent soliloquies. I choose an extract, however, which happens to be a speech at dinner, merely for the convenience of quoting something complete and not too long; it does not differ in kind or quality from any of the soliloquies:

'I see what is before me,' said Jinny. 'This scarf, these wine-coloured spots. This glass. This mustard pot. This flower. I like what one touches, what one tastes. I like rain when it has turned to snow and become palpable. And being rash, and much more courageous than you are, I do not temper my beauty with meanness lest it should scorch me. I gulp it down entire. It is made of flesh; it is made of stuff. My imagination is the body's. Its visions are not fine-spun and white with purity like Louis's. I do not like your lean cats and your blistered chimney pots. The scrannel beauties of your roof-tops repel me. Men and women, in uniforms, wigs and gowns, bowler hats and tennis shirts beautifully open at the neck, the infinite variety of women's dresses (I note all clothes always) delight me. I eddy with them, in and out, in and out, into rooms, into halls, here, there, everywhere, wherever they go. This man lifts the hoof of a horse. This man shoves in and out the drawers of his private collection.

I am never alone. I am attended by a regiment of my fellows. My mother must have followed the drum, my father the sea. I am like a little dog that trots down the road after the regimental band, but stops to snuff a tree-trunk, to sniff some brown stain, and suddenly careers across the street after some mongrel cur and then holds one paw up while it sniffs an entrancing whiff of meat from the butcher's shop. My traffics have led me into strange places. Men, how many, have broken from the wall and come to me. I have only to hold my hand up. Straight as a dart they have come to the place of assignation—perhaps a chair on a balcony, perhaps a shop at a street corner. The torments, the divisions of your lives have been solved for me night after night, sometimes only by the touch of a finger under the table-cloth as we sat dining—so fluid has my body become, forming even at the touch of a finger into one full drop, which fills itself, which quivers, which flashes, which falls in ecstasy.

'I have sat before a looking-glass as you sit writing, adding up figures at desks. So, before the looking-glass in the temple of my bedroom, I have judged my nose and my chin; my lips that open too wide and show too much gum. I have looked. I have noted. I have chosen what yellow or white, what shine or dullness, what loop or straightness suits. I am volatile for one, rigid for another, angular as an icicle in silver, or voluptuous as a candle flame in gold. I have run violently like a whip flung out to the extreme end of my tether. His shirt front, there in the corner, has been white; then purple; smoke and flame have wrapped us about; after a furious conflagration—yet we scarcely raised our voices, sitting on the hearth-rug, as we murmured all the secrets of our hearts as into shells so that nobody might hear in the sleeping-house, but I heard the cook stir once, and once we thought the ticking of the clock was a footfall—we have sunk to ashes, leaving no relics, no unburnt bones, no wisps of hair to be kept in lockets such as your intimacies leave behind

them. Now I turn grey; now I turn gaunt; but I look at my
face at midday sitting in front of the looking-glass in broad
daylight, and note precisely my nose, my chin, my lips that
open too wide and show too much gum. But I am not
afraid.'[1]

There we have, clearly drawn, the 'character' of
the surface sensualist who lives only in and for the
moment; and Mrs. Woolf drew equally clearly the
characters of the solid country woman, the riven man
who hides the shy scholar under the figure of the
successful business man, and so on. But what we are
to consider here is Mrs. Woolf's prose style. She was
one of the very few people writing in her day who
had a definite voice, whose anonymous articles in, say,
the *Times Literary Supplement* we at once (usually)
recognized as hers. It is, of course, difficult to say
exactly what it is that gives the voice its recognizable
quality, for the physical sensation is always an elusive
thing, hard to describe. The sentences are all bold,
they end firmly, but there is a kind of fragility about
them as if too harsh an intonation would shatter them.
Compare this passage with the one from George
Moore previously quoted. Both writers depend for
their effect upon the shape itself of the sentence, upon
the inner modulations, and especially upon the play
of vowel sounds, yet when you read them you find
that you are forming Mrs. Woolf's prose further
forward in the mouth, nearer the lips, than Moore's.
How or why this is it might be possible to analyse;
it is enough for us to notice it as a stylistic character.
One further thing it is fruitful to observe is that Mrs.

[1] From *The Waves*, by Virginia Woolf, The Hogarth Press, 1931.

Woolf's style was, more than anybody else's of her time, specifically lyrical; and one must hasten to say what it means when one drags in that much abused word. It means that the effect is got primarily by the sound and the rhythm, not by the sound and rhythm in addition to the images or the subject-matter. It is the rhythm ('the known effects of metre'), the lilt, the changing vowel sounds that produce in the reader the state Mrs. Woolf wanted to produce, not merely the things she brought to view; certain things she presents in the passage quoted are not such as would naturally occur in a lyric. But in that very passage of the dog, note the change from 'snuff' to 'sniff', as a very simple example. Take as a more extended example the sentence beginning 'I am volatile . . .' and ending 'flame in gold', with its ever deepening vowel sounds. And as a final clue to the lyric quality, which exists by virtue of setting going in your head a particular kind of music, there is the repetition of the phrase, 'my lips that open too wide and show too much gum'.

It is not often, however, that the novelist of today allows himself the chance of a set piece of characterization; the person drawn is usually shown by small touches in conversation, sometimes directly revealing by the comments of another person. As an example of this we may take a passage from one book of F. M. Ford's very notable tetralogy, which has not received the praise it deserves.

'Then do you mind,' Tietjens said, 'telling me if you know this road at all?'

'Not a bit!' she answered cheerfully. 'I never drove it in

my life. I looked it up on the map before we started because
I'm sick to death of the road we went by. There's a one-
horse 'bus from Rye to Tenterden, and I've walked from
Tenterden to my uncle's over and over again. . . .'

'We shall probably be out all night then,' Tietjens said.
'Do you mind? The horse may be tired. . . .'

She said:

'Oh, the poor horse! . . . I *meant* us to be out all night. . . .
But the poor horse. . . . What a brute I was not to think of it.'

'We're thirteen miles from a place called Brede; eleven
and a quarter from a place whose name I couldn't read: six
and three-quarters from somewhere called something like
Uddlemere, . . .' Tietjens said. 'This is the road to Uddlemere.'

'Oh, that was Grandfather's Wantways all right,' she
declared. 'I know it well. It's called "Grandfather's"
because an old gentleman used to sit there called Gran'fer
Finn. Every Tenterden market day he used to sell fleed cakes
from a basket to the carts that went by. Tenterden market
was abolished in 1845—the effect of the repeal of the Corn
Laws, you know. As a Tory you ought to be interested in
that.'

Tietjens sat patiently: He could sympathise with her
mood; she had now a heavy weight off her chest; and, if long
acquaintance with his wife had not made him able to put up
with feminine vagaries, nothing ever would.

'Would you mind,' he said then, 'telling me. . . .'

'If,' she interrupted, 'that was really Gran'fer's Wantways:
midland English. "Vent" equals four cross-roads: high
French *carrefour* . . . Or, perhaps, that isn't the right word.
But it's the way your mind works . . .'

'You have, of course, often walked from your uncle's to
Gran'fer's Wantways,' Tietjens said, 'with your cousins, taking
brandy to the invalid in the toll-gate house. That's how you
know the story of Grandfer. You said you had never driven

it; but you *have* walked it. That's the way *your* mind works, isn't it?'

She said: '*Oh!*'

'Then,' Tietjens went on, 'would you mind telling me—for the sake of the poor horse—whether Uddlemere is or isn't on our road home. I take it you don't know just this stretch of road, but you know whether it's the right road.'

'The touch of pathos,' the girl said, 'is a wrong note. It's you who're in mental trouble about the road. The horse isn't . . .'

Tietjens let the cart go on another fifty yards; then he said:

'It *is* the right road. The Uddlemere turning *was* the right one. You wouldn't let the horse go another five steps if it wasn't. You're as soppy about horses as . . . as I am.'

'There's at least that bond of sympathy between us,' she said drily. 'Gran'fer's Wantways is six and three-quarters miles from Udimore; Udimore is exactly five from us; total, eleven and three-quarters; twelve and a quarter if you add half a mile for Udimore itself. The name is Udimore, not Uddlemere. Local place-name enthusiasts derive this from "O'er the mere". Absurd! Legend as follows: Church builders desiring to put church with relic of St. Rumwold in wrong place, voice wailed: "O'er the mere." Obviously absurd! . . . Putrid! "*O'er the*" by Grimm's law impossible as "*Udi*"; "mere" not a middle Low German word at all. . . .'

'Why,' Tietjens said, 'are you giving me all this information?'

'Because,' the girl said, 'it's the way your mind works. . . . It picks up useless facts as silver after you've polished it picks up sulphur vapour; and tarnishes! It arranges the useless facts in obsolescent patterns and makes Toryism out of them. . . . I've never met a Cambridge Tory man before. I thought they were all in museums and you work them up again out of bones. That's what father used to say; he was an Oxford Disraelian Conservative Imperialist. . . .'

'I know of course,' Tietjens said.

'Of course you know,' the girl said. 'You know everything. . . . And you've worked everything into absurd principles. You think father was unsound because he tried to apply tendencies to life. *You* want to be a Nenglish country gentleman and spin principles out of the newspapers and the gossip of horse-fairs. And let the country go to hell, you'll never stir a finger except to say I told you so.'

She touched him suddenly on the arm:

'*Don't* mind me!' she said. 'It's reaction. I'm so happy. I'm so happy.'[1]

A good deal is accomplished even in that short passage, the process of course going on continuously throughout the book; and here is also expressed the girl's nervous condition, her sense of reaction after surviving a tense episode. This art of building up character entirely by conversation has been carried to its utmost limits by Miss Compton-Burnett, where the process is completed by so many delicate touches as to daunt quotation.[2] One may, perhaps give the flavour by citing, ' "Sarah," said Julian . . . "I have not been led into any delicacy, have I ?" ',[3] which at once reveals something of Julian. It is not, one would think, easy to distinguish much of an author's own style from the conversations he reports, but that there is a difference in styles can be judged by comparing the passage from Ford's book with the following. The mind can be guessed at by the sort of thing each writer makes his people say:

I found the Count Greffi in the billiard-room. He was

[1] *Some Do Not,* by Ford Madox Ford, Duckworth, 1924.
[2] But see later.
[3] *Brothers and Sisters,* by I. Compton-Burnett, Heath Cranton, 1929.

practising strokes, looking very fragile under the light that came down above the billiard table. On a card table a little way beyond the light was a silver icing-bucket with the necks and corks of two champagne bottles showing above the ice. The Count Greffi straightened up when I came towards the table and walked towards me. He put out his hand. 'It is such a pleasure that you are here. You were very kind to come to play with me.'

'It was very nice of you to ask me.'

'Are you quite well? They told me you were wounded on the Isonzo. I hope you are well again.'

'I'm very well. Have you been well?'

'Oh, I am always well. But I am getting old. I detect signs of age now.'

'I can't believe it.'

'Yes. Do you want to know one? It is easier for me to talk Italian. I discipline myself but I find when I'm tired that it is so much easier to talk Italian. So I know I must be getting old.'

'We could talk Italian. I am a little tired too.'

'Oh, but when you are tired it will be easier for you to talk English.'

'American.'

'Yes, American. You will please talk American. It is a delightful language.'

'I hardly ever see Americans.'

'You must miss them. One misses one's countrymen and especially one's countrywomen. I know that experience. Should we play or are you too tired?'

'I'm not really tired. I said that for a joke. What handicap will you give me?'

'Have you been playing very much?'

'None at all.'

'You play very well. Ten points in a hundred?'

'You flatter me.'

'Fifteen?'

'That would be fine but you will beat me.'

'Should we play for a stake? You always wished to play for a stake.'

'I think we'd better.'

'All right. I will give you eighteen points and we will play for a franc a point.'

He played a lovely game of billiards and with the handicap I was only four ahead at fifty. Count Greffi pushed a button on the wall to ring for the barman.

'Open one bottle please,' he said. Then to me, 'We will take a little stimulant.' The wine was icy cold and very dry and good.

'Should we talk Italian? Would you mind very much? It is my great weakness now.'

We went on playing, sipping the wine between shots, speaking in Italian, but talking little, concentrated on the game. Count Greffi made his one hundredth point and with the handicap I was only at ninety-four. He smiled and patted me on the shoulder.

'Now we will drink the other bottle and you will tell me about the war.' He waited for me to sit down.

'About anything else,' I said.

'You don't want to talk about it? Good. What have you been reading?'

'Nothing,' I said. 'I'm afraid I am very dull.'

'No. But you should read.'

'What is there written in war-time?'

'There is *Le Feu* by a Frenchman, Barbusse. There is *Mr. Britling Sees Through It*.'

'No, he doesn't.'

'What?'

'He doesn't see through it. Those books were at the hospital.'

'Then you have been reading?'

'Yes, but nothing any good.'

'I thought *Mr. Britling* a very good study of the English middle-class soul.'

'I don't know about the soul.'

'Poor boy. We none of us know about the soul. Are you *Croyant*?'

'At night.' Count Greffi smiled and turned the glass with his fingers.

'I had expected to become more devout as I grow older but somehow I haven't,' he said. 'It is a great pity.'

'Would you like to live after death?' I asked and instantly felt a fool to mention death. But he did not mind the word.

'It would depend on the life. This life is very pleasant. I would like to live for ever,' he smiled. 'I very nearly have.'

We were sitting in the deep leather chairs, the champagne in the ice-bucket and our glasses on the table between us.

'If you ever live to be as old as I am you will find many things strange.'

'You never seem old.'

'It is the body that is old. Sometimes I am afraid I will break off a finger as one breaks a stick of chalk. And the spirit is no older and not much wiser.'

'You are wise.'

'No, that is the great fallacy, the wisdom of old men. They do not grow wise. They grow careful.'

'Perhaps that is wisdom.'

'It is a very unattractive wisdom. What do you value most?'

'Someone I love.'

'With me it is the same. That is not wisdom. Do you value life?'

'Yes.'

'So do I. Because it is all I have. And to give birthday parties,' he laughed. 'You are probably wiser than I am. You do not give birthday parties.'

We both drank the wine.

'What do you think of the war really?' I asked.

'I think it is stupid.'

'Who will win it?'

'Italy.'

'Why?'

'They are a younger nation.'

'Do younger nations always win wars?'

'They are apt to for a time.'

'Then what happens?'

'They become older nations.'

'You said you were not wise.'

'Dear boy, that is not wisdom. That is cynicism.'

'It sounds very wise to me.'

'It's not particularly. I could quote you the examples on the other side. But it is not bad. Have we finished the champagne?'

'Almost.'

'Should we drink some more? Then I must dress.'

'Perhaps we'd better not now.'

'You are sure you don't want more?'

'Yes.' He stood up.

'I hope you will be very fortunate and very happy and very healthy.'

'Thank you. And I hope you will live for ever.'

'Thank you, I have. And if you ever become devout pray for me if I am dead. I am asking several of my friends to do that. I had expected to become devout myself but it has not come.' I thought he smiled sadly but I could not tell. He was so old and his face was very wrinkled, so that a smile used so many lines that all gradations were lost.

'I might become very devout,' I said. 'Anyway I will pray for you.'

'I had always expected to become devout. All my family died very devout. But somehow it does not come.'

'It's too early.'

'Maybe it is too late. Perhaps I have outlived my religious feeling.'

'My own comes at night.'

'Then too you are in love. Do not forget that is a religious feeling.'

'You believe so?'

'Of course.' He took a step towards the table. 'You were very kind to play.'

'It was a great pleasure.'

'We will walk upstairs together.'[1]

Since that is a complete portrait, it differs in method from Ford's presentation; but method apart there is a marked difference in style. Hemingway got his effects largely by repetitions, and by using the simplest words and ideas. And, oddly enough, he gives the impression of being sentimental by his avoidance of the sentimental, by being as matter of fact as possible. His lines are very simple, and it is by saying the same thing over and over again that he impresses them on you. We find that after all, although the authors wish to speak through other mouths, they are still speaking with their own voice.

There is just one more aspect of the description of persons that may be considered, and that is of the person considered as part of a background, put in not so much for his or her own sake as to help to produce atmosphere. This first extract comes directly after a description of Miss Reba's two dogs, 'small, woolly, white, worm-like dogs'.

Later Temple could hear them outside her door, whimpering and scuffing, or, rushing thickly in when the negro maid

[1] From *A Farewell to Arms*, by Ernest Hemingway, Cape, 1929.

opened the door, climbing and sprawling on to the bed and into Miss Reba's lap with wheezy, flatulent sounds, billowing into the rich pneumasis of her breast and tonguing along the metal tankard which she waved in one ringed hand as she talked. . . .

Her slightest movement appeared to be accompanied by an expenditure of breath out of all proportion to any pleasure the movement could afford her. Almost as soon as they entered the house she began to tell Temple about her asthma, toiling up the stairs in front of them, planting her feet heavily in worsted bedroom slippers, a wooden rosary in one hand and the tankard in the other. She had just returned from church, in a black silk gown and a hat savagely flowered; the lower half of the tankard was still frosted with inner chill. She moved heavily from big thigh to thigh, the two dogs moiling underfoot, talking steadily back across her shoulder in a harsh, expiring, maternal voice.

To tear extracts out of this chapter does not give the sense of the figure merging into the background; we have to read also the description of the house, with its significant noises, its 'narrow stairwell' which 'turned back upon itself in a succession of niggard reaches', the sinister clock. But we may return to Miss Reba, to see her as an object.

. . . Temple watched the door until it opened and Miss Reba stood in it, the tankard in her hand. She now wore a bulging house dress and a widow's bonnet with a veil. She entered on the flowered felt slippers. Beneath the bed the two dogs made a stifled concerted sound of utter despair.

The dress, unfastened in the back, hung lumpily about Miss Reba's shoulders. One ringed hand lay on her breast, the other held the tankard high. Her open mouth, studded with gold-fillings, gaped upon the harsh labour of her breathing.

'Oh God, oh God,' she said. The dogs surged out from beneath the bed and hurled themselves toward the door in a mad scrabble. As they rushed past her she turned and flung the tankard at them. It struck the door jamb, splashing up the wall, and rebounded with a forlorn clatter. She drew her breath whistling, clutching her breast. She came to the bed and looked down at Temple through the veil. 'We was happy as two doves,' she wailed, choking, her rings smouldering in hot glints within her billowing breast. 'Then he had to go and die on me.' She drew her breath whistling, her mouth gaped, shaping the hidden agony of her thwarted lungs, her eyes pale and round with stricken bafflement, protuberant. 'As two doves,' she roared, in a harsh, choking voice.[1]

Faulkner is going to make you see, make you understand, by his fresh use of words, their surprising applicability every time. It is the vividness of his adjectives, added to the firm, underlining stroke of every sentence, that pushes the image home: the hat *savagely* flowered, the *harsh, expiring, maternal* voice, the *thwarted* lungs; or the extended adjective, as of the rings *smouldering* in hot glints; or, the sound echoing the sense, 'gaped upon the harsh labour of her breathing'. Faulkner had the essential element of a stylist; he appreciated the colour of words.

[1] From *Sanctuary,* by William Faulkner, Chatto and Windus, 1931.

§ 3

Description of Things

I n the main, description of things can be divided into two classes, the scientific and the imaginative. With the former we shall have little to do, in its strictest form, because, though it is in its way admirable, the experts who write it can communicate only with their fellow experts. For instance, do we ordinary mortals get any impression of the friendly primrose from the following?

> Herbs, with radical leaves; the flowers either solitary or in a terminal umbel, on leafless, radical peduncles. Calyx tubular or campanulate, with 5 teeth or lobes not reaching to the base. Corolla with a straight tube, and a spreading, 5-lobed limb, each lobe often notched or 2-cleft. Capsule opening at the top in five teeth.[1]

That is probably as 'pure' description as you can get, prose which rigorously excludes any appeal to the emotion, any association. A primrose on the river's brim a simple primrose is to him, and it is *nothing more*. It is the achievement of science that it can provide description and nothing more. It can do the same thing in describing events, in the form of a railway time-table, though, of course, emotion cannot be excluded if the reader brings it with him. The words 'Arr. Paddington 3.45' may be charged with feeling for Romeo who is going to meet Juliet by that train. When scientists write 'popular science' they cease to

[1] Bentham's *British Flora*.

be scientific; popular science is a delusion, because an object, a series of operations, a theory, cannot mean the same thing to a man who has handled the material, knows the implications of the work done, and understands the reservations of the theory, as to the man who is innocent of them.

Yet there is a form of prose which approaches the scientific, the prose written by field-naturalists; but they write from the love of the thing they are describing, and they want to impart their own delight to you. Nevertheless, the best form of this prose is undoubtedly that which relies upon statement of fact to produce delight rather than upon any exterior decoration; the art, in fact, is to get the effect without obvious aids.

To these Northern dawns, as surely as to the sunlight of April over the water-meadows of the South, belongs for me that dominant sound of spring skies, the drumming of the snipe. Wherever I may hear it, the thoughts it brings with it are of the same things, of cloud and blue reflected in water, of the smell of wet earth and of growing plants, of birds gone wild in the mating months. And whenever I hear it, the sound comes fresh and new and insistent; I wait for it in the intervals of silence and know as I listen that there is no other like it that I shall ever hear. For snipe drum in the breeding season; and of the three species that we may call British, two, the great snipe and the jack snipe, only visit us in the winter. And no other bird but the snipe drums as he does—though drumming is not the best word for the sound made not by striking but vibration; humming, perhaps, would be a better.

And to understand the sound you must watch the bird, as I have watched snipe for hours together, and have caught

from them some of the new pulses stirring them. The centre
of the bird's life is its nest, or the chosen spot where its nest
is to be, and where, perhaps, its mate sits among the rushes.
Above the nest it flies up and round, high and fast, soars up
with beating wings, slants down again sideways with wings
half closed and tail spread, and—these are the tiny points to
pick up with the field-glasses—the two outer feathers of the
tail rigid and at right angles to the body. Up again move the
beating wings, down again slides the bird aslant, again sounds
the drum. And it is the rushing air that fans the web of those
stiff feathers that is the snipe's drumming. For many years,
a decade or two ago, there were disputes as to how the drumming was done, some said by the wings, some in the throat;
but there is really no doubt about it, as anyone can prove for
himself by sticking the two tail feathers at right angles into
the shaft of an arrow and shooting it into the air. The sound
as the arrow descends is the very sound of the drumming, the
sound that has named the bird in country places the heather-
bleater. There must be many Englishmen in any year who
walk by the marshes and meadows and hear the sound and
look about them to find a goat.[1]

That is admirably clean, and in a curious way Mr.
Parker has been able to suggest the stillness of the
watcher, perhaps quite unaware. One would say,
though one might be ludicrously wrong, that Mr.
Parker speaks with a soft voice. It is certainly through
his prose voice that he conveys the thing, and, without ever expressing it, his joy in the existence of the
thing. How far he depends for his effect on our
associations it is hard to say; those of us who have
actually looked round for a goat when we heard a

---

[1] From *English Wild Life*, by Eric Parker, Longmans, Green & Co.

snipe drumming will experience the pleasure of recognition on reading his last sentence; we cannot avoid being influenced by the happiness we have had of marshes under clear or cloud-flecked skies: but that is only evidence of how well Mr. Parker has described the thing. It is all perfectly simple; the proportion of monosyllables is unusually high, yet Mr. Parker manages to avoid the wooden effect that so often goes with that style of writing: the whole is sustained by the cadences which come naturally to him as he speaks.

I would venture to say that his description is perfect, but that there are some who would not agree with that verdict. Among them would be Paul Elmer More, who considered that 'Mere description, though it may at times have a scientific value, is, after all, a very cheap form of literature', because 'too much curiosity of detail is likely to exert a deadening influence on the philosophic and poetic contemplation of nature'. This raises too many issues to be considered here, but as a comment on More's 'after all' we might ask 'after all what?' Let us see, however, how More considered a description of nature should be treated: it is extremely interesting as showing what actually does happen:

Dear as the sound of the wood thrush's note still is to my ears, something of charm and allurement has gone from it since I have become intimate with the name and habits of the bird. As a child born and reared in the city, that wild, ringing call was perfectly new and strange to me when, one early dawn, I first heard it during a visit to the Delaware Water Gap. To me whose ears had grown familiar only with the

rumble of paved streets, the sound was like a reiterated unearthly summons inviting me from my narrow prison existence out into a wide and unexplored world of impulse and
adventure. Long afterwards I learned the name of the
songster whose note had made so strong an impression on my
childish senses, but still I associate the song with the grandiose
scenery, with the sheer forests and streams and the rapid river
of the Water Gap. I was indeed almost a man—though the
confession may sound incredible in these days—before I
again heard the wood thrush's note, and my second adventure
impressed me almost as profoundly as the first. In the outer
suburbs of the city where my home had always been, I was
walking one day with a brother, when suddenly out of a grove
of laurel oaks sounded, clear and triumphant, the note which
I remembered so well, but which had come to have to my
imagination the unreality and mystery of a dream of long ago.
Instantly my heart leapt within me. 'It is the fateful summons
once more!' I cried; and, with my companion who was
equally ignorant of bird-lore, I ran into the grove to discover
the wild trumpeter. That was a strange chase in the fading
twilight, while the unknown songster led us from tree to
tree, ever deeper into the woods. Many times we saw him
on one of the lower boughs, but could not for a long while
bring ourselves to believe that so wondrous a melody should
proceed from so plain a minstrel. And at last, when we had
satisfied ourselves of his identity, and the night had fallen, we
came out into the road with a strange solemnity hanging over
us. Our ears had been opened to the unceasing harmonies of
creation, and our eyes had been made aware of the endless
drama of natural life. We had been initiated into the lesser
mysteries; and if the sacred pageantry was not then, and
never was to be, perfectly clear to our understanding, the
imagination was nevertheless awed and purified.[1]

[1] From *A Hermit's Note on Thoreau* from *Shelburne Essays* I. i
(Houghton Mifflin).

I submit that what happens when a writer eschews 'mere description' in favour of philosophic or poetical contemplation, is that he fails to be either philosophic or poetic, and gives us a portrait of himself. The only salvation for any writer is to keep his eye on the object. If the object is a thrush, let him keep his eye on the thrush; if philosophy, let him keep his inward eye on philosophy: in either instance he may achieve art, which he will certainly not do if he keeps it on poetry. The passage, we need have no doubt, is an excellent portrait of More. He was an incurable romantic, trying to extract more out of a definite thing than that thing has to give, and he betrayed this by his continual forcing of the note. To my ear, though perhaps not to others', More's style here is weak because it is false: he is not speaking in his natural voice: there is falsification everywhere, a stringing together of word associations. We may pass by the ejaculation 'It is the fateful summons once more!' More may have uttered it; we may doubt it, but we were not there to hear. We suspect that he said, 'There's that bird again!' Such a phrase, however, as 'had come to have to my imagination the unreality and mystery of a dream of long ago' rouses profound suspicions. When we come to 'the unceasing harmonies of nature' and 'the endless drama of natural life' those suspicions are confirmed. It is phrase-making, for we feel that the endless drama of natural life is hardly exhibited by a thrush flitting about from bush to bush. All philosophy, I hope, and all poetry I am sure, depends upon a vivid sense of actuality; thus Mr. Parker's 'mere description' has both more poetry and more

philosophy than More's brooding. Mr. Parker gives
us the material for both poetry and philosophy, and we
prefer to bring our own philosophy to nature, not to
have indicated to us what we should feel. If the object
of the description of a thing is to give us the thing
and the sensations that belong to it, Mr. Parker suc-
ceeds, More fails. This is not to say, however, that
More may not have written a good emotive passage;
that is a question that would require another analysis.
All we can be certain of is, that he has not given us
a good description of nature, of a thing.

The word 'thing', of course, is not used here to
denote only physical objects, but rather as a con-
venient word which will convey neither events nor
persons. In the following passage there is, indeed, a
faint trickle of event; persons are part of the 'thing',
but neither is what matters. It is a state of affairs that
is being described, and what conduces to it is merely
incidental:

Stumbling and splashing up a communication trench known
as Canterbury Avenue, with the parcel of smoked salmon
stuffed into my haversack, I felt that smoked salmon wasn't
much of an antidote for people who had been putting up with
all that shell-fire. Still, it was something. . . . Round the next
corner I had to flatten myself against the wall of that wet
ditch, for someone was being carried down on a stretcher.
An extra stretcher-bearer walking behind told me it was
Corporal Price of 'C' company. 'A rifle-grenade got him . . .
looks as if he's a goner. . . .' His face was only a blur of
white in the gloom; then with the drumming of their boots
on the trench-boards, Corporal Price left the war behind him.
I remembered him vaguely as a quiet little man in Durley's

platoon. No use offering *him* smoked salmon, I thought, as I came to the top of Canterbury Avenue, and, as usual, lost my way in the maze of saps and small trenches behind the front line. Watling Street was the one I wanted. Finding one's way about the trenches in the dark was no easy job when one didn't live up there. I passed the dug-outs of the support company at Maple Redoubt. Candles and braziers glinted through the curtain-flaps and voices muttered gruffly from the little underground cabins (which would have been safer if they had been deeper down in the earth). Now and again there was the splitting crack of a rifle-shot from the other side, or a five-nine shell droned serenely across the upper air to burst with a hollow bang; voluminous reverberations rolled along the valley. The shallow blanching flare of a rocket gave me a glimpse of the mounds of bleached sand-bags on the Redoubt. Its brief whiteness died downward, leaving a dark world; chilly gusts met me at corners, piping drearily through crannies of the parapet; very different was the voice of the wind that sang in the cedar tree in the garden at home. . . .

Pushing past the gas-blanket, I blundered down the stairs to the company headquarters' dug-out. There were twenty steps to that earthy smelling den, with its thick wooden props down the middle and its precarious yellow candlelight casting wobbling shadows. Barton was sitting on a box at the rough table, with a tin mug, and a half-empty whisky bottle. His shoulders were hunched and the collar of his trench-coat was turned up to his ears. Dick was in deep shadow, lying on a bunk (made of wire-netting with empty sandbags on it). It was a morose cramped little scene, loathsome to live in as it is hateful to remember. The air was dank and musty; lumps of chalk fell from the 'ceiling' at intervals. There was a bad smell of burnt grease, and the frizzle of something frying in the adjoining kennel that was called the kitchen was the only evidence of ordinary civilization—that and Barton's shining pince-nez, and the maps and notebooks which were on the table. . . .[1]

What Mr. Sassoon was doing here was to create atmosphere, evoking it skilfully by means of contrasts of things stated in contrasting series of vowel-sounds —'voluminous reverberations rolled along the valley'; 'lumps of chalk fell from the "ceiling" at intervals'. And as you read the latter end of this book (a short extract hardly gives the effect), you become conscious of being spoken to in a voice of sadness and utter resignation. This sense seems to be conveyed almost entirely by the plain statement of the existence of things—'that and Barton's shining pince-nez, and the maps and notebooks which were on the table'.

But what makes the statement different from other possible statements is the way the sentences are modelled. You find on looking into this that the main stresses all come at the beginning of each sentence; they become less and less emphatic towards the end; the sharply marked rhythmic beats die away. And only when, twice, he ends on the word 'redoubt' does Mr. Sassoon end on a firm, sharp syllable. Either he concludes on a weak one—'valley', 'bottle', 'table' —or on a long one, preferably with an open vowel— 'platoon', 'there', 'home'. Consciously? That is most unlikely. He could speak in no other way when he was saying that kind of thing.

Imaginative description of things, one is led to suppose, consists chiefly in the creation of atmosphere. An object only becomes 'imaginative' when it is seen

[1] From *Memoirs of a Fox-Hunting Man*, by Siegfried Sassoon, Faber and Faber, 1928.

through an atmosphere. Create the latter, and you can put almost any object in it, and the object will appear imaginatively described. What, for instance, London in May will look like, or feel like, will depend entirely upon the state of mind of the person describing it:

The whole city was in flower. The first impression was one of blossoming. And over all and above all sounded the magnificent, lion-mouthed roar of the traffic. The grey, busy streets and circuses, ablaze with the swift, raucous yellow and red flames of the omnibuses, were further sprinkled with the gigantic, Victorian bouquets of the flower-women. Through the elegant screen at Hyde Park Corner, through the graceful arches between the pearly stone-pillars, the old trees could be seen once more waving their green fingers on the spring breeze, that struggled under them like a bird. Beneath this quivering shade, the first warm sun of the year had caused to flutter out from their cells and hives every kind of brilliantly coloured insect. The drone of talk lingered on the warm, cigarette-scented air, while not far away there sounded a continous accompaniment in the muffled thudding of cantering hooves. Almost extinct specimens, boasting every kind of check, gaiter and whisker, were trotting sternly up and down, as though this action of theirs must convey a vast amount to a great many people, as though, for example, they were carrying an all-important despatch to the Commander-in-Chief, while every now and then a riding-master would go past, instructing the cluster of children round him just as a duck teaches her young to swim. In the great yellow squares, the crooks and dry sticks of the shrubberies were breaking into little rosettes of shrill green or posies of pink-and-white that spread their ephemeral wings on the mild spring air, while the innumerable soot-stained iron-railings that guarded the faint, Persian torches of the lilac, already a little burning down, for once clearly showed themselves too solid for their delicate work. The statue in the centre of each garden had assumed a new and wistful coyness, as it struck its heavy, oratorical pose in the midst of so much lightness of leaf and petal. Even the houses seemed to be blossoming—a great smell of paint being the scent that these ponderous flowers exhaled—for the residences of the rich had just been dizened for them, while in some cases the process had not yet been finished, and up ladders, on planks and round the tops of houses, the white-coated workmen were still forming their own ever-shifting but hieratic friezes. This smell of paint fought against the country scents gently breathed out by every young leaf and crinkled blossom, and mingled with that of tar and petrol, for cars and taxicabs were purring softly over the watery black surface of the roads, shining and smooth as canals, through the amber and clouded heat of a hot London morning. Outside one square block of a house, a red and white awning was already being erected; large, rectangular vans drove up on their tiny wheels, and men hurried in and out. And Tristram thought of how, in the evening, the gondola-like cars would glide up to houses with a lacquered inevitability, and cascades and showers of golden light would splash and shiver down from the wide-open windows into the darkness. From them, too, would float the over-sympathetic hooting and sobbing of saxophones, as they gurgled and throbbed out those tunes which, in spite of their self-satisfied brazen rhythms and savage gorilla-like drummings that pretend to constitute an incitement to worship before Venus, have yet under them a good solid bottom of hell-fire! For beneath every jazz rhythm was hidden the mournful whining of the Wesleyan Chapel, the austere howlings of the Pilgrim Fathers, as much as the comfortable self-righteousness of 'Hymns Ancient and Modern': as dance-music, it was, in fact, comparable to the daughter of a clergyman who earns renown by playing an unexpectedly daring part on the music-hall stage. Still, the traffic, even at this hour, would roar loud above such melodious thumpings and moanings. At night its waves would arrange themselves into their wonted tiers, each one serving a different need or pleasure of the town: there would be the after-theatre wave, the later one of the pleasure-seekers returning home, both westward: and then the lorries, piled up with vegetables and provisions, would pound and lumber eastward.[1]

The atmosphere of lightness, of liquid, cool air trembling into heat, of brilliant colour, is attained by continually keeping the mind alert to fancy. Every physical object is made the starting-point of an idea. This is not an instance of a passage overburdened with metaphor, for the whole point of the passage is to release you from the actuality of things. Normally, metaphor or simile point at the object; here the object points the way to a metaphor. There is indeed one flaw in the paragraph; the passage about the Wesleyan chapel is amusing enough in itself, and true, but it is out of key, for there the mind is asked to be something more than the organ of sense, it is to be that of criticism and memory. The sentences are long, but there is an alert gait about them, the rhythm is a springy one; there is a constant play of vowels and consonants; a certain amount of what used to be called 'imitative harmony', such as 'would pound and lumber east-ward': it is difficult to determine how much it is the things presented to us, and how much the voice in which they are presented, that produces atmosphere in the reader.

This way of description by creating the atmosphere,

[1] From *The Man Who Lost Himself*, by Osbert Sitwell, Duckworth, 1929.

a result arrived at by bringing inanimate things to
life, can, however, be done much more simply and
directly, not so much by presenting the reader with
the atmosphere ready-made, as by giving him the
objects and relying on his sensibility to evoke the
atmosphere for himself; or rather, seeming to, for
here again the rhythm is really the decisive factor, a
rhythm which alternately soothes and jerks the reader
into the right state of receptive consciousness. To the
reader who respects himself, and is unwilling to be
altogether passive, some of the pleasure he gets from
books is due to a direct collaboration with the author.
The method is perhaps superior, but all that this
means is that it is addressed to a slightly different
class of reader. This is what is done in the following
passage. We have been told that tapestries previously
described are to be sunk in the river for cleaning:

It would be the most beautiful experience imaginable to
float down the river and be brought by the stream against
one after another of the tapestries, to have to pass down their
histories, moving from end to end of their length, to hear the
water flowing though them, pass by their paper thickness,
look back to the ghostly forms hardly discernible out of that
voice of water sounding from them, and to see plumes and
then helmets rising out of the next grave of heroes, for as they
come nearer they never move and are as dead as in the tomb.
The swords flashing in the water, the glint of the armour,
come up in their turn out of this passing of time through their
bones, and before the tapestry has been touched by the boat
even the little flowers of the ground can be seen starring the
meadows. The field is powdered with daisies, and with little
blue flowers as small as the blossom of the water-weeds that
have been banked against the tapestry by the force of the

stream, and that cannot pass through it with the water that carried them. They are piled up in a heap of trodden garlands, with twigs of wood, blades of grass, and all the refuse of the stream, and twine themselves on the rope that supports all this imagery in the river. It can be lifted with an oar and thrown over to the other side, when it drifts down towards the next tapestry and lets in a still clearer light to fall upon the place that it has freed.

The banks have become a thicket of ropes, every few yards, and the whole river is pitched and divided with this tent-like machinery set up in order to clean the tapestries. Further down, when this set has been passed, come the other hangings that these pages have described. The Hunting tapestries, the Shepherds and the Shepherdesses, the Wood-cutters, all these are in the river, breaking the swift flow with their coloured nets.

The figures come out fresh and clear as new; the tongues of the hounds hang red from their mouths; the jewels upon the horse-trappings glitter in the false sunlight sifted to them through the water; and the young man whose sleeve and shoulder are worked with the device of a cloud shedding drops of rain, or tears, is young once more. Blood runs in his veins, the hounds tug at their leash, and the rain, or tears, upon his sleeve shake with his breath and seem to dance like the motes in a beam of light. The Royal Hunt is in the shallow woods, stirring the fallen leaves with their press of hoofs. The horns wind and rumble in the distance; the cranking waterwheel lifts and falls, and the miller's daughter comes out of the house again to talk to the fisherman.[1]

Apart from the gradual change from describing tapestries to describing the real life the tapestries have brought into being, there is in that passage another deliberate attempt to confuse realms, namely

[1] From *The Visit of the Gypsies*, by Sacheverell Sitwell, Duckworth, 1929.

that of sight and sound. We are asked to see the forms through the voice of the water sounding from them: but this is not illegitimate, not mere trickery, something divorced from experience, for sound can confuse the sight. What we can notice, however, in comparing this passage with the last, is that the rhythms of this one, instead of keeping us alert, tend to make us dreamy. This is the effect of 'to see plumes and then helmets rising out of the next grave of heroes, for as they come nearer they never move and are as dead as in the tomb', as it is that of the two long sounds of 'move' and 'tomb', and the flat sound of 'dead'. Compare the effect of that with, to choose at random, 'as it struck its heavy, oratorical pose in the midst of so much lightness of leaf and petal'. With the former we glide (the sounds come from the back of the throat), with the latter we dance (the words are composed of dentals and labials): in doing each we lay open a different part of our sensibilities.

In these two last examples the 'thing' has been imaginatively described so as to create a state of mind in you which will release the imagination to play over something which seems to be a little to one side of the object; really you only half attend to the object; you are all the time catching at connexions outside it. More is implied than is actually stated, but that more you must add for yourself; it is something that you must produce out of your experience, not out of the object. Previous extracts quoted have tried to give you the object itself. They cannot, of course, give it you completely, for black marks on white paper cannot be a snipe or a dug-out; you must make them real by thinking of a snipe or a dug-out, and it is in this way that the objects themselves have been given you. These may be within your experience, at all events they will be enough in your experience to enable you to construct the object, and from that the emotion proper to the object. But suppose it is outside your experience? Then the imaginative description must enable you to construct from outside it:

The wind by now was more than redoubled. The shutters were bulging as if tired elephants were leaning against them, and Father was trying to tie the fastening with that handkerchief. But to push against this wind was like pushing against rock. The handkerchief, shutters, everything burst: the rain poured in like the sea into a sinking ship, the wind occupied the room, snatching pictures from the wall, sweeping the table bare. Through the gaping frames the lightning-lit scene without was visible. The creepers, which before had looked like cobwebs, now streamed up into the sky like new-combed hair. Bushes were lying flat, laid back on the ground as close as a rabbit lays back his ears. Branches were leaping about loose in the sky. The negro huts were clean gone, and the negroes crawling on their stomachs across the compound to gain the shelter of the house. The bouncing rain seemed to cover the ground with a white smoke, a sort of sea in which the blacks wallowed like porpoises. One nigger-boy began to roll away: his mother, forgetting caution, rose to her feet: and immediately the fat old beldam was blown clean away, bowling along across fields and hedgerows like some one in a funny fairy-story, till she fetched up against a wall and was pinned there, unable to move. But the others managed to reach the house, and soon could be heard in the cellar underneath.[1]

[1] From *A High Wind in Jamaica*, by Richard Hughes, Chatto and Windus, 1929.

There the attack is quite different; the voice is urgent. We are not to be made receptive, but, as it were, to be hurtled into the very turmoil of the hurricane. The short, sharp sentences, nearly all beginning with a short, sharp noun—'The wind', 'Bushes', 'Branches'—the vivid similes and metaphors which seem to owe nothing to fancy but to be almost direct photographic likeness, give us no time to think or muse: one image comes close on the top of another. It is our eyes, not our minds or our imaginations, that are alert. We see things that we never saw before. There is no artifice in this as there is in the Sitwell passages, but that is not to say there is no art. It is imaginative description written in the same direct manner as the scientific kind, but the intent relates it to the former.

It is, then, possible to make us 'see' things with the imaginative eye; but can we be made to see them more directly, as we might think, without atmosphere? The difference, possibly, is only one of emphasis, or perhaps of the thing you are expected to see. It will be admitted that the descriptions of things so far quoted are obviously written by literary men, men, that is, for whom the word is the great evoker of ideas. But is it possible to use the word to evoke simply the thing itself, as a painter might see it?

If you follow the valley of the Manzanares below Madrid you come to a pleasant banlieue. The road is lined by trees, and, standing a little way back from it are *guinguettes* with arbours where the Madrilenes come of Sunday afternoons and evenings. Striking up from the valley one passes through a little wood and comes out on to a landscape that somehow came to represent for me the peculiar character of Madrid. Low hills slope upwards in gentle and varied undulations, with here a scrap of cornland, there a sewage-farm, and elsewhere almost barren sandy soil; a glaring dusty road winds gently upwards towards the flat ridge, which is crowned by a line of modern flats and factories stretching a long arm out from the town into the bare upland country, and against all this one great cypress draws a black bar across the dazzling sky and the rolling earth-waves. The cypress and the dazzle proclaim that one is in the South, and yet all the rest seems familiar and Northern, like the elm wood one has just traversed. For that is the peculiarity of Spain: in so meridional a light the vegetation belongs almost entirely to the North. Elms, ashes, sycamores, so little thinkable in Provence, become once more the rule in this land, which is none the less even more arid and more Southern in its other aspects. That cypresses flourish in Spain is evident from their height and growth. But how rare they are, and how much they would improve the landscape if they were common—for nothing can be more appropriate than the contrasts of their black green on the ochres and umbers of Spanish town and hillside. As some compensation the Northern trees tend to take on a certain blue metallic hardness which makes them stand out stark and clear-cut on the tawny and grey of the earth. Velasquez seized on that and summarized it brilliantly in those all-too abstract and decorative backgrounds of his portraits of princes in hunting costume.

The path skirts the edge of the rolling hills where they descend into the flat of the Manzanares valley, and a strangely delightful country unrolls itself. On one side is the valley woodland slightly formalized by having once been laid out as a park and subsequently neglected, on the other the succession of bare rolling hillocks, with here and there a lonely ash or elm; and where the hills end in low sand-cliffs, old ruined walls are held up by huge crumbling buttresses; and further

on neglected tanks and weedy fountains reflect the cypresses
and sky. A quite peculiar land, as though the Villa Medici
and Hampstead Heath had been rolled into one. One strikes
into a pastoral and idyllic little valley, climbs a small hill, and
there is the long, low, two-storied villa or small palace of
Moncloa, standing on the level brow of the hill. From the
terrace wall one looks plumb down on to lower terraces and
walled gardens and, over them and the Manzanares valley, to
the distant snow-line of the Guadarrama.[1]

That is, possibly, as close as we can get; and it is probable that only a painter could have written it, would
have seen, for example, the cypress drawing a black
bar across the dazzling sky and rolling earth-waves.
When you come to think about it, this is an extraordinarily tactful piece of writing: though the word
is important, it is never allowed to take your eye from
the physical picture. It is an evocative passage, but
just evocative enough, no more. The emotion is carefully damped, by such phrases as 'that cypresses
flourish in Spain is evident by their height and
growth', and the technical reference to Velasquez.
Nothing but the eye is ever appealed to, and the tone
of the voice, with its low modulations, is that of a man
showing you things, adding words which point you
out their visual significance alone. Roger Fry had the
great virtue of reticence: he would not try to force you
farther than you were willing to go.

[1] From *A Sampler of Castille*, by Roger Fry, Hogarth Press, 1923.

PART II
EXPLANATORY PROSE

§ I

Science

THE object of explanatory prose is to set out *how* things happen, not to describe them *as* they happen. The purest form of it is scientific description, which should be, one supposes, as impersonal, as voiceless as possible. One can invent it for oneself: 'When the piston working in the cylinder has compressed the petrol vapour to a certain point, the make and break in the magneto causes a spark to fly from one point to another of the sparking plug, and thus produces an explosion which drives the piston back. The piston rod . . .' and so on.[1]

There is, no doubt, plenty of such description to be found in a thousand and one text-books, but it is of no interest to us here, simply because the voice of the human being is not to be heard in it; and if science were no more than description (which some people maintain), description, moreover, only of things so carefully sifted that the describer cannot make any choice, scientific writing would all be of the order to which the extract from Bentham given in the last chapter belongs. But science is more than description;

---

[1] I do not wish to be held responsible for the mechanical accuracy of this description.

it is showing the relation of things, and not to other things alone, but to concepts also. Sometimes it consists altogether of formulating concepts, and in these days when once more 'Physics from metaphysics begs defence', it is often difficult to distinguish between science and philosophy.

At all events, science today explains in a degree that mere description will not satisfy: it is concerned with hypothesis as much as with fact, and although it still has to do with the 'how' and not the 'why' of things, the moment the mind is concerned with hypothesis, personality enters in. One can nearly always tell this at once by the tinge of eagerness that creeps into the voice. Still, there is some prose free of this slightly higher pitch, prose which can definitely rank as scientific, purely expository prose, yet from which personality is not excluded because hypothesis is at the basis of the explanation. Here, for instance, is a passage:

The excitation of the calcium atom is performed by light of two particular wave-lengths, and the atoms in the chromosphere support themselves by robbing sunlight of these two constituents. It is true that after a hundred-millionth of a second a relapse comes and the atom has to disgorge what it has appropriated; but in re-emitting the light it is as likely to send it inwards as outwards, so that the *outflowing* sunlight suffers more loss than it recovers. Consequently, when we view the sun through this mantle of calcium the spectrum shows gaps or dark lines at the two wave-lengths concerned. These lines are denoted by the letters H and K. They are not entirely black, and it is important to measure the residual light at the centre of the lines, because we know that it must have an intensity just strong enough to keep calcium atoms floating under solar gravity; as soon as the outflowing light is so weakened that it can support no more atoms it can suffer no further depredations, and so it emerges into outer space with this limiting intensity. The measurement gives numerical data for working out the constants of the calcium atom including the time of relaxation mentioned above.

The atoms at the top of the chromosphere rest on the weakened light which has passed through the screen below; the full sunlight would blow them away. Milne has deduced a consequence which may perhaps have a practical application in the phenomena of explosion of 'new stars' or novae, and in any case is curiously interesting. Owing to the Doppler effect a moving atom absorbs a rather different wave-length from a stationary atom; so that if for any cause an atom moves away from the sun it will support itself on light which is a little to one side of the deepest absorption. This light, being more intense than that which provides a balance, will make the atom recede faster. The atom's own absorption will thus gradually draw clear of the absorption of the screen below. Speaking rather metaphorically, the atom is balanced precariously on the summit of the absorption line and it is liable to topple off into the full sunlight on one side. Apparently the speed of the atom should go on increasing until it has to climb an adjacent absorption line (due perhaps to some other element); if the line is too intense to be surmounted the atom will stick part-way up, the velocity remaining fixed at a particular value. These later inferences may be rather far-fetched, but at any rate the argument indicates that there is likely to be an escape of calcium into outer space.[1]

That is impersonal enough, yet it could, one sees, have been done in another way: that is to say that only Sir Arthur Eddington could have written it as it is

[1] From *Stars and Atoms*, by A. S. Eddington, Oxford University Press, 1929.

written. But the easiest way to see that it has a special quality of its own is to put it beside another passage:

Images are of various sorts, according to the nature of the sensations which they copy. Images of bodily movements, such as we have when we imagine moving an arm or, on a smaller scale, pronouncing a word, might possibly be explained away on Professor Watson's lines, as really consisting in small incipient movements such as, if magnified and prolonged, would be the movements we are said to be imagining. Whether this is the case or not might even be decided experimentally. If there were a delicate instrument for recording small movements in the mouth and throat, we might place such an instrument in a person's mouth and then tell him to recite a poem to himself, as far as possible only in imagination. I should not be at all surprised if it were found that actual small movements take place while he is 'mentally' saying over the verses. The point is important, because what is called 'thought' consists mainly (though I think not wholly) of inner speech. If Professor Watson is right as regards inner speech, this whole region is transferred from imagination to sensation. But since the question is capable of experimental decision, it would be gratuitous rashness to offer an opinion while the decision is lacking.

But visual and auditory images are much more difficult to deal with in this way, because they lack the connexion with physical events in the outer world which belongs to visual and auditory sensations. Suppose, for example, that I am sitting in my room, in which there is an empty arm-chair. I shut my eyes, and call up a visual image of a friend sitting in the arm-chair. If I thrust my image into the world of physics, it contradicts the usual physical laws. My friend reached the chair without coming in at the door in the usual way; subsequent inquiry will show that he was somewhere else at the moment. If regarded as a sensation, my image has all the marks of the supernatural. My image, therefore, is regarded as an event in me, not as having that position in the orderly happenings of the public world that belongs to sensations. By saying that it is an event in me, we leave it possible that it may be *physiologically* caused: its privacy may be only due to its connection with my body. But in any case it is not a public event, like an actual person walking in at the door and sitting down in my chair. And it cannot, like inner speech, be regarded as a *small* sensation, since it occupies just as large an area in my visual field as the actual sensation would do.[1]

The difference is that Lord Russell is being persuasive whereas Eddington did not seem to care a rap whether you believed him or not, with the result that in the end you are more likely to consider what he said. His aloofness is more telling in the end than Lord Russell's familiar buttonholing of you, with his 'Suppose, for example . . .'. No one will deny that Lord Russell's is far more pleasant prose; as a vehicle of communication, that is, it is better; but what Eddington was aiming at is not communication so much as presentation. We must grant, of course, that in the first extract we were asked to look at the external universe, and in the second to peer, to some degree, into ourselves; but what we are aware of is that Lord Russell is trying to communicate something of his warmth to us, his intellectual excitement. He does not put us off as Sir Arthur did, pull us up, so to speak, with 'apparently' and 'may be rather far-fetched'. Not that Sir Arthur's passage is

> seraphically free
> From taint of personality,

[1] From *The Analysis of Mind*, by Bertrand Russell, Allen and Unwin, 1921.

but you feel that all the time he was being carefully restrained and keeping his excitement out of his voice; he was rigorously balancing the ups and downs, and would not emphasize one thing more than another. Lord Russell's sentences, however, have a natural run: he is not observing with you, he is telling you. Perhaps we may express the difference by saying that Sir Arthur trusted to his subject to keep you interested, while Lord Russell is keeping you alert by his prose, by the varied length, the varied impact, of the phrases and sentences.

However impersonal science may be, no man, who is a man, can help his attitude towards facts being coloured by his general attitude towards life: man cannot help being a moral being. What one looks for, however, in scientific prose, is the exclusion *as far as possible* of the writer's attitude towards life, for when this is allowed to enter too much into it, the prose ceases to become scientific, and appears as something else:

. . . What we perceive as present is the vivid fringe of memory tinged with anticipation. This vividness lights up the discriminated field within a duration. But no assurance can thereby be given that the happenings of nature cannot be assorted into other durations of alternative families. We cannot even know that the series of immediate durations posited by the sense-awareness of one individual mind all necessarily belong to the same family of durations. There is not the slightest reason to believe that this is so. Indeed if my theory of nature be correct, it will not be the case.

The materialistic theory has all the completeness of the thought of the middle ages, which had a complete answer to everything, be it in heaven or in hell or in nature. There is a trimness about it, with its instantaneous present, its vanished past, its non-existent future, and its inert matter. This trimness is very medieval and ill accords with brute facts.

The theory which I am urging admits a greater ultimate mystery and a deeper ignorance. The past and the future meet and mingle in the ill-defined present. The passage of nature which is only another name for the creative force of existence has no narrow ledge of definite instantaneous present within which to operate. Its operative presence which is now urging nature forward must be sought for throughout the whole, in the remotest past as well as in the narrowest breadth of any present duration. Perhaps also in the unrealised future. Perhaps also in the future which might be as well as the actual future which will be. It is impossible to meditate on time and the mystery of the creative passage of nature without an overwhelming emotion at the limitations of human intelligence.[1]

Whether this is philosophic prose, or emotive prose, whether indeed it is not religion rather than science that Whitehead was speaking of in his chapter on 'Time' is a matter that can, perhaps, be decided only by the individual. What we do know, however, is that the writer of the last passage was not in a mood of scientific detachment when he wrote it. He is not standing outside his subject as Eddington was, nor appealing for honest observation as Lord Russell does; he is surrounding you with the atmosphere with which his consciousness is at the moment full. He urgently wants you to hate trimness and love mystery as much as he does. Take such phrases as 'the *vivid fringe* of memory *tinged* with anticipation'; '*be it* in heaven or in hell or in nature'; 'vanished *past*', '*remotest* past',

[1] From *The Concept of Nature*, by A. N. Whitehead, Cambridge, 1920.

'meet and *mingle*'. All the italicized words and forms (they could easily be added to) have a colour of their own in a thousand associations in our minds, producing an emotional aura in which such phrases as 'the creative force of existence . . . . Its operative presence which is now urging nature forward . . .' may seem to have some definite meaning: and we do not pause to ask how big an emotion has to be before it becomes 'overwhelming'.

Thus of the three writers Whitehead tells us most about himself, Eddington least; and here the question intrudes whether our original analysis of our judgement of prose will hold water. Are we going to assess the virtues of scientific prose in the same way as we do the virtues of other prose, that is, by the sound of the voice? The test is whether we can find scientific prose as admirably detached as Eddington's, yet quite different in sound. Can we, in spite of the fact that the most satisfactory scientific form seems impersonal, yet establish contact with a personality? Let us look at this:

Perhaps it may seem to be pushing the definition too far if, when we find no evidence of any regular structure in a substance like glass, we say that it ought to be classed as a liquid. But, indeed, there is good sense in so defining glass. The molecules of the glass are not quite satisfied: they are trying, all the time, to substitute order for disorder. They are very slow about it under ordinary conditions, but if the glass is raised to a temperature which is not quite enough to make it run, the molecules begin to arrange themselves, the crystalline state appears, or, as is often said, devitrification sets in. The tendency in all things is to the crystalline state, as to the natural state. A moderate amount of vibration, a proper temperature, and time help this tendency to assert itself; great forces and great heat tend, of course, to break the crystals up. The crystalline state of a body, for example an iron girder, is often altered by vibration.

The difference between the three principal states, gaseous, liquid, and crystalline—it is better to say crystalline rather than solid—is brought about generally by an alteration in temperature. When the temperature is high enough, the atoms and molecules are endowed with so much individual energy of movement that they lead a more or less independent existence as a gas. When the temperature sinks somewhat, the forces begin to get the upper hand, and the atoms and molecules join up to make a liquid, but not so tightly as to bind neighbours together permanently and in a definite way. That comes about as a consequence of a still further lowering of temperature, when the molecules lay themselves up against one another for good and form the crystalline pattern: their mutual attractions having now obtained complete control.

The new condition brings the properties of the solid in its train. The structure is rigid because of the many ties which bind its parts together. Even the body which is made of a mass of minute crystals, such as a piece of steel, derives its mechanical properties from the properties of the individual crystals, modified by actions at crystal boundaries which are not yet perfectly understood. Arrangement, therefore, is at the bottom of the characteristic behaviour of steel. It is at the bottom, too, of almost every other physical property that a solid possesses: its greater or less capacity for the conveyance of heat and of electricity; its magnetic properties; its hardness, brittleness, optical qualities, and so on. When we pass from the consideration of gas and liquid to that of the crystal solid we meet with an entirely new condition which profoundly affects the properties of the new phase.[1]

[1] From *The Crystalline State,* by William Bragg, O.M., Oxford University Press, 1925.

No one would say that the last beautifully lucid passage was coloured by emotion, yet we are at once aware of a very definite personality. There seems something more human, more benign as a scientist, about Bragg than, say, about Eddington. He is less removed from us, yet his detachment from his subject is complete. He seems all the same to sympathize with the bits of matter he examines and describes so accurately. The effect is given by the phrases he uses more than by anything else: 'they are trying all the time'; 'lead a more or less independent existence'; 'lay themselves against one another', and various others: but what we have to ask ourselves is whether the formation of the phrases, apart from the words they are made of, itself produces anything of this effect. If we compare Bragg with Eddington we do indeed notice a difference: the latter is more nervous: there is just a slight tinge of protestation in his prose, a hint of a Lucretian 'positive assertion of his opinions'. He begins his sentences on a sharper note. Put, for example, 'Owing to the Doppler effect' against 'When the temperature is high enough . . .'; or 'The excitation of the calcium atom' against 'The new condition brings the properties of the solid . . .'. The difference is really very subtle, far harder to analyse than to perceive. It would be exaggerating to say that the first extract gives a sense of strenuousness, the last of contentment: but all the same there is something about the two passages that gives that impression.

LEGAL prose is nearest to that of science, perhaps because both deal with laws. It does not matter that the laws of science are merely formulations of what is supposed always to happen in certain conditions, and that the laws of the courts are arbitrary, what man wants them to be; they proceed in the same way, that is, they relate isolated instances to a general principle. We would therefore expect the prose of one to have much the same quality as that of the other, the quality of being detached, impersonal, and of arguing that certain parts belong to certain wholes. We look in both for clear-headedness, for the exact use of words (which we do not always get in prose which claims to be scientific), and for a voice which we feel might belong to anybody. That all legal prose does not read in the same way is merely another proof that you cannot keep the person out of the style; the voice is part of the physiological make-up. But let us look at just one example. Here is part of a judgement selected for me by an eminent lawyer as being representative of the best prose of his profession:

Each decision seems clear enough, but to fit them all into their places in the theory of negligence is not so easy. We may put aside the questions, When is a child capable of and guilty of contributory negligence?—When does the contributory negligence of the injured child's attendant disentitle it to recover? It is also not directly germane to the present case to investigate the duty which a person owning a public

place owes to a child who is there as of right, or the obligation
of a person who leaves about, in a place known to be fre-
quented by children, objects in themselves capable of causing
injury if meddled with, and which children are likely to
meddle with. Loaded guns and heaps of lime left in play-
grounds are almost a class by themselves. It is plain that the
responsibility of the owner of a close into which an infant
strays in circumstances not consistent with a bare trespass
might be very formidable if the law stopped here. The child
must take the place as he finds it and take care of himself;
but how can he take care of himself? If his injury is not to
go without legal remedy altogether by reason of his failure to
use a diligence which he could not possibly have possessed,
the owner of the close might be practically bound to see
that the wandering child is as safe as in a nursery. The way
out of the dilemma was found in *Burchell* v. *Hickisson* by
deciding that the circumstances may evidence the attachment
of a condition to the licence or permission to enter, namely,
that the child shall only enter if accompanied by a person in
charge capable of seeing and avoiding obvious perils and thus
of placing both himself and his charge in the position of an
ordinary licensee both able and bound to look after himself.
Lindley J. says: 'There could be no duty on the part of the
defendant towards the plaintiff' (aged four) 'further than that
the defendant must take care that no concealed danger exists.
. . . The defendant never invited such a person as the plaintiff
to come unless he was taken care of by being placed in the
charge of others, and if he was in charge of others there was
no concealed danger.' In other words, there was no invitation
to the plaintiff if he was not guarded, and if guarded then
there was no trap. Logically this principle is applicable to all
cases of infirmity or disability and not to infants only. It
was of *Burchell* v. *Hickisson*, I take it, that Scrutton J. was
thinking when he put to the jury question No. 2. His observations almost repeat the words used in the case. Furthermore,

the summing up and his questions not only covered the attachment of a condition to the lease and licence, but also the point whether in any case the plaintiff was more than a bare licensee. Of invitation in the strict sense, there was and could be no evidence. When he afterwards came to enter judgment the learned judge, not having his actual words before him, assumed that the jury only meant that there was no invitation to this particular child unaccompanied, though there was to others. Even so, the effect of an answer in an action brought by this child would be the same, but I think he hardly did justice to the intelligence of the jury. It was impossible in face of the clear direction given them that they should have meant more than this. Their verdict on this point places the plaintiff in the position of a bare licensee and no more. Whether it places her position so high, or how a person whose presence is licensed only on a condition can be a licensee if that condition is not performed, need not be considered, for it was not argued that the plaintiff was a trespasser in this case.[1]

The real difference between legal prose and strictly scientific prose is that the former is, in the nature of things, more authoritative. Lord Sumner definitely laid down the law; you can hear it in his voice: it was his business to say 'This is so', not to describe an event or sequence of events, and deduce what are known as causes. And in legal prose we necessarily come upon jargon, technical terms, more often than we do in scientific; one would not like to bet that after reading the judgement we should all of us know exactly how far we were responsible for the injury an infant did to himself when playing on our ground; nevertheless it is to scientific prose (rather than purely technical) that legal prose can best be attached.

[1] Judgement by Lord Sumner, K.B.D.I., 1913.

§ 3

Philosophy

SCIENTIFIC prose, we probably agree, aims at being as impersonal as it can be; the scientist studies truth and reality, and should be indifferent to what they may turn out to look like. The philosopher also studies truth and reality; but whereas the scientist is (or ought one again to say 'should be'?) content to confine himself to what he can observe, and with the inferences he can check from his observations, the philosopher aims at ultimate truth, and cannot be indifferent to what he discovers, or to the scheme he finds himself led to construct. It is his nature to find a meaning in things—otherwise he would spend his time doing something other than philosophizing—and, since he is human, the meaning must to some extent be gratifying to man. Indeed there is a strong suspicion that he often creates what he wants to find. But this is not the place to philosophize about philosophy; what we are concerned to note is that a certain quality of emotion is likely to enter into philosophic prose. It is true that Aristotle seems usually to have kept it out, also Spinoza (though this is more doubtful), and latterly there has been Wittgenstein: but philosophy is not usually accounted of much use unless it leads in the end to a way of life, and people are not as a rule to be reasoned into action or into an outlook on life, but induced to do things or to 'think' things by their feelings or prejudices. At the same time, the boundaries today between science and philosophy are so indistinct, that it is sometimes hard to tell what particular branch of investigation we are dealing with:

. . . Moreover, the mathematician can prove, by an argument which assumes nothing as to the nature of external reality, that all changes with time can be pictured in terms of wave-motion; this concept will, then, enable us to picture such changes. If a certain kind of wave-motion seems capable of describing something in reality to a very high degree of probability, we may proceed to discuss the further question— 'Waves of what?'

Here, for the first time, we are confronted with difficulties, since the real essence of the 'What' must necessarily remain unknown to us, unless it should prove to be of the same general nature as something already existent in our minds, such as a thought or mental concept, a wish or an emotion.

To anticipate for a moment, we shall find later that the waves which are most important of all in physics can quite unexpectedly be interpreted as being of this type. They are waves of something which the scientist loosely describes as 'probability', but may be more explicitly described as 'uncertainties or imperfections of knowledge'—a concept with which our minds are only too familiar. This may create a suspicion that our minds have merely forced *a priori* upon the waves one of the very few interpretations which *a posteriori* they would be able to comprehend. This may be so, and other and less easily intelligible interpretations may be possible, but in any case the 'probability' interpretation fits the facts of observation. Given the waves, we know the probabilities, so that, in a sense, the waves *really are* waves of probability. Some may wish to interpret this as showing that these waves have no existence in reality at all, but merely in our imperfect knowledge of reality.

This, however, brings us right up to the question which has been lurking in the background all the time—'What is reality?' I think it possible that science and philosophy would answer this question in slightly different ways. The metaphysician is, I think, more inclined to regard reality and phenomena as detached and distinct, like a man and his image in a mirror, or an aeroplane and its shadow on the ground: to use a number of grotesque expressions, an entity may have either an ontal or phenomenal existence, but nothing in between. On the other hand, the scientist is more inclined to regard reality and phenomena as the two ends of a continuous road, along which it is his job to travel. The metaphysician may dismiss the statement that waves *really are* waves of probability as ignorant nonsense, while the scientist applauds it as a step towards final truth.[1]

The subject-matter there is philosophic—the nature of reality—but the method is scientific; it relates concepts to things which can be measured rather than to general experience, or to other concepts. So the tone is impersonally argumentative, with a good deal of emphasis on supposed fact: 'the waves *really* are'; but it has to be detached, persuasive: 'I think it is possible . . .'; and it has all the care of legal prose: 'is more inclined'. One could extract further examples.

It is possible to discuss philosophic-scientific ideas, that of time, for instance, in far different tones, as was done by Wyndham Lewis, who could not abide the modern concept of time with its attendant time-philosophy; and he chose to criticize it in the form of dialogue in that superb fantasia, *The Childermass*:[2]

'Some fellows say that Time does not exist, sir—Are they right, sir——?'

[1] From *The New Background of Science*, by Sir James Jeans, Cambridge University Press, 1933.   [2] Chatto and Windus, 1928.

The Bailiff toasts him all over with a paternal eye till his
blush has turned tomato-red; then he grumbles genially:

'No, my dear, I've told you—there is neither Space nor
Time, now. There is only the one reality: and there is no
reality without contact. Until things touch and act on each
other they cannot be said to exist for each other, time commences for anything when it is in touch with something else.
And further, one thing commences to have time for another
when it is spatially present to it. Things are bearing down
on us from all directions which we know nothing about at
this moment, when they shall have struck us we shall term
that an *event* and it will possess a certain temporal extension.
All the times of all these potential spatial happenings are
longer or shorter paths that are timeless until they touch us,
when they set our personal clock or proper measure of time
ticking, measuring the event in question for us. You see the
idea?'

A voice so deep that it seems to fill the air with some
thickening oil as it rolls out, begins tolling: a shudder of
scandal at its alien contact shakes the assembly.

'Would it not be true, sir, to say that in your magical
philosophy there is only Time, that it is essentially with *Time*
that you operate?'

The Bailiff is electrified at the impact of the new voice, and
he lights up all over. The sounds stagger his senses like a
salvo from a gong announcing battle from the positions of
a legendary enemy. It is a hail from the contrary pole, it
opens for him by magic the universe that lies between which
before the voice came was shut and dead. With eyes of the
most velvet challenge he turns gladly to the interrupter. It is
the bearded figure but recently arrived.

'How is my philosophy magical, Hyperides? Besides, I'm
not a philosopher, as I have already said, so I don't see how
I can have a philosophy.'

They are the oldest opposites in the universe, they eye each other: all this has been enacted before countless times, on un-numbered occasions all these things they are now about to say have been uttered, under every conceivable circumstance. He blinks his eyes in veiled welcome.

The voice roars out with the consummate accent of a rôle constantly rehearsed.

'I use magician in the ordinary sense of illusionist hypnotist or technical trick-performer: and whether your ostensible approach be that of mathematics, biology, medicine, epistemology, or moralistics, is all one. Men find what they desire. You do not expect me, at least, to be superstitious about your profession! With your convex and concave mirrors and with your witches' cauldron, Time, into which you cast all the objects of sense, softening and confusing them in your "futurist" or time-obsessed alchemy, are you not faithful to the traditions of the magician? Is your art, for all its mechanical subtlety, profounder than that of Protagoras that it took the greatest intellect of the Greek World all his time to confute?'

And later Hyperides asks:

'Is not your Space-Time for all practical purposes only the formula recently popularized to accommodate the empirical sensational chaos? Did not the human genius redeem us for a moment from that, building a world of human-divinity above that flux? Are not your kind betraying us again in the name of exact research to the savage and mechanical nature we had overcome: at the bidding, perhaps, of your maniacal and jealous God?'

'No.' The Bailiff shakes his head. 'We are on the contrary providing you with more rigorous methods in your battle with nature.' (Sotto-voce, then) 'Also, don't be offensive about God, I don't mind but the others do specially the servants.'

'So you say that your physics of "events", and the cult of the "dynamical" that substitutes for the antique repose an

ideal of restless movement, is an "advance" for "us". But an
advance in what? An advance for whom?'

'An advance for science: also, Hyperides, for the mass of
men! You always leave them out of your calculations.'

That is far more energetic prose than Sir James Jeans':
Lewis did not so much want to reason you into sense
as to argue you into passion. He was not speaking *to*
you, he is speaking, even shouting, *at* you. Take the
paragraph beginning 'No, my dear . . .' and count how
often at first the letter 't' occurs, or the combination
'ck'. The sentences come with a rush, vehemently.
Jeans was presenting you with a point of view which
he hopes that you, as a reasonable, and reasoning man,
will accept: Lewis was determined to browbeat you
into thinking as he did: he knew that by nature you
are far too lazy to be a reasoning man, and he insisted,
moreover, that you should be an intelligent, full-
blooded human being, not a thinking machine. His
was a most amusing and very effective way of writing
philosophy, but an extract does not do his method
justice, nor his argument, because the effect of this
sort of prose, being largely emotive, is cumulative,
and, besides, Lewis took his issues piecemeal.

Apart from particular purposes or occasions, then,
we can suppose that philosophic writing must be
somewhere between the coldly scientific and the
emotive: the man who writes it is reasoning, certainly,
but with his whole self, not with his brain alone, rather
with that whole mind which is also a set of feelings;
for feelings too are a part of the philosophic material:

We may well say with Bradley that the good is self-
realisation; but what is the self? Certainly not the feeling or

consciousness of the moment, no the life of the world, nor pure spirit. The self that can systematically distinguish good from evil is an animal soul. It grows from a seed; its potentiality is definite and its fate precarious; and in man it requires society to rear it and tradition to educate it. The good is accordingly social, in so far as the soul demands society; but it is the nature of the individual that determines the kind and degree of sociability that is good for him, and draws the line between society that is a benefit and society that is a nuisance. To subordinate the soul fundamentally to society or the individual to the state is sheer barbarism: the Greeks, sometimes invoked to support this form of idolatry, were never guilty of it; on the contrary, their lawgivers were always reforming and planning the state so that the soul might be perfect in it. Discipline is a help to the spirit: but even social relations, when like love, friendship, or sport they are spontaneous and good in themselves, retire as far as possible from the pressure of the world, and build their paradise apart, simple, and hidden in the wilderness; while all the ultimate hopes and assurances of the spirit escape altogether into the silent society of nature, of truth, of essence, far from those fatuous worldly conventions which hardly make up for their tyranny by their instability: for the prevalent moral fashion is always growing old, and human nature is always becoming young again. World-worship is the expedient of those who, having lost the soul that is in them, look for it in things external, where there is no soul: and by a curious recoil, it is also the expedient of those who seek their lost soul in actual consciousness, where it also is not: for sensations and ideas are not the soul but only passing and partial products of its profound animal life. Moral consciousness in particular would never have arisen and would be gratuitous, save for the ferocious bias of a natural living creature, defending itself against its thousand enemies.[1]

[1] From *Five Essays*, by George Santayana, Cambridge, 1933.

All reason, it might seem: but then remember 'its fate precarious', or the rhythm of 'while the ultimate hopes and assurances of the spirit escape altogether into the silent society of nature . . .'. Santayana's tone of voice seems exactly that which a philosopher should have, the tone of a humanist who cares equally for truth and for mankind; he may be, in a way, detached, but he is not indifferent. It can be argued that the passage, strictly speaking, is not philosophic so much as moralistic: but Santayana spoke of what is, not of what ought to be: he was dealing with generalities; his remarks are based on observation and concepts; and after all Lewis also, however much he may deal with abstract ideas, is ultimately concerned with behaviour. Santayana's prose, more modelled, more sensitive than Sir James Jeans', reveals the personality far more clearly than Sir James'. You hear a person speaking as you do not in the earlier passage, and what is more, you know the sort of person it is: but is it any the less philosophic for that?

It may be suggested that the reason is that Sir James is more positive: yet the humane philosopher need not convey this flavour of kindly scepticism that we find with Santayana: there is nothing sceptical in this:

[God is speaking to Satan.] 'You are here, as in the days of Job; and yet, surely, there is no evil in heaven. But if we turn to consider the nature of man we must enter with him into that world of illusions through which he moves so doubtfully. If he have any reality at all, it must be in reference to his own world that he is real; and since that is a world of time and change and movement, his reality, which resists its immediate dissolution into this flux, will have the same nature as the reality of an act, for an act is continuous and indivisible, and its nature is unaffected by its duration. Time is movement and change, and the unit of movement or change is an act, since it is the release of energy in a definite and invariable quantity. The unit of energy will pass from one point to another in space instantaneously, that is without taking time; but even an act of which the duration may be measured from the instant when it leaps into being until the instant when it ceases to be, is complete and indivisible, for though it may traverse a whole series of movements it is not to be confused with the movement. If a man touches something with his finger the sensation travels thence to his brain, and in passing along the nerve cells occasions a slight electrical shock; but the brain, taking up only the significance of the message, is unaware of the molecular disturbance by which it was transmitted, and the nerve cell is only aware of the slight shock, which it has experienced, as an act complete and indivisible in itself: each is unaware of the function of the other, and accepts its own experience as incapable either of increase or diminution. Moreover, since the impulse launching it, and the end to which it would attain are inseparable, either from the act itself, or from each other, it is, in some sense, a synthesis of past and present, overleaping the intervals of time, to which it lends semblance of its own continuity. And in the same way it is a synthesis of all the lesser acts composing the movement which it accompanies; for movement is a succession of isolated and indivisible acts, which become generalized in the mind, losing their individual character by repetition. And the greater act in traversing these lesser acts, or carrying them along with it, does not destroy their independent action in co-ordinating them, for they remain unaware of it, each one conscious only of its own activity, and obeying only the law of its own nature. And an act has no other object than itself, for the object of living is living, and the object of loving is loving, and whatever the act may do it does with a wanton delight in doing, glorifying its own activity. And launched into being, as it overtakes, or grazes against, or coincides or collides with other acts, it will not recognize that they have the same divine nature as it has; but it sees them as mere matter, which it assimilates, or marries, or resists, and from this assimilation, and friction, and pressure are born the material forms of things, of the act itself as well as of all other acts encompassing or contained in it. For the perfect, the divine act has the nature of infinity, and seeks to extend through all space, and to master all things opposed to it; and, in the moment, when it meets with resistance, is created the self, which is all surface, where its own expression finds the limits of its form determined by its own strength in relation to the strength of other acts opposing it. But that self is no more than the expression of the act in form; and it is other than the act, in so far as it represents the limit imposed on the act by other acts, and being other, it too is material. But, at the same time, only through its skin of self, which is both one and other, and thus a medium, is the act conscious of other acts; and when they press upon this taut surface, the act becomes one with itself in resisting any encroachment upon its own sphere of activity. It is from this conflict of one-ness with other-ness in the skin of self that all divisions and oppositions of the world of time originate. The conflict is greater when the opposed acts are equal or nearly equal to each other, and the form reaches its full nature when equivalence is established between them; but there is no conflict between acts of widely different magnitude, for the lesser acts are either drawn into the system of the greater or repelled from it, without either being disturbed, and the lesser acts rain upon the surface in so rapid a succession that the mind ceases to regard them: they cause a kind of habit in it, and habit implies indifference and fatigue; and as the tendency to establish equivalence increases such habits increase with it, and the self becomes dull and gravid. It ceases to respond either to the external pressure or to the impulses of the act, and at last it falls asunder in dissolution, and the divine act escapes from it to begin again the business of creation.'[1]

In that passage you feel that the whole man is speaking. It is marvellously buoyant prose: it reminds one, in its swiftness and its vigour, of the prose of Landor, while perhaps the nearest to it in philosophic writing is Berkeley's. Before examining it more closely, let us look at a passage which deals, we shall see, with much the same range of concepts; and, besides, Manning, and Moore from whom the next passage comes, evidently held a number of ideas in common:

What, then, is to be understood by 'metaphysical'? I use the term . . . in opposition to 'natural'. I call those philosophers pre-eminently 'metaphysical' who have recognized most clearly that not everything which *is* is a 'natural object'. 'Metaphysicians' have, therefore, the great merit of insisting that our knowledge is not confined to the things which we can touch and see and feel. They have always been much occupied, not only with that other class of natural objects which consists in mental facts, but also with the class of objects or properties of objects, which certainly do not exist in time, are not therefore parts of 'Nature', and which, in fact, do not *exist* at all. To this class, as I have said, belongs what we mean by the adjective 'good'. It is not *goodness*, but only the things or qualities which are good, which can exist— can be objects of *perception*. But the most prominent members of this class are perhaps numbers. It is quite certain that two natural objects may exist; but it is equally certain that *two* itself does not exist and never can. Two and two *are* four. But that does not mean that either two or four exists. Yet

[1] From 'Apologia Dei', from *Scenes and Portraits*, by Frederic Manning, Davies, 1930.

it certainly means *something*. Two *is* somehow, although it does not exist. And it is not only simple terms of propositions —the objects *about* which we know truths—that belong to this class. The truths which we know about them form, perhaps, a still more important subdivision. No truth does, in fact, *exist*; but this is particularly obvious with regard to truths like 'two and two are four', in which the objects, *about* which they are truths, do not exist either. It is with the recognition of such truths as these—truths which have been called 'universal'—and of their essential unlikeness to what we can touch and see and feel, that metaphysics proper begins. Such 'universal' truths have always played a large part in the reasonings of metaphysicians from Plato's time till now; and that they have directed attention to the difference between these truths and what I have called 'natural objects' is the chief contribution to knowledge which distinguishes them from that other class of philosophers—'empirical philosophers'—to which most Englishmen have belonged.

But though, if we are to define 'metaphysics' by the contribution which it has actually made to knowledge, we should have to say that it has emphasized the importance of objects which do not exist at all, metaphysicians themselves have not recognized this. They have indeed recognized and insisted that there are, or may be, objects of knowledge which do not *exist in time*, or at least which we cannot perceive; and in recognizing the possibility of these, as an object of investigation, they have, it may be admitted, done a service to mankind. But they have in general supposed that whatever does not exist in time, must at least *exist* elsewhere, if it is to *be* at all —that whatever does not exist in Nature, must exist in some supersensible reality, whether timeless or not. Consequently they have held that the truths with which they have been occupied over and above the objects of perception, were in some way truths about such supersensible reality. If, therefore, we are to define 'metaphysics' not by what it has attained, but by what it has attempted, we should say that it consists in the attempt to attain knowledge, by processes of reasoning, of what exists but is *not* a part of Nature. Metaphysicians have actually held that they could give us such knowledge of non-natural existence. They have held that their science consists in giving us such knowledge as can be supported by reasons, of that supersensible reality, of which religion professes to give us a fuller knowledge, without any reasons. When, therefore, I spoke above of 'metaphysical' propositions, I meant propositions about the existence of something supersensible—of something which is not an object of perception, and which cannot be inferred from what is an object of perception by the same rules of inference by which we infer the past and future of what we call 'Nature'. And when I spoke of 'metaphysical' terms, I meant terms which refer to qualities of such a supersensible reality, which does not belong to anything 'natural'. I admit that 'metaphysics' should investigate what reasons there may be for belief in such a supersensible reality; since I hold that its peculiar province is the truth about all objects which are not natural objects. And I think that the most prominent characteristic of metaphysics, in history, has been its profession to *prove* the truth about non-natural *existents*. I define 'metaphysical', therefore, by a reference to supersensible *reality*; although I think that the only non-natural objects, about which it has *succeeded* in obtaining truth, are objects which do not exist at all.[1]

The tone of the voice is different: yet Manning handled those very ideas which Moore analysed with a pleasantly destructive air of giving the devil his due. But is the tone different merely because the approach to the material is not the same? Here, perhaps, we can get a little closer to our main theme. For if the

[1] From *Principia Ethica,* by George Edward Moore, Cambridge.

prose depends on the subject, and on the man, as well, how are we to tell where we are? But really, to philosophize a little ourselves, is not the personality revealed by the thing the person is most interested in? Ruskin does not discuss horse-racing, Surtees does not adventure into metaphysics. You write about what you want to write about, you write in the style which comes naturally to you, and thus the style, being part of you, is appropriate to the subject, which you have made part of yourself.

At all events, the difference in subject-matter (for ultimately the subject-matter is the writer's mind, not the object he fastens it on) is reflected in the way the two philosophers write. At a first glance you might not think Manning's style at all metaphorical; he takes it for granted that his ideas are facts, and without realizing it we take it for granted too. But then look at Moore, and we see that Manning is all metaphor: 'And launched into being, as it overtakes or grazes against, or coincides or collides with other acts . . . .' Moore has no metaphor at all. His is a piece of delight-fully clear argument into which emotion is not for a moment allowed to enter: and metaphor, however discreetly used, cannot help giving at least a tinge of emotion, or of slight intellectual excitement beyond that produced by the argument. Manning moreover is emotional, or at least emotive, in his whole phrasing, which borders on the rhetorical—in the good sense. Look at the way his long sustained sentences carry you on, at the way he whirls you over one idea into the next: and quite apart from such words as 'perfect', 'divine', or 'infinity', which are emotive by what they suggest, a certain ardour communicates itself to you from the crowded onrush of his words, from the way the sentences are built up, from the cadences. His sentences as a rule gather way as they move forward, and pile up in polysyllables at the end: 'its nature is unaffected by its duration'; '. . . definite and invariable quantity'; '. . . losing their individual character by repetition'. There is no tiresome insistence, yet there is enough to give extraordinary force to the quite different ending, 'and the self becomes dull and gravid'. Manning's prose, in short, has many of the qualities we associate with poetry; for one thing, a rhythmic ground-swell, with a varied surface. There is no pattern of rhythm in Moore's work, though most of the phrases come easily enough to the tongue, and his sentences have shape. Why there is no sense of pattern is that they all have a different shape. It is not merely, we see, that Moore did not work in so many polysyllables as Manning did, for he occasionally used them, but when he did so, he avoided, perhaps on purpose, the effect of piling up, of each word being urged on by the one behind it.[1] Take 'and in recognizing the possibility of these, as an object of investigation, they have, it may be admitted, done a service to mankind'. Manning, we may say, painted a picture, and he was most effective when his brush strokes were full and free; Moore was dissecting something, and was at his best when he was most trenchant: 'but it is equally certain that *two* itself does not exist, and never can.'

It would be better to compare Moore with Jeans

[1] I know all this is subjective: but what is one to do?

to find differences in tone when the same kind of thing is being dealt with. But this would inevitably develop into a comparison of their personalities—and that is not an activity it would be fruitful to conduct in this context.

§ 4

Morals

MORALISTIC prose can suitably be tacked on to the philosophic, for though philosophy need not be moralistic, morals must be based on philosophy. How you behave is determined by the views you have about life. We are not, of course, concerned here with the sort of moralistic prose which is merely exhortation or invective—that would be classed under emotive—but with the writing of men who have a clear view of life, based on observation and thought, and who try to relate conduct to this view. It goes without saying that such men have a purpose: they are not, cannot be, indifferent in the way the scientist is indifferent, for they relate what is, not to what also is, as far as can be deduced, but to what ought to be. Therefore one does not expect their prose to be so aloof, so detached from their emotions, though sometimes it comes very close to being so:

I have of course in this whole discussion [on the One and the Many] been simplifying a subject of immense difficulty and complexity at the risk of doing injustice to Plato and the other members of the Socratic group. I am not unaware of the almost inexhaustible store of wisdom in Plato. He must still be one of the chief aids to those who wish to achieve religious insight without an undue sacrifice of the critical spirit. Yet it is difficult not to have certain doubts about the Platonic and Socratic identification of knowledge and virtue. This identification is not superficial precisely—men like Plato and Socrates are never superficial. Knowledge may conceivably become so perfect that to act contrary to it would be like putting one's hand into the fire. Moreover, when one has struggled out of any maze of error, it will always seem in the retrospect that the error was due even less to a defect of will than to ignorance. Nevertheless, the Socratic thesis runs counter in certain respects to universal experience. Not only do people do what they know to be wrong, but they often take a perverse satisfaction in doing it, as Ovid,[1] anticipating the *delectatio morosa* of the theologians, was one of the first to point out. Our problem, let us remind ourselves, is to be at once self-reliant and humble. But it will not be found easy to preserve humility and at the same time to grant, after the Greek philosophy, the primacy to mind. All other forms of pride are as nothing compared with the pride of intellect; and the pride of intellect itself is most manifest in the attempt to know good and evil. So much psychological truth is, it would seem, to be found in the myth of the Fall.[2]

From this it would appear that the way to moralize without preaching is to make statements, which from the firm tone of voice in which you say them admit of no contradiction. Who would dare to deny that 'Not only do people do what they know to be wrong . . .' or that 'All other forms of pride are as nothing compared with the pride of intellect'? There is, certainly, argument running through the book, but it is not the sort of argument Moore practised so deftly; nor has it, as with Jeans, that slight tinge of urgency that tunes the voice of the man who wants to convert you.

[1] 'Video meliora proboque, deteriora sequor.' 'Nitimur in vetitum semper, cupimusque negata.'
[2] From *Democracy and Leadership*, by Irving Babbitt, Houghton Mifflin, 1924.

This way of dealing with morals is the most effective of all; there are the facts, it is for you to take them or leave them. It is not conceivable, the tone implies, that a sensible man would leave them.

It is rare to find moralistic prose so perfectly written (I am not referring to possible choices of other words, or any literary point except that of tone); and in this next passage we feel that the writer is not quite so much in control of his impulse to better mankind:

When a childish disposition is carried over into an adult environment the result is a radically false valuation of that environment. The symptoms are fairly evident. They may appear as a disposition to feel that everything which happens to a man had an internal relation to himself; life becomes a kind of conspiracy to make him happy or to make him miserable. In either case it is thought to be deeply concerned with his destiny. The childish pattern appears also as a deep sense that life owes him something, that somehow it is the duty of the universe to look after him, and to listen sharply when he speaks to it. The notion that the universe is full of purposes utterly unknown to him, utterly indifferent to him, is as outrageous to one who is imperfectly matured as would be the conduct of a mother who forgot to give a hungry child its lunch. The childish pattern appears also as a disposition to believe that he may reach out for anything in sight and take it, and that having gotten it nobody must under any circumstances take it away. Death and decay are, therefore, almost an insult, a kind of mischief in the nature of things, which ought not to be there, if everything only behaved as good little boys believe it should. There is indeed authority for the belief that we are all being punished for the naughtiness of our first grandmother, that work and trouble and death would not really be there to plague us but for her unhappy transgression;

that by rights we ought to live in paradise and have everything we want for ever and ever. Here, too, is the source of that common complaint of the world-weary that they are tired of their pleasures. They have what they yearned for; yet having it they are depressed at finding that they do not care. Their inability to enjoy what they can have is the obverse of the desire to possess the unattainable: both are due to carrying over the expectations of youth into adult life. They find themselves in a world unlike the world of their youth; they themselves are no longer youths. But they retain the criteria of youth, and with them they measure the world and their own deserts.

Here, too, is the origin of the apparent paradox that as men grow older they grow wiser and sadder. It is not a paradox at all if we remember that this wisdom which made them sadder is, after all, an incompleted wisdom. They have grown wiser as to the character of the world, wiser too about their own powers, but they remain naïve as to what they may expect of the world and themselves. The expectations which they formed in their youth persist as deeply ingrained habits to worry them in their maturity. They are only partially matured; they have become only partially wise. They have acquired skill and information, but the parts of them which are adult are embedded in other parts of their natures which are childish. For men do not necessarily mature altogether and in unison; they learn to do this and that more easily than they learn what to like and reject. Intelligence is often more completely educated than desire; our outward behavior has an appearance of being grown up which our inner vanities and hopes, our dim but powerful cravings, often belie. In a word, we learn the arts and sciences long before we learn philosophy.

If we ask ourselves what is this wisdom which experience forces upon us, the answer must be that we discover the world is not constituted as we had supposed it to be. It is not that we learn more about its physical elements, or its geography, or the variety of its inhabitants, or the way in which human society is governed. Knowledge of this sort can be taught to a child without in any fundamental way disturbing his childishness. In fact, all of us are aware that we once knew a great many things which we have since forgotten. The essential discovery of maturity has little if anything to do with information about the names, the locations, and the sequences of facts; it is the acquiring of a different sense of life, a different kind of intuition about the nature of things.[1]

The position, evidently, might have been more pithily put, and it would then have become a statement of fact —if we accepted the position; but then the effect would not have been the same. As it is do we not dimly apprehend an admonitory finger wagging at us, bidding us put away childish things? There is a deliberate stateliness about the flow of talk (or is it, perhaps, a deliberate weariness?); life, we are made to feel, is too serious to be lively about. The piece, in short, has a moralizing tone which defeats its own end, for we are at once put on our guard. No doubt Mr. Lippmann worked for this effect, put in on purpose those sentences with a dying fall: 'finding that they do not care'; 'constituted as we had supposed it to be'. There is a slight muffling of sense in such combinations as 'apparent paradox', 'more completely'; for 'paradox' already contains the idea 'apparent', and a thing is either complete or it is not. There is a kind of hypnotism, or a sensation of being lulled, induced by the repetition of 'the childish pattern', and 'Here,

[1] From *A Preface to Morals*, by Walter Lippmann, Allen and Unwin, 1929.

too', and a twinge of regret in such a construction as 'They are only partially matured; they have become only partially wise'. Yet the result is due mainly to the level flow of the sentences, nearly all much of the same length, to the even, not very quick pace, to the heightening of the voice at or near the beginning of the sentence and its gradual hushing as it draws to a close. One may not personally like this prose; but it has its uses, and is worth studying as an instrument.

§ 5

Theology

THEOLOGY is a specialized corner of philosophy, that which deals with man's relation to God, or with God's relation to the universe: it bases itself upon a group of assumptions altogether different from those upon which science is built up. It is bound to be more emotional than pure philosophy, for when a man writes theology the whole mass of his hopes and fears, as well as his intellectual being, comes into play. Yet when it is written by a man who is also a philosopher, it has all the attributes of philosophic prose.

If we make this modification, the doctrine [of contingency] seems to me to be perfectly intelligible. It means, in effect, that while everything happens in cosmic history as God ordains or permits, no event is a perfectly determined 'one-valued function' of other specific events, and that when we say that the occurrence of Y may certainly be inferred from A, B, C, . . . there is always an understood *Deo volente*. It may be that the ultimate 'pattern of the whole' demands a divergence from the most uniformly exhibited 'routine of sequence', and if it does, the sequence will not occur; the sun will, at need, 'stand still upon Gibeon'. But whether the sun stands still or 'hastes to go down', it is certain that there is a 'pattern of the whole' and that *it* will not be violated. No 'innovation' will be a capricious departure from it. But it is impossible in principle to calculate from data already in our possession whether and when an 'innovation' will take place because the 'pattern of the whole' is not and cannot be a *datum*. (Or, to take an illustration from human action, it would be manifestly fallacious to argue that a phrase found in the published work of a writer must be an 'error of the press' because the same writer has published many thousands of lines, but has nowhere else used that particular phrase. If it is the especially right and appropriate expression of the thought in his mind at the moment of writing he may use it, though he never used it before and will never use it again. A man's habits of speech have a great deal of influence on his choice of phraseology, but they never absolutely dictate it.)

It would thus be wholly consistent with theistic belief in the government of the world by God to recognize a genuine element of contingency in all historical events. You may in a sense resolve this contingency into defect of knowledge on our part, but only if you mean that we are not fully acquainted with the divine *purpose*. The defect could not be removed by any extension of our acquaintance with the details of past cosmic history, since the fullest acquaintance with them would not put us in possession of the 'whole counsel of God'. There is thus, so far, no reason to take up *a priori* an attitude of opposition to physicists who tell us they are led by their own special studies to admit a 'principle of Indeterminacy' pervading the whole physical order. They may be right or they may be wrong, but they are not saying anything which conflicts either with the inherent reasonableness of the universe, or with theistic faith. Professor Eddington, for example, is not maintaining that $\Delta \hat{\imath}\nu o\varsigma \ \beta \alpha \sigma \iota \lambda \epsilon \acute{\nu} \epsilon \iota, \ \tau \grave{o}\nu \ \Delta \iota' \ \acute{\epsilon} \xi \epsilon \lambda \eta \lambda \alpha \kappa \acute{\omega} \varsigma.$[1]

Nor do I see that the admission of contingency conflicts with the belief in the divine *omniscience*, as is often supposed. It would do so, if we impiously thought of God as inferring our future from our past much as an astronomer calculates the future positions of a planet from a record of positions it has occupied in the past. But no theologian, I take it, ever thought of God's knowledge in this fashion. To quote James Ward,

[1] 'Whirl has kicked Zeus out and now reigns.' From *The Clouds of Aristophanes*, Way's translation.

'How God knows, or even what knowledge means when attributed to the Supreme Being, few of us will pretend to understand.' But, as Ward is arguing in the context of the remark, at least it will not be imagined that He calculates the course of events like a 'Laplacean demon', from a multitude of differential equations. Whatever omniscience is, it is not this.[1]

I do not feel that that admirable passage (I do not venture to comment on the argument, I am concerned only with the quality of the prose) needs any remark: what I have suggested about philosophical prose will apply to this too; and for that reason I give only one example of this sort of writing, that is, theological prose written by professed theologians.

For theology crops up in all sorts of unexpected places—in the works of poets, historians, critics, and novelists—or perhaps we had better call it religion. Let us begin with one of the least obviously emotive:

Therefore in order to understand Keats henceforward, we must be able to contemplate him under the three aspects of mind and body and soul: to make a true contact with what he was, we have permanently to enlarge our conception of man's nature. To me, I confess, this strange proposition appears the veriest common sense. A pure poet is not an ordinary man; nor can he be, as criticism too often assumes, an ordinary man with an extraordinary faculty tacked on to him. Such portentous births, though they are apparently accepted by minds which would not accept similar phenomena in other realms, are really more incredible than Anthropophagi. An unrelated faculty is inconceivable. That we are unable to perceive the relation should be a reason not for tacitly denying that the relation exists, but for mistrusting our own knowledge. We

[1] From *The Faith of a Moralist*, by A. E. Taylor, Macmillan, 1930, Series II.

are reluctant to do that. For some reason, the Western mind has become very complacent in its knowledge. Possibly we have good right to be complacent in the knowledge of the external world. But there is not the faintest reason to suppose that we know more about the human soul than did our misty forefathers thousands of years ago. I believe that we do not know so much; that we know in truth far less; that in this realm at least—and it is an important one—our ignorance is abysmal and our pretensions childish. By our presumption we shut ourselves off from knowledge. We do not believe, we cannot believe, that poetry has really something to tell us of importance to our lives. We laugh at the old theory of direct inspiration without pausing to think whether it meant anything, and whether the belief that the poet (the *vates sacer*) brought men a message from God has not a profound symbolic significance which is not adequately replaced by the conception of him as 'abnormal', or at best the incalculable provider of some exotic thrill called an 'æsthetic emotion'. Our modern rationalism, which is so deep in our bones that we are scarcely conscious of it, will reduce everything to its own terms. There is no God, it says, therefore the poet cannot be inspired by him; there is no supra-rational truth, therefore the poet cannot declare it.

I hold, and hold fast, to a different philosophy. I have been gradually forced into it, not least through an instinctive and ineradicable conviction that pure poetry is not irrelevant to life, but on the contrary more exactly relevant to it than any other creation of the human spirit. I believe, for I have found it so by experience, that pure poetry contains a revelation, that I would far rather stand with the ancients in their belief that the poet is directly inspired by God than with the moderns in theirs that the poet is a *lusus naturae* and poetry an amusing accident. What the ancients said—though I might not care, or dare, to use their language—corresponds with my experience; their explanation is at least adequate to the revelation which pure poetry brings: what the moderns say is almost an insult to my knowledge. And the fundamental cause of this inadequacy of the modern theory to the actual reality of experience lies in our ignorance of the nature of the human soul. This is the price we have paid for the 'enlightenment' of the Renaissance. For it is all very well to turn God out of the universe rather than suffer a parody of the divine reality to remain: but if you turn out God, without taking upon yourself the full responsibility for what you have done, you run the risk of turning out also that secular human faculty which finds its exercise and purpose in the apprehension of the divine reality. Remove God from the universe, and you may very well remove a faculty from the human soul.[1]

That is a vigorous asseveration of faith. Nearly every sentence ends with a hard ring; the voice all the time is raised to the level of robust affirmation. There is no hesitancy, though there is no lack of control; yet underneath it all there is a current of excitement, the excitement of a man declaring a truth, an almost Pauline fervour. Let us compare it with a calmer statement of belief:

I often entangle myself in arguments more complicated than even those paths of Inchy as to what is the true nature of apparitions, but at other times I say as Socrates said when they told him a learned opinion about a nymph of the Ilissus, 'The common opinion is enough for me.' I believe when I am in the mood that all nature is full of people whom we cannot see, and that some of these are ugly or grotesque, and some wicked or foolish, but very many beautiful beyond any one we have ever seen, and that these are not far away when we are walking in pleasant and quiet places. Even when I was a boy I could never walk in a wood without feeling that at

[1] From *Keats and Shakespeare*, by J. Middleton Murry, Oxford, 1925.

any moment I might find before me somebody or something I had long looked for without knowing what I looked for. And now I will at times explore every little nook of some poor coppice with almost anxious footsteps, so deep a hold has the imagination upon me. You too meet with a like imagination, doubtless, somewhere, wherever your ruling stars will have it, Saturn driving you to the woods, or the Moon, it may be, to the edges of the sea. I will not of a certainty believe that there is nothing in the sunset, where our forefathers imagined the dead following their shepherd the sun, or nothing but some vague presence as little moving as nothing. If beauty is not a gateway out of the net we were taken in at our birth, it will not long be beauty, and we will find it better to sit at home by the fire and fatten a lazy body or to run hither and thither in some foolish sport than to look at the finest show that light and shadow ever made among green leaves. I say to myself, when I am well out of that thicket of argument, that they are surely there, the divine people, for only we who have neither simplicity nor wisdom have denied them, and the simple of all times and the wise men of ancient times have seen them and even spoken to them. They live out their passionate lives not far off, as I think, and we shall be among them when we die if we but keep our natures simple and passionate. May it not even be that death shall unite us to all romance, and that some day we shall fight dragons among blue hills, or come to that whereof all romance is but

> 'Foreshadowings mingled with the images
> Of man's misdeeds in greater days than these,'

as the old men thought in *The Earthly Paradise* when they were in good spirits.[1]

There we have two methods, and one cannot say that one is better than the other; both passages are very

[1] From *The Celtic Twilight*, by W. B. Yeats, Bullen, 1902.

good, written by masters in their own spheres. What
is clear, however, is that they will appeal with different
force to different sorts of people; or, if you prefer, to
the same people in different moods, when they are, in
fact, different people. Or perhaps one might say that
Murry can stir you, and may *compel* you to enter into
a mood in which you will be receptive of his ideas,
whereas to receive Yeats', you have to be predisposed
to greet them. Murry appeals to reason, Yeats to the
delicate, submerged sensibilities which Murry feared
have been atrophied in us. Yet Yeats might very well
win you to his mood. What particular qualities of
style, we ask, are these results due to?

The most obvious thing, of course, is the different
sort of words used by the two writers: Yeats could not
have said 'our ignorance is abysmal and our pretensions childish' any more than Murry could have said
'If beauty is not a gateway out of the net we were taken
in at our birth . . .'. Thus the impact is on different
parts of our personality: and the direction of this
impact is furthered, its strength made greater, by the
way the sentences are built up. We have already
noticed how Murry ended with a sharp ring, usually,
we can add, with a noun. Yeats brought his sentences
to a gentler close, sometimes with pronouns: 'upon
me', 'to them'; and if with nouns, such soothing ones
as 'nothing', 'quiet places', 'green leaves', words always, you observe, with quite general connotations,
connotations of feeling, not of thought; he does not
use words like 'philosophy', 'soul', 'Renaissance',
'childish', which are general enough, indeed abstract,
but which concentrate your attention upon the sub-

ject-matter. Yeats' lead you away. And then compare the sound of the words, apart from what they mean; consider how dulcet Yeats' are. Murry's words, one feels, would carry in a lecture hall, Yeats' are meant for the companionable ear of a fireside crony. The consequence is that Murry, you might say, asked an audience to accept his idea, whereas Yeats asked you or me to accept himself: and we do accept Yeats—at least his mood—so that the precise meaning of the words ceases to matter. We do not even stop to question whether nets usually have gateways. The emotive words he used are those that appeal to the senses, to the sensual imagination as well as to our hearing: think again of 'quiet places', and 'green leaves'. Murry's are much less directly emotive words, but he did use words of that kind, even phrases, such as 'without taking upon yourself the full responsibility for what you have done', the word 'responsibility', like 'complacent' and 'abysmal', being itself emotive. Our forefathers we regard with equanimity; they are dead; our '*misty* forefathers', however, carry with them a sense of remoteness and awe. Murry, we see, used his emotive words to stir you, not to lull you; so that, to repeat, Yeats would lure you into the world of the unseen, while Murry would marshal you in with inspiriting argument.

In realms such as these the parable or fable is still one of the most powerful methods of presentation and persuasion:

The Reverend Nicholas Grobe was drinking pleasantly. The evening had become, as near as any evening could, an everlasting one.

Mr. Grobe looked upon those things in his room that had ministered to his needs for so long. His eyes dwelt long upon his books, and he looked, too, at the picture of Alice, who used to display herself, in all her naughtiness, so merrily before him. He emptied his glass. He went to an old barometer that hung from the wall. Earlier in the evening he had noticed that the barometer was high, but now it was fallen very low.

Mr. Grobe turned to his chair again, intending to take another glass of wine, but he saw, to his great surprise, that the flagon was gone, and in its place was the great Bible.

Mr. Grobe looked at his watch. The watch was still stopped at seven. He was yet in the eternity of a long evening, when the only act that need occupy a man was the act of drinking. But where was the wine? Had he been all the evening drinking out of that great book? Had that book been Mr. Weston's Good Wine?

Some one outside in the garden opened and shut the rectory gate. Mr. Grobe threw open the window and looked out.

'Who are you?' he called.

'I am Weston, the wine merchant,' came the answer.

'Enter then,' said Mr. Grobe. 'Enter, for you know the way.'

Mr. Weston lost no time in obeying this command for he is a trader who has never failed to attend quickly to any customer who calls to him. He entered Mr. Grobe's study immediately. Mr. Grobe welcomed him with pleasure, though Mr. Weston noticed at once that the minister was very sad.

'You are sorrowful,' the merchant said compassionately. 'I fear you have not found my wine suitable to your taste.'

'It was certainly a good wine,' answered Mr. Grobe, 'and it gave my old beliefs back to me again, for I believe that my dead wife awaits me in paradise, where God is love.'

'Listen, Mr. Weston,' he said, 'I have just read this out of a book—that Moses was rather for dying where he stood than go one step without his God. I feel so too.'

Mr. Grobe looked anxiously at his watch.

'I shall lose my belief in God, in heaven, and in my Alice, if time moves again,' he said very sadly. 'I know that nothing is sure here while time lasts. The beliefs that we cherish, our loves, our hopes, all pass away and are gone like the autumn leaves, and all we have left of them are hours of rank misery.'

' "But his flesh upon him shall have pain, and his soul within him shall mourn" '.

Mr. Grobe wept.

Perhaps a merchant might be more pleased to see a customer in tears than one too bright and happy, for the latter would be less likely to give heed to a bill. Mr. Weston may have thought thus, but he now took from his pocket a small flask, that was full of a very dark wine.

Mr. Weston did not care to see a good man weep, and so he turned away. He went to the weather glass and tapped it. He shook his head when he saw how low it was fallen.

Mr. Weston took a chair beside Mr. Grobe. He drew the cork from the flask.

He spoke to Mr. Grobe very lovingly, but in a very low tone, so that no one—no, not even if there had been others in the room—could have heard him.

'I have brought another wine with me,' he said, 'that you are welcome to drink. I only give this wine to those I love, but when you drink this wine you will sorrow no more.'

Mr. Grobe held out his hand to take the flask, but Mr. Weston restrained him for a moment.

'You have something to ask of me,' he whispered.

'My Alice,' said Mr. Grobe. 'Shall I see her, shall I see her if I drink your black wine?'

'She is a little goose,' said Mr. Weston, smiling, 'and she will flap her wings at you.'

Mr. Grobe poured out a glass of wine. He drank contentedly and seemed to fall into a deep sleep. But soon he sighed happily, and his breathing stopped.

Mr. Weston raised Mr. Grobe's head and placed the cushion more easily underneath it.

The wine merchant covered the face of the dead.[1]

This is chiefly emotive, and the emotion is produced not only by the prose style, but in other ways as well. It is not our business to discuss these here, though we can note in passing the eerie effect of time standing still, of the barometer falling: but when we come to notice the occasional flavour of archaism, 'was gone' instead of 'had gone', 'sorrowful' instead of 'unhappy', we are beginning to discover in what way this prose gets its effects. 'Sorrowful' is weightier, more drawn out, than 'unhappy', and it is almost entirely by such sounds that Powys attained his ends. Take 'full of a very dark wine'; 'when he saw how low it was fallen': even his quotation is carefully chosen for his purpose: 'and his soul within him shall mourn'. That is one point; another is the evenness in the rhythmic quality of the sentences, the steady pace, possibly due to using very simple words; it is difficult to get speed into prose if you use only monosyllables: possibly Mr. Garnett (see p. 20) is as swift as you can be if you use simple language for story-telling, but compare his pace with Manning's (see p. 105). Also, with Powys, there is very little rise or fall in the voice. This is not to say that the rhythm is dull and plodding. On the contrary, it often approaches verse rhythm:

> Shall I see her,
> Shall I see her,
> If I drink your black wine?

[1] From *Mr. Weston's Good Wine*, by T. F. Powys, Chatto and Windus, 1927.

Trip it gipsies,
Trip it gipsies,
O gipsies trip it fine.

which would be more lilting still but for the long
stresses of 'drink your black wine'; or:

The wine merchant covered the face of the dead,
His cohorts all gleaming in purple and red.

The simplicity, we shall be forced to admit, is very
deceptive.

There is no need, however, to be indirect about first
and last things:

With this third part of *The Golden Bough* we take up the
question, Why had the King of the Wood at Nemi regularly
to perish by the hand of his successor? In the first part of the
work I gave some reasons for thinking that the priest of Diana,
who bore the title of King of the Wood beside the still lake
among the Alban Hills, personated the great god Jupiter or his
duplicate Dianus, the deity of the oak, the thunder, and the
sky. On this theory, accordingly, we are at once confronted
with the wider and deeper question, Why put a man-god or
human representative of deity to a violent death? Why ex-
tinguish the divine light in its earthly vessel instead of hus-
banding it to its natural close? My general answer to that
question is contained in the present volume. If I am right, the
motive for slaying a man-god is a fear lest with the enfeeble-
ment of his body in sickness or old age his sacred spirit should
suffer a corresponding decay, which might imperil the general
course of nature and with it the existence of his worshippers,
who believe the cosmic energies to be mysteriously knit up
with those of their human divinity. Hence, if there is any
measure of truth in this theory, the practice of putting divine
men and particularly divine kings to death, which seems to

have been common at a particular stage in the evolution of
society and religion, was a crude but pathetic attempt to dis-
engage an immortal spirit from its mortal envelope, to arrest
the forces of decomposition in nature by retrenching with
ruthless hand the first ominous symptoms of decay. We may
smile if we please at the vanity of these and the like efforts to
stay the inevitable decline, to bring the relentless revolution
of the great wheel to a stand, to keep youth's fleeting roses for
ever fresh and fair; but perhaps in spite of every disillusion-
ment, when we contemplate the seemingly endless vistas of
knowledge which have been opened up even within our own
generation, many of us may cherish in our heart of hearts a
fancy, if not a hope, that some loophole of escape may after
all be discovered from the iron walls of the prison-house which
threaten to close on and crush us; that, groping about in the
darkness, mankind may yet chance to lay hands on 'that golden
key that opes the palace of eternity', and so pass from this
world of shadows and sorrow to a world of untroubled light
and joy. If this is a dream, it is surely a happy and innocent
one, and to those who would wake us from it we may murmur
with Michael Angelo,

> 'Pero non mi destar, deh! parla basso.'[1]

The ideas there, and the images used—the ideas of
death and loss, of hope and desire for eternal life, the
images of the fleeting roses of youth—are themselves
ideas and images which arouse the emotions. Again
we notice the regularity of the rhythms, the long, sustained phrases: 'We may smile if we please at the
vanity of these and the like efforts to stay the inevitable
decline, to bring the relentless revolution of the great
wheel to a stand, to keep youth's fleeting roses for

---

[1] From *The Golden Bough* (The Dying God), by Sir J. G. Frazer, O.M.,
Macmillan, 1911.

ever fresh and fair.' We can notice also the effective use of alliteration, the ending of each phrase on a long sound—'decline', 'stand', 'fair', but these last are only additions to the steady sound of the voice, the muted ups and downs, which really give the sense of absorption into the idea of death, or of eternal life, which is, one imagines, at the base of much religious feeling.

§ 6

Political Science

POLITICAL writing or speaking is not usually scientific: politics belong rather to the realm of art, the art of persuasion, of rousing people's emotions so as to organize their fears or their prejudices, often their hatreds. It is not an art of which one can have a very high opinion—as writing or speaking it is to literature what musical comedy is to the drama—though in the old days oratory produced some very fine things. As literature, then, most political writing belongs to the emotive variety, though it is still sometimes based on thought. Even then, however, men usually utter their political opinions because they want something to happen, and things can only be got to happen when masses of men are persuaded that they ought to happen, and nobody who has handled masses supposes that they can be moved by reason. So we expect that political writing should make an emotional appeal, more so even than theological writing, for there the writer is eager to express his own emotion, and is not so much concerned with the emotions of other people. Still the more profound political writers or speakers base their remarks on thought; some philosophy not only of society but of being is the background of the picture they are painting:

I would not mind people fighting in a passion to get rid of all that barred some lordly scheme of life, but quarrels over political bones from which there is little or nothing wholesome to be picked only disgust. People tell me that the countryside must always be stupid and backward, and I get angry, as if it were said that only townspeople had immortal souls, and it was only in the city that the flame of divinity breathed into the first men had any unobscured glow. The countryside in Ireland could blossom into as much beauty as the hillsides in mediæval Italy, if we could but get rid of our self-mistrust. We have all that any race ever had to inspire them, the heavens overhead, the earth underneath, and the breath of life in our nostrils. I would like to exile the man who would set limits to what we can do, who would take the crown and sceptre from the human will and say, marking out some petty enterprise as the limit: 'Thus far can we go and no farther, and here shall our life be stayed.' Therefore I hate to hear of stagnant societies who think that because they have made butter well they have crowned their parochial generation with a halo of glory, and can rest content with the fame of it all, listening to the whirr of the steam separators and pouching in peace of mind the extra penny a gallon for their milk. And I dislike the little groups who meet a couple of times a year and call themselves co-operators because they have got their fertilizers more cheaply, and have done nothing else. Why, the village gombeen man has done more than that! He has at least brought most of the necessaries of life there by his activities; and I say, if we co-operators do not aim at doing more than the Irish Scribes and Pharisees we shall have little to be proud of. A poet, interpreting the words of Christ to His followers, who had scorned the followers of the old order made Him say:

> Scorn ye their hopes, their tears, their inward prayers?
> I say unto you, see that your souls live
> A deeper life than theirs.

The co-operative movement is delivering over the shaping of the rural life of Ireland, and the building up of its rural civilization, into the hands of Irish farmers. The old order of things had left Ireland unlovely. But if we do not passionately strive to build it better, better for men, for the women, for the children, of what worth are we? . . .[1]

In that passage Russell was bringing the facts of every day into relation with his vision; the facts are scientific, the vision is religious, and it is the religious element that predominates; the whole tone of the passage is emotive; he was rousing his audience to action, and to action based not on immediate necessities so much as on an ideal. As a contrast, here is a piece of purely scientific political writing:

The history of trade union organization and the communal psychology of the manual worker cannot be understood by anyone who ignores these facts. Consciously and unconsciously, in all countries where the economic and industrial system of capitalism has developed, labour has tried to organize itself so that it may eliminate the inherent weakness of its position in economic warfare in relation to the employers, and may create a weapon of economic monopoly for labour powerful enough to oppose to that of property. There are two ways in which labour can establish a monopoly power of the kind enjoyed by employers and capable of effective use in economic war. The sudden withdrawal of highly-skilled workers from certain special trades or industries may exert temporarily the same kind of pressure upon large numbers of the population as does an extensive lock-out upon the industrial workers. For instance, the labour of some electricians has a monopoly value of this kind in economic war. In practice, however, the places of even the most skilled workers in the most technical operations can be filled temporarily, so that there are

[1] From *Imaginations and Reveries*, by A. E. (G. W. Russell), Maunsel, 1915.

very few cases in which this monopoly power of labour can be successfully organised and used. In fact the only way in which the workers can create for labour a monopoly power comparable to that of the employer is by extending the field of economic warfare. The isolated employer who gives notice to all the employees in his mine or factory immediately initiates against them a most effective operation of economic war by bringing to bear upon them the immediate pressure of the cutting off of their supplies, but if the employees of a single factory or mine strike against an employer, they exert no such pressure on anyone and are striking a blow against an opponent in a strong position, for in most cases he can simply fill up the places vacated by the strikers from the reservoir of unemployed. It is only by extending the area of the strike or lock-out that a potential monopoly power is created for labour, and the wider the area the greater potentially is that power. In practice, such power only becomes effective if all the workers can be simultaneously withdrawn from an industry in which complete stoppage of work has an immediate effect upon the economic life of the country. For instance, the monopoly value of the miners' labour cannot easily be used by them and made effective as a weapon of economic war (in the way in which the mine-owner uses the monopoly value of his ownership of the mines as a weapon against the miner in a lock-out), because there are always in the country at any particular moment accumulated stores of coal, the product of the miners' labour, and it will therefore take months before these stores are exhausted and before the effect is felt of the miners' withdrawing their labour. On the other hand, in the case of an industry like transport, where the product of the workers' labour cannot be accumulated and used by the employer as a weapon *against* the workers themselves in economic warfare, the effect of a withdrawal of labour, provided that it is on a sufficiently large scale, may be immediate and considerable, because the transport workers can use the value of their labour to the community as a weapon of economic war.[1]

That is a piece of purely expository prose, scientific prose. You cannot deduce from it what Mr. Woolf's hopes are, nor if he has any fears. The voice is entirely that of a lecturer in a chemical laboratory: if you put such and such with such and such in a test-tube, and heat them up to so many degrees Centigrade, the following will happen. It is beautifully detached; the person is revealed only by the closeness of his attention to his subject. Mr. Woolf has allowed no idea of ultimate ends to intrude. But political thought does, in point of fact, always have an end, either to make men move forward, or to defend the *status quo*. It usually has a vision of some kind or other, some sort of Utopia to which it would like to see men tend. The question we can ask ourselves is, Is it possible to be the detached, scientific observer, and speak as such, and yet express your hopes, as much by the tone in which you speak as by what you actually say?

Plato. . . . But let us continue. I will grant you your physical science. But surely, by itself, it would only produce a race of ingenious animals, without any notions of Good and Bad at all, and therefore unable to cohere in any society.

Philalethes. The animals, or some of them, as we have learned to know them, are rather too much social than too little! Indeed, it is to insects that I should go to seek the best model of that order-imposing society which you professed so much to admire.

Pl. You turn the tables on me! But please confine yourself

[1] From *After the Deluge,* by Leonard Woolf, Hogarth Press, 1931.

to men and tell me further what you mean. For the insects I am content to leave alone.

Ph. That is just what we cannot so easily do now. We know too much about them. But all I wanted to say was that men's conduct does not depend, except to a small degree, on their conscious ideas of Right and Wrong. Their behaviour comes down, for the most part, from generations of animal ancestors, and from men who lived thousands of years ago; and only later, in a secondary way, is it modified by the habits and thoughts engendered in our own time.

Pl. Your physical science, then, will only give new powers to creatures whose morals, if I understand you rightly, are those of insects. Does that prospect fill you with enthusiasm?

Ph. At any rate, it answers your point that science might dissolve the social bond.

Pl. Let us grant it. But nevertheless, it seems to be true that, if conduct were bad, science would make it worse.

Ph. Or, if good, better. But I will not exaggerate my own point. Some changes do, in course of time, happen to human ideas and ideals, and science has some effect in preparing these.

Pl. How so?

Ph. By producing in some minds, a readiness to ask the question 'why' about everything, including human institutions.

Pl. In so far as that is true, it must lead towards that anarchy with which I was inclined, from the beginning, to credit your society.

Ph. Yes, in so far. But that is not so very far; not so far, indeed, as I would like it to be.

Pl. Please be more explicit.

Ph. As I see the case, it is something like this. Many minds, even those of eminent men of science, perhaps, indeed, especially of those, never apply the method of science except to the special topic with which their inquiries are concerned. On other subjects they let themselves go, in the ordinary social prejudices. For that is a kind of relaxation, like running down hill on wheels after you have been laboriously pushing up.

Pl. Science you mean, in such cases, is like a mill stream, dammed off from everything but the mill, and in no danger of overflowing the country?

Ph. Yes. And such men will be generally conservative in their political views, and will think also that, because they are men of science, some special sanctity attaches to their prejudices. So that they, at any rate, will not lead us towards anarchy.

Pl. Apparently not.

Ph. On the other hand, there is another class of men, not practitioners of science themselves, but, by its spirit, which is that of free inquiry, set free to criticise, without mercy, a system of society which has not offered to them the opportunities of influence and power which they think they deserve. These men condemn all institutions, as the others defend them, and it is they who, when or if they get their way, produce the anarchy you fear.

Pl. Yes?

Ph. But both of these are very small classes. Elsewhere there is, on the one hand, a great mass of ignorance and indifference; and on the other hand, what I think most important, a minority, which may become a majority, of educated people who are sceptical without being revolutionary.

Pl. You mean?

Ph. That they look critically at social customs and institutions, asking what purpose they serve and ready to hear all that may be reasonably advanced for or against them. When they come to a conclusion they do so on good grounds, and when they seek a remedy they do so disinterestedly and with reasonable care not to produce greater evils, by changes sudden and unprepared, than those they desire to remedy. It is to this class of men that I look to bring science to bear, safely and usefully, upon society.

Pl. I understand. But even so, this group of reformers, I must insist, if they are indeed to reform and not destroy, must have a clear and true notion of what is bad and what is good.

Ph. No doubt. But they do not think that that is the point of difficulty.

Pl. What is, then?

Ph. The disagreements of people as to who is to have the good things. . . .[1]

That is beautiful prose, sinewy but never sharp, in no way overweighted, yet bearing all that it wants to bear. It carries conviction more than Russell's does, because it has none of the urgency that tends to make hope override fact, yet the hope is there. The tone is quiet and reasonable; there is no declaration about it, no telling us that men have the heavens above them, and the breath of life in their nostrils. Compare the rhythm of that last phrase I have taken from Russell with that of 'must have a clear and true notion of what is bad and what is good'. Lowes Dickinson's prose is far less stressed, it breathes the wisdom of the sage rather than that of the man of action: there is nothing rhetorical about it. The calm length of the sentences imposes a calm upon you as you read them. Or compare the simplicity of the diction with the more knotted effect Mr. Woolf gives. The latter's sentences are long, but the words he uses (perhaps they were unavoidable) make them a little rough and jerky: 'The sudden withdrawal of highly-skilled workers from certain special trades or industries may exert

[1] From *After Two Thousand Years,* by G. Lowes Dickinson, Allen and Unwin, 1930.

temporarily the same kind of pressure . . . .' The result is that this prose is not so persuasive as Dickinson's, it does not sink so readily into the consciousness. But to be able to write prose at once so warm and so detached as Dickinson's, is a high achievement of art.

§ 7

History

I SUGGESTED earlier in this book that history was the most impure of all literary forms, and by this I meant that not only does the historian want to produce various effects at various times, but that he often wants to produce them at the same time. We need not bother here to decide the constant argument as to whether history is art or science; let us say that it is like architecture in being a science out of which art can grow. In so far as it must examine into, and deal with, facts, where possible connecting them together or comparing them, it is science; in so far as it aims at imaginative reconstruction, and involves selection, it is art: and so far as it is communication it is art. Moreover, a historian who had no prejudices or passions, no intellectual preferences, would be a monster, and his work would probably be unreadable. We can see what an impure art it is when we consider that we might, perhaps, have done without this section altogether, and left historians to be represented under narrative— description of events, description of things, description of people (see, for example, Namier's 'Newcastle', p. 41)—or again under philosophic or emotive. Froude went so far as to say that the historian had to have all the gifts of the dramatist—and something else as well. So the manner of writing history, within the limits of the historian's own style, will vary with what he wants to do.

But still, I think, one can defend giving a section to historians, for there is a special job which they alone have to do. They are concerned, not only with what happened, but why it happened, and the way it happened—after they have made up their minds that it really did happen. Their peculiar task seems to be to bring a great number of considerations to bear upon one event; they have to concentrate upon it all that wide reading, a clear and as far as possible impartial brain, with a knowledge of human beings, can gather together, and illuminate it with imaginative sympathy.

You can, of course, simply state your results:

The motive behind the party passions and political manœuvres of the age of Anne was religious, or if not religious in the higher sense, at least denominational. The world of Marlborough and St John, of Defoe, Swift and Sacheverell does not appear religious in the same sense as the world of Laud and Baxter, of Cromwell and George Fox. The chief actors in Anne's reign, even when they are beating the drum ecclesiastic, do not seem to have essentially religious minds. Doctrine and ritual are no longer undergoing transmutation in the crucible of war and parliamentary debate. The House no longer divides on Arminianism or the use of the surplice. The doctrine and ritual of the Church of England has become a fixed quantity that no one proposes to alter. The Dissenting Sects hold with easy minds the doctrines that their grandfathers sought after sorrowing, and reached with doubts and divisions, groans and tears. And the Puritans no longer aspire to capture the Church of England. Controversy, therefore, has limits set within which it must move, yet within these limits the rivalry of Church, Dissent and that vague *tertium quid*—Free Thought—is the very pulse of the machine of politics. As in the Ireland of to-day, so in the England of Anne, although men no longer debated doctrine and ritual as the subject-matter of politics, the framework of the rival political parties was formed on a confessional basis, and dislike of the smell of one's neighbour's religion seemed the prevailing passion of man as a political animal.[1]

The whole thing is presented with that finality and conciseness which goes with statement of fact: 'The House no longer divides on Arminianism or the use of the surplice.' Each sentence is short, and ends decisively: there are no subsidiary clauses. Trevelyan was simply *telling* us; that is all. Yet when we look more closely, we see that he is doing far more than tabulating results: he is colouring them by purely literary means so as to give some idea of the feelings of the time: 'doctrines that their grandfathers sought after sorrowing, and reached with doubts and divisions, groans and tears'; making it alive for us today by such a phrase as 'the smell of one's neighbour's religion'. It is science and art combined.

We can follow this with a passage which shows not only what happened, but how it happened (by a freak of luck it largely explains the results Trevelyan tells us about):

In the year 1690 appeared a pamphlet entitled *A Discourse of Trade*, by *N. B.*, *M.D.* Notable for its enlightened discussion of commercial theories for the balance of trade, it is a good specimen of an indifferent *genus*. But its authorship was more significant than its argument. For N. B. was Dr Nicholas Barbon; and Dr Nicholas Barbon, currency

[1] From *England under Queen Anne*: vol. i, *Blenheim*, by G. M. Trevelyan, O.M., Longmans, 1930.

expert, pioneer of insurance, and enthusiast for land-banks, was the son of that Praise-God Barebones, by the parody of whose alluring surname a cynical posterity recorded its verdict on the brief comedy of the Rule of the Saints over Laodicean Englishmen. The reaction from Puritan rigour to Restoration licence is the most familiar of platitudes. The reaction to a mundane materialism was more gradual, more general, and ultimately of greater significance. The profligacy of the courtier had its decorous counterpart in the economic orgies of the tradesman and the merchant. Votaries, not of Bacchus, but of a more exacting and more profitable divinity, they celebrated their relief at the discredit of a too arduous idealism, by plunging with redoubled zest into the agreeable fever of making and losing money.

The transition from the anabaptist to the company promoter was less abrupt than might at first sight be supposed. It had been prepared, however unintentionally, by Puritan moralists. In their emphasis on the moral duty of untiring activity, or work as an end in itself, on the evils of luxury and extravagance, on foresight and thrift, on moderation and self-discipline and rational calculation, they had created an ideal of Christian conduct, which canonized as an ethical principle the efficiency which economic theorists were preaching as a specific for moral disorders. It was as captivating as it was novel. To countless generations of religious thinkers, the fundamental maxim of Christian social ethics had seemed to be expressed in the words of St Paul to Timothy: 'Having food and raiment, let us be therewith content. For the love of money is the root of all evil.' Now, while, as always, the world battered at the gate, a new standard was raised within the citadel by its own defenders. The garrison had discovered that the invading host of economic appetites was, not an enemy, but an ally. Not sufficiency to the needs of daily life, but limitless increase and expansion, became the goal of the Christian's efforts. Not consumption, on which the eyes of the earlier sages had been turned, but production, became the pivot of his argument. Not an easy-going and open-handed charity, but a systematic and methodical accumulation, won the meed of praise that belongs to the good and faithful servant. The shrewd calculating commercialism which tries all human relations by pecuniary standards, the acquisitiveness which cannot rest while there are competitors to be conquered or profits to be won, the love of social power and hunger for economic gain—these irrepressible appetites had evoked from time immemorial the warnings and denunciations of saints and sages. Plunged in the cleansing waters of later Puritanism, the qualities which less enlightened ages had denounced as social vices emerged as economic virtues. They emerged as moral virtues as well. For the world exists not to be enjoyed, but to be conquered. Only its conqueror deserves the name of Christian. For such a philosophy, the question 'What shall it profit a man?' carries no sting. In winning the world, he wins the salvation of his own soul as well.[1]

That has not, we feel, quite the detachment of science. Tawney had discovered a truth, and he wanted us to share it; but we can hear from the way he told it that this truth pleases him enormously: it is with delighted zest that he pursued the puritan and exposed him. He was simply explaining how a thing happened, yes, but he could not keep his delight out of his voice. Nor need we want him to have. We do not ask for our historians to be dictaphones; we demand that they should be men, for unless they colour history for us with their own personalities, we shall not read them, however regrettable this may seem. There is a sharpness about his sentences that admirably conveys the

[1] From *Religion and the Rise of Capitalism*, by R. H. Tawney, Murray, 1926 (1st ed. 1922).

tone he wished, a steely quality: 'the shrewd, calculating commercialism' for instance. A slight flavour of scorn runs through the whole, occasionally defining itself as in the gentle hiss of 'on work as an end in itself': there are hardly any deep-toned sounds at all. It is the sort of passage that convinces us that Clio, after all, is a muse.

Both Trevelyan and Tawney had conclusions they could state: the former had a set of facts, the latter a set of justified inferences. Sometimes an historian allows us to see him getting his facts, unravelling conflicting evidence: then the prose is much more scientific, comes near to legal prose, in fact, as in the following extract:

The Empire at this time seemed lost among the Slavs. Just to the north lay the great kingdom of Bulgaria, by now predominantly a Slav kingdom; to the west of that were the Slav Serbians and Croatians; further north was Sviatopulk's huge Moravian Empire, and still further north, Poland and Bohemia; on the east on the Dnieper was the growing power of Russia. And in addition the Empire itself was filled with unruly Slavs. The Hungarians came as a deliverance. About 895 the Emperor Leo, at war with Symeon of Bulgaria, called in the Hungarians to take Bulgaria in the rear—he found it more pious and less expensive to use them to fight against his co-religionists. During the Hungarians' absence in Bulgaria, the Petchenegs, with whom Symeon managed to ally himself, raided and destroyed their homes; and on their return the Hungarians were obliged to move elsewhere. Accordingly, about the year 900, under their chief Prince Arpad they crossed the Carpathians and fell upon the plain of the Danube and the Theiss, and the hills of Transylvania, then shared between the Moravian and the Bulgarian monarchs. By 907 the Moravian kingdom had vanished, and the Hungarians were firmly settled in the empty place.

The Anonymous Hungarian historian declares that they met with opposition from the Bulgarians and from a small body of Greeks. That the Bulgarians opposed them is certain; but the Greeks can scarcely have objected to the fall of Moravia and the loss to Bulgaria of half its territory. The Hungarians were still close enough to raid the Empire, but now they had the tempting riches of Western Europe near by, to divert their attention; and Byzantium must have relished the disappearance of Slav Moravia and the partial isolation of the Bulgars. Once settled in their new home, the Hungarians raided freely and successfully. It was Germany and Italy that suffered most; but France was not unspared, and the terrible cavalry rushed down as far as Andalusia. About the time of Arpad's death (907) a band of Hungarians under two prominent princes crossed south as far as Macedonia, to the terror of Bulgars and Macedonians, and raided Rascia and the theme of Durazzo. This band lingered so long that at last it forgot the way home, and stayed to be a new ingredient in the ethnological hotchpotch of the Balkans.

For about twenty-five years the Balkans seem to have rested; though during all the Bulgar war Byzantine diplomats were busy among the princes of the Magyars. Then soon after 930 the invasions of the Empire recommenced, with details hard to be deciphered. The account in all the Greek chronicles—an account that there is no reason to doubt—is that in April, 934, the Hungarians, for the first time, ravaged Thrace on the way to Constantinople. The Protovestiarius Theophanes went out to meet them and to arrange terms. This he managed with great success, satisfying both Greeks and Hungarians—though the former paid heavily, while Romanus, from the goodness of his heart, spared no money in the redemption of captives. The Hungarian historians are vaguer; one version, dating the invasion in the twenty-first year (from the conquest of Moravia, i.e. about 928) says that the Hungarians captured Adrianople (Hydropolis) and besieged Constantinople, and then tells the story of a single combat and of perfidy on the Emperor's part. Eventually the Hungarians retreated, devastating all Greece. The other version, dating it in the twentieth year, merely says that Constantinople was too strong to take, so the Hungarians ravaged the rest of Greece: while the Anonymous Hungarian, without dating the legend, merely states that it was untrue that the Hungarians ever burnt the Golden Gate of the City. Thus far, the stories fit well enough; the difficulty arises with the version of the contemporary Maçoudi. According to him, on the frontiers of the Greek Empire, in a strong position between the mountains and the sea, lay the important town of 'Valander'. The 'Turks' could not penetrate through here. Owing, however, to a squabble kindled by an insulted Moslem merchant from Ardebil, the population of Valander raided into Turkish territory. The Turks therefore formally united —and the context implies that this was a union of Hungarians with Bashkirs and Petchenegs, under a Petcheneg chieftain— and set out with 60,000 horse against Valander. The Emperor 'Armenus' (Romanus) sent 50,000 Greek troops with 12,000 newly converted Christians against the Turks; but there was a terrific Greek defeat, and the Turks were so sated with captives that a woman could be bought for a silk dress. Then after lingering a little outside the walls of Valander, the Turks moved off to Western Europe. All this Maçoudi dates in the year 932.

The obvious, and usually admitted, theory is that these stories refer to the same raid. Marquart, who went fully into the question, accepts, though with surprise, the union of Magyars with Petchenegs, and identifies Valander with Develtus, on the gulf of Burgas. But he does not overcome certain difficulties. Develtus, it is true, was in a key position

on one of the main routes to Constantinople, the route that
the Petchenegs, though not the Magyars, would certainly use;
it was also situated close to the Greek frontier, and was, I
believe, a Greek city. But if its citizens wished to raid 'Turkish' territory—even Petcheneg territory—they would have to
journey at least a hundred and fifty miles through Bulgaria
and then cross the Danube. There was no place where the
imperial frontier impinged on the 'Turkish', whether Magyar
or Petcheneg. Indeed, how the Empire could play the rôle
ascribed to it is very hard to see. Neither in 932 nor 934
could Romanus, busily engaged in both years in conducting
grand campaigns in the East, have managed to produce an
army of such size so quickly in Thrace. Moreover, it is
inconceivable that the Greek chroniclers should have omitted
so sensational an event when giving their quite coherent
version of the invasion. And finally, though it is possible to
envisage a union between the Magyars and the Petchenegs,
such a union is inherently highly improbable.[1]

Sir Steven Runciman, we see, is clearing the way
towards fact. His prose is necessarily more complicated than Trevelyan's. There is not, there could
not be, the same conciseness of statement, except
where he is judicially summing up. I suggest it should
be compared with the extract from Lord Sumner's
judgement (p. 95).

Sometimes, however, argument of this sort is required so as to elucidate some train of events, or some
reaction that without the argument does not seem clear:

. . . It is hardly credible that Godfrey met Coleman on
September 28, 1678 with any other object than to discuss
with him the charges made by Oates. Still less is it credible

[1] From *The Emperor Romanus Lecapenus*, by Steven Runciman,
Cambridge, 1929.

that Coleman failed to point out Oates' perjury in this matter. It need not be supposed that a definite statement passed from him. A hint would have sufficed. In some way, it may be conjectured, Coleman disclosed to the magistrate that which he should have concealed. Such understandings are abrupt in origin but swift in growth. Beyond doubt the secret, the shadow of which Godfrey saw stretching across the line of his life, was that the Jesuit congregation of April 24 had been held in the house and under the patronage of the Duke of York.

And hence arose the perplexity and depression of mind from which he is said to have suffered during the last days of his life. He was possessed of information which, if published, would infallibly ruin the cause of the Duke of York and of the Catholics, to whom he was friendly. It had come to him in private from his friend, and to use it might seem an act almost of treachery. Yet with these sentiments Godfrey's duty as a magistrate was in absolute conflict. It was undoubtedly his business at once to communicate his knowledge to the government. Not only was it illegal not to do so, and highly important that such a weighty fact should not escape detection, but Godfrey found himself at the centre of the investigation of Oates' discovery, and to reveal his news was probably the only way of exposing Oates' perjury. Nor did Godfrey underestimate the danger into which this knowledge brought him. He feared that he would be assassinated. The Jesuits were confronted with the fact that a secret of unbounded value to their enemies had come into the hands of just one of the men who could not afford, however much he might wish, to retain it. All the tremendous consequences which would ensue could not then be prevented or palliated. The only possible remedy was to take from Godfrey the power of divulging the secret. His silence must be secured, and it could only be made certain by the grave. To the suggestion that the motive to the crime was not sufficient, it need only be answered that at least nine men preferred to die a horrible and ignominious death rather than prove their innocence and purchase life by telling the facts. Godfrey's death was no ludicrous act of stupid revenge, but a clear-headed piece of business. It was a move in the game that was played in England between parties and religions, and which dealt with issues graver than those of life and death.[1]

The tone of that passage is slightly more argumentative than the tone of the previous one. You are aware all the time that Pollock was intent upon making you see eye to eye with him. The effect is given, I think, by bringing a heavy stress on the last word, which is a key one: 'by the grave', '. . . telling the facts', '. . . piece of business'. This, of course, must be led up to by beginning the sentence with a running, though not very marked rhythm: 'His silence must be secured . . .', 'To the suggestion that the motive . . .', 'Godfrey's death was no ludicrous act of stupid revenge . . .'. It is true that Sir Steven Runciman also tends to have a stress on the last word, but he has equally strong stresses at the beginnings of his sentences. Let us take a whole one. 'The obvious, and usually admitted, theory is that these stories refer to the same raid.' Once more, perhaps, I must repeat the warning that such modellings of sentences are probably not conscious: they are the way the man reveals himself by the quality of his voice.

Nevertheless, it may be argued, the historian ought to be detached. Cannot we have material in all its complication shown us without having to listen to an argument as well? Is it not possible to be as detached

---

[1] From *The Popish Plot*, by John Pollock, Duckworth, 1903.

as Trevelyan seems to have been, and yet not simplify
the material to the extent that he does? The achievement may be difficult, but is it out of reach?

... Although the avowed object of the quadruple alliance and
its proposed extension was the defence of Bohemia, it was
notorious that the subsidies of the English and Dutch would
be employed by Austria and Saxony in the re-conquest of
Silesia and possibly in the dismemberment of the electorate
of Brandenburg, though the full extent of the prospective dismemberment could not be determined until the two active
powers had agreed as to how the bear's skin should be divided
after the animal had been killed. The peace overture from
Berlin cut right across all such designs. At the same time
came the news that Frederick had spiked his enemy's guns
at St. Petersburg by a flattering invitation to the Tsaritsa to
terminate the war as mediator. If Russian aid was not forth-
coming, it might be well to make some use of the Prussian
overture. From one point of view it was not unattractive. If
Maria Theresa could be induced to accept it, and England,
as the paymaster, claimed some right of dictation, she would
once more be free, as in 1743, to concentrate her whole forces
against the house of Bourbon. On the other hand it could be
argued that Frederick was not to be trusted, that he had
broken one treaty and would as easily break another, that the
overture was a sign of weakness, and that it might be safer in
the end that he should be reduced to impotence, a consumma-
tion that would equally set free the Austrian forces, while
these would at the same time be immensely increased. The
elimination of Prussia from its newly-won position among the
great powers would be a disaster of the first magnitude to
France, and would force that state to make a humble peace.
Between the two alternative methods of getting rid of the
Prussian bugbear, by conciliation or by humiliation, neither
Newcastle nor Chesterfield could see their way to a decided

course. The tacit decision of the English ministers was to wait upon events. If Austria and Saxony came to an agreement (as they did in May), and if their invasion of Silesia was successful (as Chesterfield seems to have expected), then the league of Warsaw would be justified and Prussia would cease to trouble Europe. If on the other hand they failed to agree, or if the invasion was unsuccessful (as it was), then it would be necessary to fall back upon the renewal of the treaty of Breslau. Meanwhile they put off Frederick with evasive but conciliatory answers.[1]

Perhaps nobody who has not waded through the diplomatic correspondence of the period (as I happen to have done) can appreciate what a brilliant piece of compression that is, or what clarity of thought it meant to produce such a limpid statement of the issues. Before discussing it as prose, let us look at another piece of elucidation.

As in February Louis had been careful to show the Provisional government that his return to exile was to be regarded as a concession and not a surrender, so now he made it known in more unmistakable terms that his refusal to come forward at the general election did not in any way imply a permanent withdrawal from political affairs. Had he stood, he wrote on May 11, in an open letter to one of his friends, his antecedents would have made him against his will the man to whom all the dissatisfied would turn as leader. But 'if France had need of me,' he continued, 'if my part were clearly traced, I should not hesitate to override all secondary considerations in order to fulfil my duty. . . . Meanwhile voluntary exile is pleasant, just because I know it is voluntary.' Louis had, in fact, during these months, two scarcely reconcilable objects

[1] From *The Private Correspondence of Chesterfield and Newcastle, 1744–1746*, Introduction, by Sir Richard Lodge, Royal Historical Society, 1930.

in view. It was necessary that he should give the people an occasional lead, and allow them clearly to understand that there was no height which he was not prepared to venture, if they would follow him. But it was also necessary that the Assembly should be propitiated, the Assembly which might consign him again to exile, or at any rate exclude him from political life. On May 24 he wrote another letter, this time to the president of the Assembly, protesting against the maintenance of the law of banishment against him. How had he deserved it? By declaring that France was not the appanage of any man, family, or party? By his sufferings at the hands of the Government which the Republic had overthrown? By his deference to the Provisional Government in February? By his disinterested refusal to come forward in April? It was in championship of universal suffrage that he had attacked Louis Philippe; the same cause would ensure his services to the Assembly should they be required. 'In the presence of a king elected by two hundred deputies, I could remember that I was the heir of an empire founded by four million Frenchmen. In the presence of the national sovereignty, I can and will claim only my rights as a French citizen.' These two letters are typical of Louis Napoleon's cleverness in dealing with the situation; it is noteworthy that even the letter intended for the people contained a phrase which would soothe the Assembly, while even the letter intended to propitiate the Assembly contained an allusion designed to appeal to the people.[1]

Lodge's method was that of compression, Mr. Simpson's that of slight expansion, perhaps because the first, we feel, was written for fellow historians, the latter for laymen. That is, Lodge expected you to grasp the implications of what he said, Mr. Simpson

[1] From *The Rise of Louis Napoleon, 1808–1848*, by F. A. Simpson, Longmans, 1925.

skilfully makes them for you. Yet both are admirably clear. There are further points of likeness. Both are pleased with their subject, both reveal a sense of humour, both stick to the point. Where then does the marked difference lie? It is not in the relative length of the sentences or clauses, nor in any marked distinction between the kind of words they use: again it is in the tone of the voice, the way the phrases run. This requires close analysis, on the lines of prose prosody; but the difficulty of this sort of analysis, whether of prose or of poetry, is that though you can mark stresses, you cannot, without a far too complicated system of notation, show the variation in the weight of stresses; and though you can show some syllables as long and others as short, you cannot show how long or how short. There are infinite gradations both in stress and in length. Try to carry out some such scheme with the first sentence of each passage quoted, and with the notation we can use they will seem much the same: yet everybody's ear will recognize them as being different. It has something to do with the impact of the idea: it is the difference between 'it was notorious that' and 'so now he made it known . . . that'. It is, we can feel, the difference between someone telling you something and someone showing you something. Lodge was stating, Mr. Simpson explaining; yet at the same time the former explains and the latter states. It is a shifting of emphasis, of which has the priority, statement or explanation, a difference in stressing which becomes clearer if you read the passages aloud, a variation which does not defy the analysis of tasting, but does defy that of the printed symbol.

§ 8

Criticism

THE criticism of literature, as suggested earlier, may lead you anywhere—to metaphysics, to theology, as we have already seen with Middleton Murry (p. 120), to morals, to politics, or to making a magnificent splash with your own emotions. Ultimately, of course, literature has to be judged by its value to humanity: an appraisal of literature must in the end be an appraisal of values, though not of the everyday practical ones, nor of the obvious ones. The critic has to answer such questions as 'How far does literature enable mankind to live more happily, more intensely, more profoundly, more wisely?' These questions are extremely complicated, for everyone will differ from everyone else as to what he means by happy, profound, or wise. Moreover there is a further complication, for literature, especially poetry, *is* not always what it *is about*: the method of art is indirect. What, for instance, really is *The Rape of the Lock*? We know that it is about a young beau cutting a lock of hair from a belle, and that a variety of aerial sylphs are concerned in the matter: in fact, the story is extremely silly. But that is not the poem. What it is, is the sort of thing criticism makes it its business to discover and explain.

But leaving the question of ultimate values aside, there are still a number of directions in which criticism can work. It may choose to deal with the general nature of poetry, or, on the other hand, with questions of technique; that is, either with the nature of the poetic communication, or the means by which that communication is attained. The critic may discuss the way a poet proceeds, together with the make-up of poets in general, or with that of a special poet; or he may dissect a piece passage by passage, line by line, as Johnson and Landor did, a type of very useful criticism which hardly ever seems to be practised now; for romantic feeling seems to regard this as impious, on a line with trying to measure the influence of the Pleiades or to loosen the bands of Orion. The critic, again, may deal with general principles of writing, or with some particular literary point. All work of this sort is properly speaking literary criticism: its edges are not clearly defined, because, as we know, questions of value are bound to creep in at the end. Perhaps this is because critics and writers in general sometimes feel the need to justify their way of life. The world as a whole is not convinced of the worth of books as it is of the worth of, say, pigs: no one accuses you of wasting your time if you discuss pig-breeding—even Prime Ministers have done so—but you will still find a great many people who do not see 'the use' of reading Shakespeare. This may account for the frequent invasion of the moral sphere by critics, an adventure to which pig-breeders are not notably prone.

Criticism, indeed, is such a dubious business, that even people who, one supposes, would feel differently, often ask the question, 'What is the use of criticism?'[1] You cannot, they say, lay down rules,

[1] Sufficiently well answered by Mr. T. S. Eliot, in his *The Use of Poetry and the Use of Criticism*, Faber and Faber, 1933.

because genius always breaks them triumphantly; so why bother? Why not just enjoy what you read, and express your enjoyment? They then write passages with the object of creating in the reader just those emotions they felt when reading some book or poem, or the complete works of some great writer:

And so it is, I think, the Browning who feels, that matters; not the Browning who speculates about the Universe. For his speculations were rather a South Sea Bubble, however brightly coloured. But just as Tennyson outlives his own prophecies, as a painter of sky and earth, a musician of wave and tree, so Browning becomes worth hearing when he turns from his preaching to catch the leap of a lover's pulse or the answering flush on a girl's face. It is his lovers that live, just as the loves of Horace have outlived all the laws of Augustus—happy or tragic, faithful or faithless; triumphant in their brief pride above the dust of a dead city, while the sheep-bells tinkle where its belfries tolled; or saddened amid the desolate indifference of the Roman Campagna; or stepping gaily from a gondola in Venice to meet the dagger gleaming in the archway's gloom; now watching the alchemist pound the blue poison for a rival's lips, or quietly strangling a fickle mistress, so as to keep her always, with her own long, coiling hair; now pressing a rose-leaf for remembrance in a dead girl's hand, or riding for the last time on earth with a woman loved in vain, or remembering sadly, yet gladly, on a death-bed the stolen meetings of long ago. . . .[1]

No one will deny that that is extremely good of its kind; as a piece of emotive prose it is admirable, with its long-sustained sentence which carries you without pause from one passionate or sentimental position to

[1] From *Eight Victorian Poets*, by F. L. Lucas, Cambridge, 1930.

another, with its skilful use of consonants as in 'stepping gaily from a gondola in Venice', or of vowels as
in 'with her own long, coiling hair'. Such literature has
its value: in expressing his own emotions in this way
Mr. Lucas communicates something to his readers:
but the question we have to ask ourselves is, 'Is this
criticism?' What does it do to make clear to us the
peculiar quality of what Browning has to give? Might
not the same be said, perhaps, of Boccaccio? We
know a great deal about Mr. Lucas after reading that
passage, but do we know anything about Browning?
This sort of criticism has been called, justly I think,
'etiolated creation', for Mr. Lucas is creating something, not an object so much as an atmosphere, not
from life, but from literature, that is, life already at
one remove. One objection to it as criticism is that it
assumes that the reader has exactly the same sensibilities as the critic, not merely the same sort of mental
apparatus, similar physical sensations, and comparable standards of, and capacity for, judgement—these
have always to be assumed—but identical suscepti-
bility and associations. It is, in a way, dangerous, because it may give you the impression that after reading
it you know something about Browning; it will serve
as a substitute for him, so you need never read him:
and Mr. Lucas would be the first to agree that it is far
better that people should read the poets than anything
written about them. Finally, it is not criticism because
it does not give you the peculiar pleasure of criticism,
but that of experiencing some general emotion with
a vague reference to life.

For criticism—perhaps I may say it again—is a

M

pleasurable activity (otherwise I should not have written this book, and you would not be reading it), and
its peculiar pleasure lies in its function of making distinctions, of getting things clear, of enabling you to
see your way through the wood. It can make distinctions of many kinds, distinctions of sensibility, of
forms, of periods, between one kind of poetry and
another, between poetry and prose, as to the nature of
one kind of writer as compared with another.[1] If you
ask what 'the use' of all this may be, one can only
answer that apart from the pleasure it gives—and
pleasure is a positive value—it leads you to a finer
appreciation of writing, and makes you realize more
clearly, more completely, what any given writer
meant. It is true that there are some who object with
James Thomson that

> If you will analyse the bread you eat,
> The water and the wine most pure and sweet,
> Your stomach soon must loathe all drink and meat:

but I cannot for the life of me see why. Because you
understand radiation and convection does the fire
warm you any less? By analysing his sensations,
which is the critic's basic work, he does not impo-
verish them: on the contrary, they gain a richness
from being brought into harmony among themselves,
thus forming a composite whole, instead of a series of
isolated emotions.[2]

---

[1] There is also 'historical criticism': this is a sub-department of socio-
logy.
[2] See *Principles of Literary Criticism*, by I. A. Richards, Kegan Paul,
1925.

Here, then, we shall confine our examples of critical prose to what we can describe as 'literary criticism'. Let us begin with a simple piece of exposition:

The first and most obvious peculiarity which every one notices in poetry is its *metre*—the marked rhythm or beat of the sound of its words; for this seems to put it most distinctly apart from all other ways of using language. With the peculiar distinction of *metre*, we are familiar from the very first, long before we ever thought of noticing how its effect comes about. For our nursery rhymes are always admirable specimens of metre. For example:

> Zinty tinty tuppenny bun,
> The cock went out to have some fun.
> He had some fun: he beat the drum.
> Zinty tinty tuppenny bun.

Now of course the metre is not the only thing which those lines give us; but it is the thing in them which first and most strongly takes hold of our minds. And it seems pretty clear, that the very peculiar *sense* of these lines would not hold together at all, if it were not for the metre. From which it appears, that you can say things in metre which could hardly be said otherwise: in this rather special case, you can give irresistible currency to what is roughly called *nonsense*.

Now, even in such a simple example of metre as this, it is worth while noticing how it makes its effect. Part of the effect of the whole *quatrain* (which is the name often used for a distinct group of four lines) is due to the fact that the rhythm of the first and fourth lines is not quite of the same kind as the rhythm of the second and third lines. I will explain the difference a little later on. What is even more important is this: the rhythm or beat of the words runs right through the first, second, and fourth lines without a stop; but in the third line the rhythm is strongly divided by a pause in the middle into two equal halves, which throws this line into marked contrast with the others and makes it the climax of the four. Of course, the rhythm pauses in the middle of the line because the sense pauses there also; but it is precisely because the stop in the sense is accompanied by this stop in the rhythm that the quatrain makes its point. If you say the lines aloud, you will find that this metrical effect in the third line enables you to make the fun which the cock actually did have a matter of some excitement:

He had some fun: he beat the drum.

After the brief suspense of the rhythm on the word 'fun', does it not seem inevitable that you should raise your voice and put special emphasis on 'he *beat* the *drum*'? It is the metre which both induces you to do that and makes the doing of it so effective.[1]

It seems easy to do this sort of thing, yet this extreme clarity and simplicity can only be achieved by a man who knows his subject-matter both intimately and profoundly: it is extraordinarily easy to confuse issues when writing on a subject of this kind. Professor Abercrombie is, of course, explaining to beginners, but that makes it all the harder, because he can take nothing for granted. The passage is a model of expository prose; and it is because criticism is expository that one classes its prose with the scientific. Abercrombie allowed no emotional issue to cloud his reasoning here: but what follows is something from which emotion cannot altogether be kept away, because we are bound to have some feeling about the subject.

[1] From *Poetry; its Music and Meaning*, by Lascelles Abercrombie, Oxford, 1932.

The novelist, I am supposing, is faced with a situation in his story where for some good reason more is needed than the simple impression which the reader might have formed for himself, had he been present and using his eyes on the spot. It is a case for a general account of many things; or it is a case for a certain view of the facts, based on inner knowledge, to be presented to the reader. Thackeray, for example, has to open his mind on the subject of Becky's ambitions or Amelia's regrets; it would take too long, perhaps it would be impossible, to set them acting their emotions in a form that would tell the reader the whole tale; their creator must elucidate the matter. He cannot forget, however, that this report of their emotions is a subjective affair of his own; it relies upon his memory of Becky's or Amelia's plight, his insight into the workings of their thought, his sense of past action. All this is vivid enough to the author, who has seen and known, but the reader stands at a further remove.

It would be different if this consciousness of the past, the mind which holds the memory, should itself become for the reader a directly perceptible fact. The author must supply his view, but he might treat his view as though it were in its turn a piece of action. It *is* a piece of action, or of activity, when he calls up these old recollections; and why should not that effort be given the value of a sort of drama on its own account? It would then be like a play within a play; the outer framework at least—consisting of the reflective mind—would be immediately in front of the reader; and its relation to the thing framed, the projected vision, would explain itself. So long as the recorder stands outside and away from his book, as Thackeray stands outside Vanity Fair, a potential value is wasted; the activity that is proceeding in his mind is not in itself an element in the effect of the book, as it might be. And if it was thus drawn into the book it would do double duty; it would authenticate and so enhance the picture; it would add a new and independent interest as well. It seems that there is everything to be said for making a drama of the narrator himself.[1]

Moreover, another emotion besides that due to one's memories is added, the emotion one feels about craftsmanship: it need not be very warm, but it is there. There is also a slight, a very slight, tinge of feeling communicated by the prose. Take the sentence beginning 'It *is* a piece of action . . .' and ending with a query to the reader. Mr. Lubbock is involving you in the discussion, so that you cannot remain indifferent to the 'wastage' of a 'potential value'. Abercrombie very carefully kept you outside. He is showing you something, pointing out certain aspects of an object: Mr. Lubbock is inviting you to think, not to see; and this difference in the effect on you is due to a difference in the speed of the prose. Abercrombie was brisk: he would never let you pause in a sentence unless he wanted to emphasize what is to follow. There are no implied parentheses, such as 'I am supposing', or 'the projected vision'. He would say 'of course', to make you feel easy, but he would not ask you a question. He makes you less contemplative than Mr. Lubbock does, because he ended his sentences hard: 'about', 'minds', 'stop', 'four', 'point': not with 'might be' or 'as well'. Abercrombie's prose is more limpid than Mr. Lubbock's; it runs more readily, but then Mr. Lubbock is dealing with something far more complex, something you cannot run over rapidly, though at the same time we must remember that it is Abercrombie's drastic simplification that

[1] From *The Craft of Fiction*, by Percy Lubbock, Cape, 1921.

makes his subject seem easier. Both passages are good pieces of exposition, and the matter of the one requires treatment different from the matter of the other. But is that the whole story? Not quite. In the first example we hear the voice of a man surveying his subject, in the second of a man probing into it: and beyond that again is the natural speech accent of the different individuals.

It is not unusual to find a combination of the two attitudes of surveying and probing, what the probing brings forth being continually added to the survey. Should we not then expect a style midway between the two last exemplified?

Dryden's gift for adapting his rhythmical emphasis to his meaning amounted to genius. Alliteration, effective rhyme, antithesis, and the use of polysyllables were only auxiliaries to that. It was that which gave him rapidity without the appearance of haste and flexibility without the loss of strength. Bound by the laws of a syllabic system of versification and condemned to a narrow metrical range, he succeeded in manipulating his measures so that he could speak directly and easily yet with dignity. He was more than a believer in mere variety of accent, though he stressed that too as early as the *Essay of Dramatic Poesy*, where Neander observed, 'Nothing that does *Perpetuo tenore fluere*, runs in the same channel, can please always. 'Tis like the murmuring of a stream, which not varying in the fall, causes at first attention, at last drowsiness. Variety of cadences is the best rule.' Dryden was a believer in significant variety of accent. Pope, in a letter to his friend Henry Cromwell, recognised three places within the heroic line where pauses might come: after the fourth, after the fifth, and after the sixth syllables. Dryden knew no limits of the kind. The freedom of blank verse seems to have been in his thoughts. His pauses come anywhere; and often they do not come at all, as in these lines:

> Drawn to the dregs of a democracy, . . .
>
> Of the true old enthusiastic breed, . . .
>
> To the next headlong step of anarchy, . . .
>
> But baffled by an arbitrary crowd.

He kept himself free to distribute his emphasis where the sense demanded it. The result was what might be called a speaking voice in poetry. Some one seems actually to be reciting *Absalom and Achitophel*:

> Others thought kings an useless heavy load,
> Who cost too much, and did too little good;
> They were for laying honest David by,
> On principles of pure good husbandry.

And the voice of a flesh and blood Prologue is plainly heard here:

> Lord, how reformed and quiet are we grown,
> Since all our braves and all our wits are gone! . . .
> France, and the fleet, have swept the town so clear
> That we can act in peace, and you can hear. . . .
> 'Twas a sad sight, before they marched from home,
> To see our warriors in red waistcoats come,
> With hair tucked up, into our tiring room.
> But 'twas more sad to hear their last adieu:
> The women sobbed, and swore they would be true . . .

Everywhere Dryden's personal presence can be felt. Pope lurks behind his poetry; Dryden stands well forward, flush with his page and speaking with an honest voice if not an honest heart.[1]

[1] From *John Dryden*, by Mark Van Doren, Harcourt Brace and Howe, 1920; The Minority Press, 1931.

Here you are invited both to think and see. The sentences are statements, ending hard, and therefore
expressed with conviction. They also begin forcibly.
Mr. Van Doren does not say, 'Dryden's personal presence can be felt everywhere', but 'Everywhere Dryden's personal presence can be felt'. The emotivity,
if there is any, is that of exhilaration, of a sense of
glory, as in the last sentence quoted, and it is conveyed
by the form of the sentences as well as by the meaning
of the words. The tone is expository, but it is not so
detached as Abercrombie's: we are to be made to see
by being awakened to sight. Yet all the while we are
being shown as well as being told, we are present at
the probing, and sometimes the tone changes a little
in conformity with the different sense: 'The freedom
of blank verse seems to have been in his thoughts.'
We can imagine infinite gradations in the tone of
exposition, the particular one being determined by
the character of the writer.

   This next piece of critical prose is not expository:
it tells, yes, but it is a summing up, to which is added
an explanation of the judgement:

If one English poet might be recalled to-day from the dead
to continue the work which he left unfinished on earth, it is
probable that the crown of his country's desire would be set
on the head of John Keats, for he was smitten down in his
youth, in the very maturing of powers, which, having already
produced work of almost unrivalled beauty, held a promise of
incredible things.
   Had his marvellous genius fully matured, it is impossible
to surmise what Keats might not have done: but concerning
the poetry that he has actually left us, the general verdict is

that, while the best of it is of the highest excellence, the most of it is disappointing. Nor is this judgment likely to be overset, although some may always unreservedly admire him on account of his excellences,—and this because his fault is often the excess of a good and rare quality,—and others again as unreservedly depreciate him on account of that very want of restraint, which in his early work, besides its other immaturities, is often of such a nature as to be offensive to good taste, and very provocative of impatient condemnation.

Among Keats' poems, too, a quantity of indifferent and bad verses is now printed, not only from a reverence for his first volume, which he never revised, and which is very properly reprinted as he issued it, but also from a feeling which editors have had, that since anything might be of value, everything was; so that any scrap of his which could be recovered has gone into the collections. Concerning which poor stuff we may be consoled to know that Keats himself would have had no care; for, not to speak of what was plainly never intended for poetry at all, he seems to have regarded at least his earlier work as a mere product of himself and the circumstances, now good now bad, its quality depending on influences beyond his control and often adverse, under which he always did his best. On one point only was he sensitive, and that was his belief that he sometimes did well, and would do better. The failures he left as they were, having too much pride to be ashamed of them, and too strong a conviction of an everflowing, and, as he felt, an increasing and bettering inspiration, to think it worth while to spend fresh time in revising what a younger moment had cast off.[1]

What follows is, in a sense, a summing up too, but the explanation is of greater importance:

It will seem to some readers hardly fair to compare a poem like *In Memoriam*, which, if in places the staple of its feeling

[1] *A Critical Introduction to Keats*, by Robert Bridges, Oxford, 1929.

and thought wears a little thin, is entirely serious throughout, with poems which have so much the character of an intellectual *tour de force* as Donne's *Anniversaries*, but it is easy to be unjust to the sincerity of Donne in these poems. Their extravagant eulogy did not argue any insincerity to Sir Robert and Lady Drury. It was in the manner of the time, and doubtless seemed to them as natural an expression of grief as the elaborate marble and alabaster tomb which they erected to the memory of their daughter. The *Second Anniversarie* was written in France when Donne was resident there with the Drurys. And it was on this occasion that Donne had the vision of his absent wife which Walton has related so graphically. The spiritual sense in Donne was as real a thing as the restless and unruly wit, or the sensual, passionate temperament. The main thesis of the poem, the comparative worthlessness of this life, the transcendence of the spiritual, was as sincere in Donne's case as was in Tennyson the conviction of the futility of life if death closes all. It was to be the theme of the finest passages in his eloquent sermons, the burden of all that is most truly religious in the verse and prose of a passionate, intellectual, self-tormenting soul to whom the pure ecstasy of love of a Vondel, the tender raptures of a Crashaw, the chastened piety of a Herbert, the mystical preconceptions of a Vaughan could never be quite congenial.[1]

The first thing that strikes us about these two last passages is that whereas Bridges was proclaiming something you will disbelieve at your peril, Grierson was persuading you to think as he himself did. Bridges had taken up a position: he even hectored you a little, so that you feel inclined by way of reaction, even if you did not think so before, to protest that the things which are offensive to his taste may not be so to yours.

[1] *Donne's Poetical Works*, ed. by H. J. C. Grierson, Oxford, 1912.

Bridges was speaking *ex cathedra*; there can be no per-
missible doubt as to what 'good' taste is, about what
is silly in Keats, about what is best: he permitted himself a Johnsonian hammer-blow—'very provocative
of impatient condemnation'. He showed you that
you are to make a sharp division between your feelings
for the man and your judgement of the poet, for in
the first part he slips in emotive words or ideas: Keats
left work 'unfinished *on earth*', not simply unfinished:
he was 'smitten down', he did not merely die. Except
in the first short paragraph there is nothing of this.
He spoke like a dictator, and there is a superb certainty in everything that he said: he drove home his
meaning in a way to jolt you into conviction: he did
not brutally subdue your mind, rather he surprised
you into agreement by a flat statement which contrasts
with his seemingly irresistible motion forward. Take,
'but also from a feeling which editors have had, that
since anything might be of value, everything was'.
Grierson is more sympathetic to Donne, he makes us
feel, than Bridges was to Keats. His passage is far less
abrupt: the sentences all end in a weak syllable, not
with 'was' or 'care' or 'best': suppose, for instance, he
had written 'so graphically related' instead of 'related
so graphically': even that would have made a difference to the impact of his ideas on your mind, though
still the last syllable is unstressed. One understands
Donne better after reading the passage about him,
whereas Keats remains as distant as ever. But then
Bridges meant you to approach the poetry direct,
while Grierson wanted you to arrive at it through the
poet. But here again subject or intention will not by

themselves account for the difference: we know as well as we can know anything that Grierson could not for the life of him have written as Bridges did, nor could Bridges have written like Grierson: the latter was too interested in the ideas he was pursuing to want to strike an attitude about them: he was too aware of the complexity of his subject to be dictatorial about it. We feel this especially when he wrote 'quite congenial' instead of 'congenial'. He refused to speak out of his own authority, as Bridges dared to do: he was far more tender of his readers' sensitive spots. Yet there was nothing feeble about him: he thought what he thought, but he supposed also that you might have different views.

The particular end of criticism, we suggested, was to distinguish, and a step towards this is analysis. We can begin with a piece of general analysis which comes near historical criticism at the end, but still remains literary criticism:

Clarissa trembles on the edge of the ridiculous. Pomposity, smugness, and fatuity are always just round the corner. And yet it would not be fair to dismiss it as merely pompous, smug, or fatuous. In it there is a remarkable refinement of observation, and an amazing insight into all the corners of a small but ardent mind. Richardson's sympathies, for all the narrowness of their range, were extraordinarily acute, and so completely does he live in and through the soul of Clarissa that one is compelled to admit that one at least knows what Dr. Johnson meant when he said that there was 'more knowledge of the human heart' in one letter of *Clarissa* than in all of the novels of Fielding. In it readers could recognize themselves to an extent which was impossible in any previous novel. Experiences such as might possibly happen to them were here happening to people like themselves, and they could live with Clarissa on the terms of an intimacy impossible in the case of any other heroine of fiction. No one could possibly *behave* like Don Quixote or Robinson Crusoe, but thousands must have asked themselves what Clarissa (or Lovelace!) would have done in these circumstances or those.

Thus their creator at once restricted and enlarged the field of fiction. He eliminated all extraordinary adventures and all passions more exalted than those within the range of the more ordinary sort of person, but he examined the emotions appropriate to bourgeois existence with a minuteness never known before, and he did for the middle-class heart what Defoe had done for the externals of daily life—he examined, that is to say, all its little hopes, scruples, and perturbations, with an eye which delighted to note and respect them. Hence it was thanks more to his influence than to that of any other man that the novel could become, as it did, a dominant influence in moulding the opinions, the manners, and the modes of feeling cultivated by a very large section of any literate public.[1]

The tone of that is quite impartial: treating things on such a large scale does not lend itself to emotion, not even the emotion that peeps through Grierson's accumulating sentences, for though Krutch's sentences are long, they are not cumulative; they present the same consistency throughout. But one need not be detached to say something general: often, even, detachment would nullify what you have to say:

Like leaves imprisoned beneath thick ice, which the poet mentions in a passage I have transcribed above, Mallarmé's *concetti*, his *Petits Vers*, inscriptions for fans, enigmatic and melodious stanzas to be copied into the pages of an album,

[1] From *Five Masters*, by Joseph Wood Krutch, Cape, 1931.

verse epistles, rhyming envelopes, are less fluttering and ephemeral than from the nature of such productions we usually expect. Imagine a clear sheet of ice, solid, unflawed, allowing the passer-by to look down and examine its depths, the ingenuous aspirations which lay immobilized there, the combed-out tresses of the stream, drowned refuse and all the wrack and wastage of circumstance. . . . Yet under this translucent covering, to-and-fro moves an inconstant, small brilliant flame, glowing through its coffin-lid, momentarily transforming the icy, motionless fronds among which it is immured. 'Il détient le génie, la puissance, la gloire,' Mallarmé said after visiting Victor Hugo, 'mais il lui manque une petite flamme que j'ai et que je voudrais lui donner.' The consciousness of genius, Mallarmé's preoccupation with the Word, its lofty obsession,—'donner un sens plus pur aux mots de la tribu',—so irradiates his verse that although, during his search for a poetic formula which should have enabled him to put his hands on the essential part of every poet's inspiration—(the long-drawn melancholy cadence of Baudelaire's autumnal dirge, what critics have called his *miaulement* or voluptuous feline wail)—he seems to have destroyed the sententious magniloquence of the ancient poetry by excluding its rhetorical basis, equally he would seem to have re-endowed it with that interior dispassionate glow which, if not altogether lost, it was then in some danger of losing. Convinced that literary expression had grown too elastic, that its channels were too accommodating, the writer was concerned to erect fresh obstacles, since we can best achieve solitude by retreating on to a plane where the larger number of our contemporaries will not care to follow. Yet it was no mere immunity from latter-day contacts that Mallarmé sought; the sympathies which actuated him had little or nothing in common with that cultivated depravation of literary taste, summed up in the protagonist of Huysmans' lugubrious romance. Mallarmé, we should remember, was a student of English verse; he had

learned to appreciate the magical *immediacy* of effect which is
the occasional, precarious, and hard-won privilege of certain
English writers. After a thousand beauties, so many of them
cumulative, which the fulness of time brings into being, which
their context gradually matures, the sudden emergence of
some felicitous image, springing like a group of sea-gods
where a moment earlier there was vacancy, flowering like a
wave where we could distinguish only the bare, uneventful
swelling and subsiding movement of the verse, is startling and
peculiarly delightful to a foreign ear:

> He question'd every gust of rugged wings
> That blows from off each beaked promontory,
> They knew not of his story
> And sage Hippotades their answer brings,
> That not a blast was from his dungeon stray'd,
> *The air was calm and on the level brine*
> *Sleek Panope and all her sisters play'd.*[1]

In this ornate passage Mr. Quennell is explaining
what Mallarmé was doing, or did, just as Krutch was
making up the ledger of Richardson's achievement.
Mr. Quennell is writing poetically, I do not mean
indulging in that bastard style which borders on
poetry in its rhythms and is known as 'poetic prose',
but that he is getting his results by imagery, so that
you shall arrive at his conclusions, at his analysis, by
intuition rather than by reason. The method is justi-
fiable (every method is, if you can bring it off), but
it has its obvious dangers, the plainest one being that
the means will become more important, to reader and
writer alike, than the end, unless it is well nourished
with fact. At all events we might call Krutch's prose

[1] From *Baudelaire and the Symbolists*, by Peter Quennell, Chatto and
Windus, 1929.

'scientific': we cannot give that adjective to Mr. Quennell's, for he appeals to your emotions all the time. The very beginning, with its inverted sentence 'Like leaves imprisoned beneath thick ice . . . Mallarmé's *concetti* . . .', with the use of the word 'imprisoned' to reinforce the tone, sets the emotions stirring. The suggestive word is continually used: 'enigmatic', 'fluttering', 'wrack and wastage', 'immured'; and towards the end the whole effect of the image of the group of gods, borne so to speak on the crest of a rising sentence-wave, works us up to feel, not just to note intellectually, the point of the quotation which follows. The test of such a piece of writing *as criticism* must be whether we begin to understand what Mallarmé was after when we have read it, as well as beginning to understand Mr. Quennell; or whether we understand Mr. Quennell to the exclusion of Mallarmé. But we are not here dealing with the virtues and vices of critics as critics; we are trying to see what they are doing with their prose, and how they do it. I have already suggested what Mr. Quennell does; he stirs your intuitive capacity into play: and I have partly suggested how he does it. We still have to listen to his 'voice', notice with what kind of emphasis he modulates his sentences. He has not the calm, even tone of Dr. Krutch; his voice is continually shifting its level, the emphases gradually rise towards the middle of the sentences and then sink down again. Take the one beginning 'Yet under this translucent covering . . .' or the one which sets off 'Convinced that literary expression . . .'. He likes to bring his first stress on his second syllable: 'Like léaves . . . Yet

únder . . . Convínced that . . .', and to spread out the
stresses towards the end: '. . . among which it is immured', '. . . will not care to follow', spread out too,
we notice, among rather long vowels, preferably
sonorous. Krutch ended firmly: '. . . just round the
corner', '. . . any other heroine of fiction', as he begins
equally firmly, '*Clarissa* trembles . . .', 'In it readers
would recognize . . .', and keeps up much the same
motion all the way through, being firm, but never
attaining the finality of Bridges.

Here is a manner far less stylized than Mr. Quennell's, though it deals with much the same subject, the
force of the word:

Sometimes these writings of Gertrude Stein make us laugh:
her humor is perhaps the one of her qualities which comes
through in her recent books most clearly; and I should
describe them as amusing nonsense, if 'nonsense' were not a
word which had so often been used in derogation both of the
original Symbolists and of the contemporary writers dealt
with in this book. If I should say Miss Stein wrote nonsense,
I might be thought to be implying that she was not serious or
that she was not artistically successful. As a matter of fact,
one should not talk about 'nonsense' until one has decided
what 'sense' consists of—and one cannot investigate this
without becoming involved in questions which go to the
bottom of the whole Symbolist theory and throw further light
on the issues it raises.

The original Symbolists supposed themselves to be defending the value of suggestion in literature as against the docu-
mentation of Naturalism and the logic of rationalism—and
both they and their opponents seemed to tend to take it for
granted that the suggestion was all on one side and the sense
all on the other. We have already noted this tendency in

Valéry, in Eliot and in Yeats, and we have stumbled over the difficulties it leads to. Now, as a matter of fact, all literature, all writing, all speech, depends equally upon suggestion; the 'meaning' of words is what they suggest. Speaking accurately, it is impossible to say that one kind of writing suggests, whereas another kind proves or states. Any literary work, if it accomplishes its purpose, must superinduce in the reader a whole complex of what we are accustomed to call thoughts, emotions and sensations—a state of consciousness, a state of mind; it depends for its effectiveness upon a web of associations as intricate, and in the last analysis as mysterious as our minds and bodies themselves. Our words themselves are the prime symbols and the only originality of the Symbolists consisted in reminding people of the true nature and function of words. It is of course possible to think of words abstractly so that they shall seem to have pure definite meanings, but the fact remains that as soon as we begin to use them, we cannot help pouring them full of suggestion by our inflections, our pauses, our tones or by their order and collocation on the page, and in any case selecting them in such a way as to bring out certain previous associations.[1]

It is often complained that criticism is dogmatic (a condition of affairs assumed to be intolerable), that it states where it should suggest, that it claims omniscience when in the nature of things it can only know a part. In some people's view criticism only becomes interesting when it approaches the dogmatic, when, that is to say, the critic has come to the stage where he can make some general statement, some observation which covers a great deal of ground. Mr. Wilson's is such a statement. It is quite true, of course, that you cannot 'state' anything nakedly, that you cannot

[1] From *Axel's Castle*, by Edmund Wilson, Scribner's, 1931.

strip words to their skeletons, but at the same time
we can mean something when we say that Mr. Wilson
makes a statement, and that Mr. Quennell does not.
It is in the tone of the voice. Mr. Quennell also states,
but he does not give us the impression of doing so:
he disguises his action by appealing to something
other than our knowledge and our reason, while Mr.
Wilson, through tact, is not so downright as he might
be, and softens the tone by putting in parentheses. It
is curious to note how the phrase, 'as a matter of fact',
which should, one supposes, be the sign that a dogmatic axiom is coming, brings about this softening
effect. Mr. Wilson uses it once in each of the two
paragraphs quoted: take it away and see what happens.
The tone becomes harsher. Length of sentence also
helps to make the tone milder, as does the occasional
'of course' which never means 'of course', or hardly
ever, but 'I concede you'. What Mr. Wilson says is
very apposite to our discussion. It is true that you
cannot state without suggesting, or suggest without
stating: what makes one passage differ from another is
the emphasis laid on statement or suggestion, and the
secret of this lies in the tone of the voice. Mr. Wilson
on the whole states; he gets the atmosphere of suggestion by the softening effects which we have noted.

But to be suggestive it is not necessary to be pliant
in this way, ready, it would seem, to bow to the
reader's superior judgement. You can be suggestive
in quite a different way, by being hard, by keeping the
reader's mind alert to what you are saying. We can
take a piece of detailed criticism to show how it can
be done.

I shall now list four eighteenth-century puns, in order of increasing self-consciousness.

> Let such raise palaces, and manors buy,
> Collect a tax, or farm a lottery;
> With warbling eunuchs fill a licensed stage,
> And lull to servitude a thoughtless age.
>
> (*London*, Johnson.)

Licensed refers, I understand, to the passing of the Licensing Act, and adds with a peculiarly energetic sneer that they had all kinds of goings-on. This, I take it, is a joke, one would say it with an accent on *licensed* and look knowingly at the listener to make sure he saw the point. You may say this is only the use of a technical word in a generalized sense, but it is not a metaphor; the two meanings are different and he means to say both of them.

> Most manfully besiege the patron's gate,
> And, oft repulsed, as oft attack the great,
> With painful art, and application warm,
> And take at last some little place by storm.

Place is hardly more than an ambiguity by vagueness; it is only because the ornamental comparison is between such different activities (one 'poetical', the other prosaic and considered sordid) that the political and military meanings of the word seem different enough to be funny.

> The watchful guests still hint the last offence,
> The daughter's petulance, the son's expense;
> Improve his heady rage with treacherous skill,
> And mould his passions till they make his will.

This is a careful, very conscious pun, which had to be dovetailed into its setting; but still it does not stand out from its setting and seem the point of it; the pun is thought of as the same kind as the other devices employed. Consider the word *heady*, which means both that he was head of the family and that his passions soon come to a head; it is the same sort of pun as the conscious one about the *will*, and yet one can absorb it without recognizing it at all.

> Where Bentley late tempestuous wont to sport
> In troubled waters, but now sleeps in port.

The pun is sustained into an allegory by the rest of the couplet: *tempestuous* and *sport* are satirical in much the same way as the last word. But here, I grant, we have a simply funny pun; its parts are united by derivation indeed, but too accidentally to give dignity; it jumps out of its setting, yapping, and bites the doctor in the ankles.[1]

It is true that Professor Empson is helped to be light and even brittle here by his subject; but what really makes his style light and vivacious throughout the whole of his enticing book of detailed criticism, is that he has to keep your attention alert all the time. He too uses 'poetic' means, as when the pun becomes a dog biting Dr. Bentley in the ankles. And as he is all the time making a point, his prose lends itself to argument. His voice has more ups and downs than even Mr. Quennell's, and more abrupt ones. Take, with the end of the sentence which comes before it, 'But here, I grant, we have a simply funny pun.' It is odd to notice here how the 'I grant', which should, one would think, have a conciliatory effect, has precisely the opposite. It conveys 'Surely I needn't point out such an obvious thing as that to you!' This prose is perhaps more stimulating than Mr. Wilson's, but it lacks the calm assurance which makes Mr. Wilson's passage so effective. The latter seems to penetrate

---

[1] From *Seven Types of Ambiguity*, by William Empson, Chatto and Windus, 1930.

below the mind: Professor Empson's fertilizes only the intellect.

Calm assurance is a most powerful tone of voice in which to speak, but it need not be dogmatic or brutal. It seems to come when a critic's thought is really based on great knowledge and actual practice: you get it in Dryden sometimes. It seems to occur most often when a large generalization is drawn from minute observation, and we welcome it, because the large generalization is one of the most illuminating, most delightful things in criticism. It enables us to get our bearings in so much that is confusing. It is not the business of the critic to make rules (which nobody of any originality would follow) because criticism is concerned with what has been: it organizes the material into a coherent whole for our better and more adept enjoyment of the parts. In this sense criticism discovers laws, but they are no more rules than scientific laws are rules. Perhaps it is the highest achievement of criticism to propound a law which throws a beam of light on something which we had not in the least realized:

Certain qualities are to be expected of any type of good verse at any time; we may say the qualities which good verse shares with good prose. Hardly any good poet in English has written *bad* prose; and some English poets have been among the greatest of English prose writers. The finest prose writer of Shakespeare's time was, I think, Shakespeare himself; Milton and Dryden were among the greatest prose writers of their times. Wordsworth and Coleridge may be cited, and Keats; and Shelley—not I think in his correspondence, but certainly in his *Defense of Poetry*. This is not a sign of versatility but of unity. For there are qualities essential to good prose which are essential to good verse as well; and we may say positively with Mr. Ezra Pound, that verse must be at least as well written as prose. We may even say that the originality of some poets has consisted in their finding a way of saying in verse what no one else had been able to say except in prose written or spoken. Such is the originality of Donne, who, though employing an elaborate metric and an uncommon vocabulary, yet manages to maintain a tone of direct informal address. The talent of Dryden is exactly the same: the difference is only that the speech which he uses is that of a more formal age. Donne makes poetry out of a learned but colloquial dialogue speech, Dryden out of the prose of political oratory; and Pope out of the most polished drawing-room manner. And of Goldsmith and Johnson we can say the same: their verse is poetry partly because it has the virtues of good prose.

Those who condemn or ignore *en bloc* the poetry of the eighteenth century on the ground that it is 'prosaic' are stumbling over an uncertainty of meaning of the word 'prosaic' to arrive at exactly the wrong conclusion. One does not need to examine a great deal of the inferior verse of the eighteenth century to realize that the trouble with it is that it is not prosaic enough. We are inclined to use 'prosaic' as meaning not only 'like prose', but as 'lacking poetic beauty'— and the Oxford and every other dictionary gives us warrant for such use. Only, we ought to distinguish between poetry which is like *good* prose, and poetry which is like *bad* prose. And even so, I believe more prose is bad because it is like bad poetry, than poetry is bad because it is like bad prose. And to have the virtues of good prose is the first and minimum requirement of good poetry.

If you look at the bad verse of any age, you will find most of it lacking in the virtues of prose. When there is a period of good verse, it has often been preceded by a period in which verse was bad because it was too poetic, too artificial; and it is very commonly followed by such another period. The development of blank verse in the hands of Shakespeare and some of his contemporaries was the work of adapting a medium which to begin with was almost intractably poetic, so that it could carry the burdens and exhibit the subtleties of prose; and they accomplished this before prose was highly developed. The work of Donne, in a lesser form, was the same. It has prose virtues, and the heavy toil of his minor imitators was wholly to degrade the idiom of Donne into a lifeless verse convention. Speech meanwhile was changing, and Dryden appeared to cleanse the language of verse and once more bring it back to the prose order. For this reason he is a great poet.[1]

That passage contains no appeal to the emotions, though it does appeal to your memory, not only of what you have read, but of what you have felt in reading it. It is extraordinarily persuasive, and we have to ask ourselves why. Partly, I think, because of its extreme simplicity, its invariable clarity. Yet it is also partly because of the *kind* of emphasis with which the important word is brought out, usually at the end of the phrase, not with a ring, nor with a thump, but with something very like a lilting lift of the voice. Is this not so, say, in '... which to begin with was almost intractably poetic, so that it could carry the burdens and exhibit the subtleties of prose;'? It is rather slow prose, enough to make you consider as you go along, but not at all heavy; there is little rise or fall in the voice compared with Professor Empson's, little crush of emphasis as compared with Bridges'. Yet it is not

[1] Edition of *London* and *The Vanity of Human Wishes*, by T. S. Eliot, The Haslewood Books, 1930.

monotonous, because there is not a superfluous word:
the prose is as clean cut, as precise as the thought;
your thought cannot slumber, and monotonous prose
is prose which sends your mind, if not your body, to
sleep. If there is a tinge of emotion, and I think there
is some, it is not conveyed by any imagery, or any
piling up of sentences, or any tricks of rhythm, but
by the feeling communicated to you that Mr. Eliot
cares very much for what he is writing about; and you
catch this feeling from Mr. Eliot because as you read
you in your turn cannot help caring very much about
the subject. This happens, I fancy, because by his
moderation he compels you to follow his mind in the
same close way that it moves over his matter; and, the
human mind being as naturally lazy as it is, this closeness is only procured when the driving force behind it
is one of interest amounting to emotion.

PART III

EMOTIVE PROSE

Rousing the Emotions

Pure emotive prose, if one can imagine such a thing, would make the reader experience an emotion without direct relation to anything in life: it would work as music does—or at least as it does with semi-musical people, that is, with the majority of those who listen to music, among whom I number myself. Yet writing cannot be utterly unrelated to experience. Unless the words used carry with them some suggestion of moving events or things, they have very little effect, as anybody can tell who has listened to poetry in a language he does not know at all. There may be some degree of pleasure or emotion, but it is very slight. Therefore the purest examples of emotive prose one can find, turn out to be those which deal with ideas whose very vastness makes them diffuse as well as portentous:

Of all the arts, Tragedy is the proudest, the most triumphant; for it builds its shining citadel in the very centre of the enemy's country, on the very summit of his highest mountain; from its impregnable watchtowers, his camp and arsenals, his columns and forts are all revealed; within its walls the free life continues, while the legions of Death and Pain and Despair, and all the servile captains of tyrant Fate, afford the burghers of that dauntless city new spectacles of beauty. Happy those sacred ramparts, thrice happy the dwellers on that all-seeing eminence. Honour to those brave warriors who, through countless ages of warfare, have preserved for us the priceless heritage of liberty, and have kept undefiled by sacrilegious invaders the home of the unsubdued.

But the beauty of tragedy does but make visible a quality which, in more or less obvious shapes, is present always and everywhere in life. In the spectacles of Death, in the endurance of intolerable pain, and in the irrevocableness of a vanished past, there is a sacredness, an overpowering awe, a feeling of the vastness, the depth, the inexhaustible mystery of existence, in which, as by some strange marriage of pain, the sufferer is bound to the world by bonds of sorrow. In these moments of insight, we lose all eagerness of temporary desire, all struggling and striving for petty ends, all care for the little things that, to a superficial view, make up the common life of day by day; we see, surrounding the narrow raft illumined by the flickering light of human comradeship, the dark ocean on whose rolling waves we toss for a brief hour; from the great night without, a chill blast breaks in upon our refuge; all the loneliness of humanity amid hostile forces is concentrated upon the individual soul, which must struggle alone, with what courage it can command, against the whole weight of a universe that cares nothing for its hopes and fears. Victory, in this struggle with the powers of darkness, is the true baptism into the glorious company of heroes, the true initiation into the overmastering beauty of human existence. From that awful encounter of the soul with the outer world, renunciation, wisdom and charity are born; and with their birth a new life begins. To take into the inmost shrine of the soul the irresistible forces whose puppets we seem to be— Death and change, the irrevocableness of the past, and the powerlessness of man before the blind hurry of the universe from vanity to vanity—to feel these things and know them is to conquer them.[1]

[1] From *Mysticism and Logic*, by Bertrand Russell.

There is very little, if any, intellectual idea to be wrested from that passage: its main, one might say its only, effect is to arouse some emotion in the reader (perhaps a temporary suspension of the judgement is necessary), an emotion which need not be in the least like the one that impelled the writer. It does not direct the mind to anything in particular, unless you say that to suggest to the reader that tragedy is a comprehensive art form is to direct the mind particularly; for to induce musings on the universe is not to guide a mental process.

There are several interesting things to notice about that passage if we are to try to arrive at any general notions as to how emotive prose is written. The first, to choose at random, though it seems to be one of the most important, is the use of archaic words and expressions (for I need not stress the emotivity of the suggestions), 'burghers', 'dauntless', 'brief hour', 'thrice happy', just as we find Whitehead used such an expression as 'ill accords with'. There is, of course, all the romantic imagery of the shining citadel and the impregnable watchtowers; and there are the abstract words such as pain, death, and fate. Then there are the adjectives that add nothing to the actual meaning, because it is otherwise stated: '*brave* warriors', '*strange* marriage', words which are, however, valuable in the effect; for consider the difference in the context between writing 'some strange marriage' and 'a marriage'. But possibly more important than all of these is the way the rhythms are sustained. Take the sentence 'Honour to those brave warriors who, through countless ages of warfare, have preserved for us the priceless heritage of liberty, and have kept undefiled by sacrilegious invaders the home of the unsubdued.' As keynote take the first clause, 'Honour to those brave warriors who, through': for if Lord Russell had written 'Honour to those brave warriors, who through . . .' the effect would be quite different, until at the very end you came on the very weakened effect of 'the home of the unsubdued'. It is, perhaps, humiliating to think that the placing of a comma may be much more important than any of your ideas. Then again there are the burdened phrases such as 'the dark ocean on whose rolling waves we toss for a brief hour', and a reminiscence or two, an echo of other moving passages, 'from vanity to vanity'. Also we can note the words 'does but'. This is common in emotive prose; it serves as a kind of warning bell to tell us that it is our emotions that are going to be attacked. It does indeed have a curious effect. Suppose Lord Russell had written the beginning of his second paragraph: 'But the beauty of tragedy makes visible a quality, which in . . .' instead of 'But the beauty of tragedy does but make visible a quality which, in . . .': we might then feel more certain that the author of *Mysticism and Logic* really was identical with the writer of *The Analysis of Mind* (see p. 88).

For it is extremely curious how a man's style will change according to what he is doing with it: to note this is once more to present us with the problem of how much it is subject-matter and how much it is personality that decides how a man shall write. Look back, for instance, at the example of Trevelyan's historical prose (p. 144), and then read this:

The morning hours slipped by, and still with impassive countenance he watched the men he treasured fall under the cannon shots. Messenger after messenger galloped off to hasten Eugene, struggling through marsh and woodland far away. But till his colleague was ready to attack, the Duke would not give the word. What were his thoughts as he lunched among his staff in the open field, perhaps for the last time? He well knew it was the day that either made or undid him quite: his fortunes could not survive defeat. And with his own ambitions, the liberties of England and of Europe had come to the last hazard, to be decided, not in any famous city or crowded meeting-place of men, but here in a naked plain of reaped stubble, between villages and farms of names unknown—that tallest spire was called Blindheim, the guides said—places where unlettered peasants had for ages tilled the soil and for ages more would till it, caring nothing what the great world in its madness had come there to do that day—save only that their poor houses and barns would assuredly be burned. Yet in this uncouth, rustic spot, the texture of Eighteenth Century civilization and thought was to take its colour for good or ill. Hasten, Eugene! Flesh and blood can no longer stand still under this carnage of a cannonade, and the very gods are impatient to see the invisible event. Here at last comes his messenger galloping from the north. He is ready: and we are more than ready. It is past noon, but August days are long. Cutts, the Salamander, is to lead the British and Dutch against Blindheim. And everywhere, along four miles of the Nebel's course, the regiments and squadrons shake themselves and move down towards the marshy edges of the brook.[1]

There again we at once notice the use of archaic expressions: 'undid him quite', 'to the last hazard',

[1] From G. M. Trevelyan, *England Under Queen Anne*: vol. i, *Blenheim*, Longmans, 1930.

'tilled the soil', 'assuredly', 'rustic spot'. But apart
from that there is not much likeness between the two
passages quoted in this chapter. Trevelyan did not
manage to sustain his rhythms, and the long sentence
in the middle of the passage is broken by the spire of
Blindheim. Of course, the purpose of the two passages
is different. Trevelyan was trying to move his readers
not by purely literary means so much as by sitting him
next to Marlborough, and trying to make him share
his hopes and his fears. 'Hasten, Eugene!' (the archaic
word again) does not, in me at least, provide the
emotional jolt evidently hoped for, and I must confess
that the invisible event leaves me unexcited. What
this would seem to suggest is that prose to be emotive
must be written with long, sustained rhythms, and
abstract words heavily weighted with association. I do
not mean that the sentences need be long, for you
can maintain rhythm across sentences, as is done in
one of the finest emotive passages known to me, in
De Quincey's *Levana and Our Lady of Sorrow*:

The second sister is called *Mater Suspiriorum*—Our Lady
of Sighs. She never scales the clouds, nor walks abroad upon
the winds. She wears no diadem. And her eyes, if they were
ever seen, would be neither sweet nor subtle; no man could
read their story, they would be found filled with perishing
dreams, and with wrecks of forgotten delirium. But she raises
not her eyes; her head, on which sits a dilapidated turban,
droops for ever, for ever fastens on the dust. She weeps not.
She groans not. But she sighs inaudibly at intervals. Her
sister, Madonna, is oftentimes stormy and frantic, raging in
the highest against heaven, and demanding back her darlings.
But Our Lady of Sighs never clamours, never defies, dreams

not of rebellious aspirations. She is humble to abjectness. Hers is the meekness that belongs to the hopeless. Murmur she may, but it is in her sleep. Whisper she may, but it is to herself in the twilight. Mutter she does at times, but it is in solitary places that are desolate as she is desolate, in ruined cities, and when the sun has gone down to his rest.

These two latter passages at least give one some concrete imagery, and the words still have meaning. We are not left with questions in our minds such as when, with Whitehead, we want to know when an emotion is big enough to be overwhelming, or, with Lord Russell, how you can endure pain that is intolerable. That is, in the earlier passages words have ceased to have any precise meaning, and are only suggestive.

In a sense, naturally, all prose is emotive, but I hope there is no confusion here about the kind of prose we are at the moment discussing: it is prose which aims directly at the emotions of the reader, not at his mind. One would naturally expect to find this prose most commonly among novelists, but it is rather curious that today the passages which strike me as being addressed to the feelings rather than to the mind are to be found in England mainly among the scientists, philosophers, historians, and critics. It is easier to find the sort of prose we are talking about here among American novelists than among English ones; for reasons I must leave to sociologists. I will begin with a short example:

On the sea the helmsman suffered the downpour, and on the high pastures the shepherd turned and drew his cloak closer about him. In the hills the long-dried stream-beds began to fill again and the noise of water falling from level to

level, warring with the stones in the way, filled the gorges.
But behind the thick beds of clouds the moon soared radiantly
bright, shining upon Italy and its smoking mountains. And
in the East the stars shone tranquilly down upon the land that
was soon to be called Holy and that even then was preparing its
precious burden.[1]

The archaic 'suffered' prepares us, and again the effect
is produced largely by the extent of the view, which
by its size is necessarily vague, first a vision of Italy,
and then a historical glimpse of Christianity, the note
of remoteness once more being struck at the very end
with a familiar echo in 'precious burden'. But we need
not be taken quite so far away from actuality:

The Mother Superior and Magdalena and Bernard attended the sick man. There was little to do but to watch and
pray, so peaceful and painless was his repose. Sometimes it
was sleep, they knew from his relaxed features; then his face
would assume personality, consciousness, even though his eyes
did not open.

Toward the close of day, in the short twilight after the
candles were lighted, the old bishop seemed to become restless, moved a little, and began to murmur; it was in the
French tongue, but Bernard, though he caught some words,
could make nothing of them. He knelt beside the bed: 'What
is it, Father? I am here.'

He continued to murmur, to move his hands a little, and
Magdalena thought he was trying to ask for something, or to
tell them something. But in reality the Bishop was not there
at all: he was standing in a tip-tilted green field among his
native mountains, and he was trying to give consolation to a
young man who was being torn in two before his eyes by the
desire to go and the necessity to stay. He was trying to forge

[1] From *The Woman of Andros*, by Thornton Wilder, Longmans, 1930.

a new Will in that devout and exhausted priest; and the time was short, for the *diligence* for Paris was already rumbling down the mountain gorge.

When the Cathedral bell tolled just after dark, the Mexican population of Santa Fé fell upon their knees, and all American Catholics as well. Many others who did not kneel prayed in their hearts. Eusabio and the Tesuque boys went quietly away to tell their people; and the next morning the old Archbishop lay before the high altar in the church he had built.[1]

That is almost free of archaisms: there is just a faint flavour given by the phrase 'the close of day', and perhaps by 'in the French tongue', instead of 'in French'. But otherwise the method is as different as possible from that of the passages already quoted. It is that of extreme simplicity and direct statement. The voice is kept deliberately dry. You are made to feel that nothing that the voice can do, nothing that words crammed with association might suggest, could increase the poignancy, the sorrow, the acceptance, of the fact. It goes without saying that the theme itself is moving, for however common death may be, it can never be commonplace. Yet the method breaks down unless you feel that the event described really is so stupendous that it needs no more than the bare telling of it to produce the effect (as in Biblical stories, especially in the New Testament): and it breaks down here because the death of this particular archbishop cannot be important enough to you to carry a very great emotion with it. So Miss Cather slips your mind back

[1] From *Death Comes to the Archbishop*, by Willa Cather, Heinemann, 1927.

to an earlier crucial moment of the dying man's life: she is giving you a complete view—like Mr. Wilder's map of Italy—as Lytton Strachey did in his (regrettably) often-quoted Death of Queen Victoria. In the main, however, simplicity of statement is relied on, but the words are very carefully chosen, with an ear for alliteration—'so peaceful and painless was his repose', and the sentences are very carefully balanced to give an effect of quietness. The monosyllables make for slow prose. A certain effect of sonority suggested here and there in the earlier paragraphs is rigorously kept out of the last.

Writers, novelists especially, would find it too limiting to confine emotive passages merely to vast, distant, or quiet things, and we find that in describing emotion authors often try to make you feel what their characters felt. They are describing something immediate, vivid, part of life at the moment, at the moment for you just as much as at the moment for their characters. Here any trace of the archaic would be disastrous:

From the throats of the ragged black men, as they trotted up and down the landing-stage, strange haunting notes. Words were caught up, tossed about, held in the throat. Word-lovers, sound-lovers—the blacks seemed to hold a tone in some warm place, under their red tongues perhaps. Their thick lips were walls under which the tone hid. Unconscious love of inanimate things lost to the whites—skies, the river, a moving boat—black mysticism—never expressed except in song or in the movements of bodies. The bodies of black workers belonged to each other as the sky belonged to the river. Far off now, down river, where the sky was splashed with red, it touched the face of the river. The tones from the throats of black workers touched each other, caressed each other. On the deck of the boat a red-faced mate stood swearing as though at the sky and the river.

The words coming from the throats of the black workers could not be understood by the boy, but were strong and lovely. Afterwards when he thought of that moment Bruce always remembered the singing voices of the negro deck-hands as colors. Streaming reds, browns, golden yellows coming out of black throats. He grew strangely excited inside himself, and his mother, sitting beside him, was also excited. 'Ah, my baby! Ah, my baby!' Sounds caught and held in black throats. Notes split into quarter-notes. The word, as meaning, of no importance. Perhaps words were always unimportant. There were strange words about a 'banjo dog.' What was a 'banjo dog'? 'Ah, my banjo dog! Oh, oh! Oh, oh! Ah, my banjo dog!'

Brown bodies trotting, black bodies trotting. The bodies of all the men running up and down the landing-stage were one body. One could not be distinguished from another. They were lost in each other.[1]

That is without echoes from other things, and while being as free of archaisms as the piece quoted from De Quincey (allowing for the passage of a hundred years or so), it does not take you into either a strange visionary realm, or an abstract one. At the same time it gets its poetic effects: and realizing that emotive prose is primarily poetic, we may remember Mr. Eliot's belief that more prose is bad because it is like bad poetry, than poetry is bad because it is like bad prose. Good emotive prose is very rare, and it seems likely that Mr. Eliot has hit upon the reason why it is

[1] From *Dark Laughter*, by Sherwood Anderson, Jarrolds, 1926.

so. However, let us look at the poetic effects here. They are almost entirely caused by repetitions. Look how often the word 'river' is repeated at the end of the first paragraph, or how often the word 'body' is repeated in the last. The words, separately, are not moving ones; they have no profound associations. Colour is a most important element in this passage: black, red, brown; a touch of white; then the stream of reds, browns, golden yellows, and black again at the end. It is clear, I think, that Mr. Anderson's intention in writing this passage was to give you some emotion; but what the precise emotion was to be, even what it was to be about, is not so clear. In the previous passages, except for Lord Russell's and De Quincey's we know both these things: the absence of that knowledge makes for more purely emotive writing.

We still feel here, that although the subject is immediate and modern, some vast issue lies behind the words: we are intended to get a glimpse of a world more primitive (and thus, it is suggested, superior, more intuitive, more in tune with the infinite) than the one white men live in. The piece which follows narrows the issue down to an intellectual attitude:

This talk of sincerity, I confess, fatigues me. If the fellow was sincere, then so was P. T. Barnum. The word is disgraced and degraded by such uses. He was, in fact, a charlatan, a mountebank, a zany without shame or dignity. His career brought him into contact with the first men of his time; he preferred the company of rustic ignoramuses. It was hard to believe, watching him at Dayton, that he had traveled, that he had been received in civilized societies, that he had been a high officer of state. He seemed only a poor clod like those around him, deluded by a childish theology, full of an almost pathological hatred of all learning, all human dignity, all beauty, all fine and noble things. He was a peasant come home to the barnyard. Imagine a gentleman, and you have imagined everything that he was not. What animated him from end to end of his grotesque career was simply ambition— the ambition of a common man, to get his hand upon the collar of his superiors, or, failing that, to get his thumb into their eyes. He was born with a roaring voice, and it had the trick of inflaming half-wits. His whole career was devoted to raising those half-wits against their betters, that he himself might shine. His last battle will be grossly misunderstood if it is thought of as a mere exercise in fanaticism—that is, if Bryan the Fundamentalist Pope is mistaken for one of the bucolic fundamentalists. There was much more in it than that, as everyone knows who saw him on the field. What moved him, at bottom, was simply hatred of the city men who had laughed at him so long, and brought him at last to so tatterdemalion an estate. He lusted for revenge upon them. He yearned to lead the anthropoid rabble against them, to punish them for their execution upon him, by attacking the very vitals of their civilization. He went far beyond the bounds of any merely religious frenzy, however inordinate. When he began denouncing the notion that man is a mammal even some of the hinds at Dayton were agape. And when, brought upon Darrow's cruel hook, he writhed and tossed in a very fury of malignancy, bawling against the boldest elements of sense and decency like a man frantic—when he came to that tragic climax of his striving there were snickers among the hinds as well as hosannas.

Upon that hook, in truth, Bryan committed suicide, as a legend as well as in the body. He staggered from the rustic court ready to die, and he staggered from it ready to be forgotten, save as a character in a third-rate farce, witless and in poor taste. It was plain to everyone who knew him, when

he came to Dayton, that his great days were behind him—
that for all the fury of his hatred, he was now definitely an
old man, and headed at last for silence. There was a vague,
unpleasant manginess about his appearance; he somehow
seemed dirty, though a close glance showed him as carefully
shaven as an actor, and clad in immaculate linen. All the
hair was gone from the dome of his head, and it had begun to
fall out, too, behind his ears, in the obscene manner of the
late Samuel Gompers. The resonance had departed from his
voice; what was once a bugle blast had become reedy and
quavering. Who knows that, like Demosthenes, he had a
lisp? In the old days, under the magic of his eloquence, no
one noticed it. But when he spoke at Dayton it was always
audible. . . .

That is, so far. The Fundamentalists, once apparently
sweeping all before them, now face minorities prepared for
battle even in the South—here and there with some assurance
of success. But it is too early, it seems to me, to send the
firemen home; the fire is still burning on many a far-flung
hill, and it may begin to roar again at any moment. The evil
that men do lives after them. Bryan, in his malice, started
something that it will not be easy to stop. In ten thousand
country towns his old heelers, the evangelical pastors, are
propagating his gospel, and everywhere the yokels are ready
for it. . . .[1]

That, to the curious, is an extremely interesting passage. It is, if you like, journalism, but if all journalism
was of that quality we should not hear so many com-
plaints about it. What is so odd about it is, that although it seems a piece of straight hard hitting, it is
not emotive as invective is emotive, but in some quite

[1] From *Prejudices*, by H. L. Mencken, Cape, 1921. (In Memoriam
W. J. B.)

different way. There is, of course, a slight feeling of pity for the decayed Bryan, but only very slight, because of the biting picture we are given of his 'grotesque' career. There are one or two emotive turns of speech, such as 'headed at last for silence', 'so tatterdemalion an estate' (instead of 'such a tatter-demalion state'), 'many a far-flung hill', and the repetition of 'he staggered'; but I do not think the effect is in the main traceable to them. What makes it so puzzling to find out the way the effect is produced is that we are not quite certain what the effect is. It is not pity, it is not scorn, or derision, or anger, or fear, certainly not a vague brooding. One wonders if it may not be accidental, or I should say that I wonder whether it is not peculiar to myself. As I read the last sentence an echo came into my mind of, of all things, Browne's *Garden of Cyrus*: 'The huntsmen are up in America, and they are already past their first sleep in Persia.' There is something of the same movement. And if we look again at Mencken's prose, we see that it has a continuous rhythm which quickens the pulse: the vigour behind it imparts a kind of excitement which has nothing to do with the subject-matter. What then is really happening to you is that you are being made warmly sympathetic, not towards Bryan, or any anti-Fundamentalist cause, but towards Mencken. There is a continual change of speed, with a kind of lilt which gives the main pace, that of 'anthropoid rabble against them', 'clad in immaculate linen', 'minorities prepared for battle'. There may follow a pause, a drop in the voice; in fact we realize that what is working upon us is a sort of oratory. I do

not defend it as classic prose, yet I submit that of its
kind it is worth studying.

Given that emotive prose is a sort of poetry, one
would expect that poets would write it best, and that
the place where it might most legitimately be found
would be the drama. It is certainly to be met with at
its highest level in Shakespeare. Till recently, with
drama divorced from poetry, no one went to the
theatre to hear the words. And even now, notwith-
standing Mr. Eliot and Mr. Christopher Fry, the
words are usually lamentably thin. Shaw had at least
superb phrasing it is a delight to listen to. Occasionally, however, a poet does take to the theatre—usually
to be repulsed—and then we sometimes get speeches
worth paying attention to. Here Samuel, old and dis-
appointed, is praying:

. . . I eat bread, but my soul faints, and wine will not heal
my bones. Nothing is good for me but God. Like waters
He moves through the world, like a fish I swim in the flood
of God Himself. Answer me, Mover of the waters, speak to
me as waves speak without mouths. Saul has fallen off, as a
ripe fig falls and bursts. He, anointed, he moved in the flood
of power, he was God's, he was not his own. Now he is cast
up like a fish among the dry stones, he beats himself against
the sun-licked pebbles. He jumped out from the deeps of the
Lord, the sea of God has seen him depart. He will die within
the smell of his own violence. Lord, Lord, Ocean and Mover
of Oceans, lick him into the flood of Thyself. Wilt Thou not
reach for him with the arm of a long wave, and catch him
back into the deeps of living God? Is he lost from the sway
of the tide for ever and for ever? When the rain wets him,
will it wet him Godless, and will the wind blow on him without God in it? Lord, wilt Thou not reach for him, he is

Thine anointed? Bitter are the waters of old age, and tears fall inward on the heart. Saul is the son whom I anointed, and Saul has crawled away from God, he creeps up the rocks in vanity, the stink of him will rise up like a dead crab. Lord, is it verily so with Saul, is he gone out from Thee for ever, like a creeping thing crawled in vanity from the element of elements? I am old, and my tears run inward, they deaden my heart because of Saul. For Saul has crawled away from the Fountain of Days, and the Ancient of Days will know him no more. I heard the voice of the Lord like waters washing through the night, saying: *Saul has fallen away and is no more in the way of the power of God.* Yea, what is love, that I should love him! He is fallen away, and stinketh like a dead crab, and my love stinks with him. I must wash myself because of Saul, and strip myself of him again, and go down into the deeps of God. Speak, Lord, and I will obey. Tell me, and I will do it. I sink like a stone in the sea, and nothing of my own is left me. I am gone away from myself, I disappear in the deeps of God. And the oracle of the Lord stirs me, as the fountains of the deep. Lo! I am not mine own. The flood has covered me and the waters of the beginning sound in the shell of my heart. And I will find another King for Israel, I shall know him by the whispers of my heart, Lo. I will fill the horn with oil again, with oil from the body of Him, and I will go into the hills of Judah. I will find out one, in whom the power sleeps. And I will pour potency over his head and anoint him with God's fecundity, and place him beyond forgetting. I will go into the hills of Judah, where the sheep feed among the rocks, and find a man fresh in the morning of God. And he shall be King. On the morrow I will gather myself and go, silently, carrying the kingship away from Saul, because the virtue is gone out of him. And Saul will kill me with a spear, in one stroke, for rage he will kill me, if I tell him. But I shall not tell him. I shall say: I must away to the land of Judah, it is the time to sacrifice in the place of Bethlehem, the appointed time is at hand.——So I shall go away from Saul for ever, and never shall I see his face again. I shall hide myself away from his face, lest he hurt himself, slaying me. I shall go in the morning with sure feet, but the shell of my heart will be weary. For I am the Lord's and servant of the Lord, and I go in obedience, even with the alacrity of willingness. But alas, that I should have loved Saul, and had pride in him! I am old.[1]

The difficulty there is to assess the effect of the archaistic style, because in this place it is perfectly fitting, and does not give any impression of quaintness. It can probably be discounted. What we get instead is the emotive effect of Biblical English, which, from the enormous weight of its associations, impresses the atheist as much as it does the believer. Over and above this, Lawrence used every art of the poet; a decided pattern of rhythm, varied according to need; poetic imagery——'Wilt Thou not reach for him with the arm of a long wave', or 'the stink of him will rise up like a dead crab'; a good deal of repetition or refrain. The vividness of these things increases as the prayer goes on: the imagery gets more rapturous——'a man fresh in the morning of God'——and the phrase chosen for refrain is more striking, while together with these things the rhythm becomes more insistent, so that you cannot be unaware of the variations in it: 'The flood has covered me and the waters of the beginning sound in the shell of my heart', followed later by 'I shall go in the morning with sure feet, but the shell of my heart will be weary'. The whole passage is almost free verse, though it very rarely falls into actual verse

[1] From *David*, by D. H. Lawrence, Secker, 1926.

rhythms. What makes this passage particularly striking is that Lawrence combined the poignancy of something actually moving, the old disillusioned prophet stretching out to God for help, with all the vague apprehensions of eternity and infinity which are Lord Russell's whole stock-in-trade; yet he never lets these get out of hand, but focuses them almost at once by a physical image. Saul, for instance, moved in the flood of power; that is a vast abstract idea: then immediately he is cast up like a fish among the dry stones. This continual shifting of the level of vision, so to speak, is very disturbing; and it is in this way that Lawrence brings into play so many more of your intellectual and emotional faculties than any other of the authors I have quoted do. That, of course, is what makes his passage real poetic prose, not sham poetry written in prose form. There are plenty of other things one could point out as making this extract still more moving: for instance, all of us, however young we may be, are to some extent open to the suggestion of 'Bitter are the waters of old age, and tears fall inward on the heart', of which we are reminded when Samuel says 'I am old, and my tears run inward'; and again when the idea comes at the end, but still more shortened and so more compressed, with the final, utterly final, 'I am old.' There is another observation I should like to make. I said in reference to Miss Cather's prose, and earlier, that monosyllables make for slowness; they make for it, but do not necessarily impose it. Lawrence's passage is as swift as Manning's polysyllabic one (see p. 105): it has, indeed, much the same rhythmic beat, but Lawrence did not let monosyllables interfere with it or delay it: 'I sink like a stone in the sea, and nothing of my own is left me.' Where he does not use the polysyllable (which usually has a small proportion of stressed syllables, e.g. 'in vanity from the element of elements') he uses his small words to make feet, one might say, of triple measure: 'I sínk like a stóne in the séa', and so on, not, after Miss Cather's manner, making shall we say iambic feet: 'a yoúng mán who was being tórn in twó befóre his eýes'. The more one looks at Lawrence's passage, the more one is struck with its consummate artistry.

When I said that emotive prose might most 'legitimately' be found in the drama, I did not wish to suggest that it is not successfully used in other forms of writing, only that it tends to arouse our suspicions when we find it in critical, philosophic, scientific, or historical work. For as a rule, when we analyse these passages, we find, not necessarily that they mean very little, but that they mean one thing while pretending to convey another. Sometimes, however, the art critic can use no way but that of arousing the emotions to make you understand what he is talking about. Is it any good trying to describe low-relief carving by telling you what the subjects are, giving you the measurements (if you could), and so on? The only possible way, though it may be full of dangers, is to try to describe it emotionally, as Mr. Adrian Stokes does in dealing with the sculpture of Agostino di Duccio in the Tempio Malatestiano:[1]

. . . On an island of jungle land surrounded by the dolphin-populated flux, the elephant and the lion have walked down

[1] In *Stones of Rimini*, Faber and Faber, 1934.

to join the inspired flood and to vouchsafe the secret places of the wood. Mountains jump up in mid-ocean, scattering the sea. Now Diana re-enters her pagan grave and submits to being resurrected as the sods are upturned by the process she has set in motion. Her place in the sky is taken by the Crab who has stolen up out of the Adriatic over Rimini. Due to the ineluctable union of water and air, under the aegis of Diana, natural forces are suspended, in the flood of moonlight trees may root in the sea, dolphins sport the land, and ships brush their rigging against the fortress, moonlight twanging at the spars. Now Diana has mounted her chariot, and as she climbs the sky to displace the Crab, fish slip off the board, their metallic bodies strike the moonlight. For all is molten silver, and up from the earth comes a bucolic Mercury, his sodden garments limp and worn by the grave to single threads. Immediately he assumes his position, one foot on land, one in water, and to give the effect of continuity, as if no interruption had occurred, he has gathered the cock of vigilance to him, also several spirits of the dead; and now he ties on his winged sandals and fixes a cloud to his knee as if he had this moment (forgetting the spirits of the dead) rushed down from Olympus. The influence at work sets the lute he carries a-whirring, and two serpents hasten to join his caduceus.

Diana is at her height. Sea and sea-life mount the shore still higher without harm to the land because of the infusion of air and moonlight in the heavy water. The mysteries of ocean and of earth, taut now and exemplified to the last atom, at peace, together they are forging the new element which shall the better sustain the offspring of dust and water, the living form, their offspring of a now-remembered marriage before the feud. Entranced human forms flash up, their sex alone indistinct as with the alert and hypnotised Mercury, as with Jupiter. Here are the Twins, hand in hand: their young bodies glisten beneath the filmy draperies that guard their breasts like administering clouds that hasten to tend the moon, to hide her tired eyes some night when her laborious tears of cold silver shall not fall into gravity; and thus she cannot set influence to work as now she does. Indeed, Diana is at her height, and in an excess of hypnotic power she summons the yet remaining lords of the universe. Saturn comes in haste, his beard unkempt, a Phrygian night-cap upon his head. But Mars has never unhammered his armour since the ancient times, his chariot is ready, and it needed but one word from him to set the wolf baying at his horses' feet. They hasten to enrich the element that sustains the human form to its greatest glory. The mountains rise and drop in the even, chorded light, a god in ecstasy on every peak as, breaking the leaf of tuneful silver, Venus comes reborn out of the further sea into the new element, her chariot drawn this time by two white swans. Trees stand upon the tallest waves that move in procession behind her. Doves descend to give her greeting and to inspect the open shell, her birthplace, that she flourishes. As she touches land she disappears. Infusion is complete. Nothing remains to the outer senses, all is music now, imperceptible to the ear, loud in the blood.

It is easy enough to say 'That is "literature"; it has nothing to do with sculpture'. Yet you will note that unlike most 'literature' of this kind, it does not attempt to interpret the artist, to arrive at his metaphysics: it limits itself to imaginative description, which, to judge from the illustrations in the book, does not seem at all too fanciful. Mr. Stokes is not trying to convey his emotion to you, so much as directing your attention to the things from which you may derive emotion.[1] What kind of emotion it is, he leaves to you. This makes us feel more easy, for we

[1] 'All emotion depends on real solid vision or sound. It is physical.' 'But in *rhetoric* and really exceptional prose, we get words divorced from any real vision.' T. E. Hulme.

resent prose which has a palpable design upon us, especially critical prose. We prefer to be left to ourselves
so far as our feelings are concerned.

At the same time it is emotive prose, and Mr.
Stokes does not attempt to hide his emotion from us.
Like all the examples we have taken, this sort of prose
deals with something vast and eternal, but in this
instance, only at second hand: what it deals with
primarily is the sculpture, hard rock you can touch
and see. And Mr. Stokes is so much in control of his
emotion that he never lets you forget this: he does not
let you drift off into cosmic musings. Nevertheless
this passage has characteristics in common with others
of the sort we are discussing. There is repetition:
'Diana is at her height . . .' There are words which, if
not archaic (there is no hint of this throughout the
passage) are curiously used: the elephant and the lion
vouchsafe the secret places of the wood: the dolphins
sport the land. These are examples of modern syn-
tactical compression. But again, as always, it is the
voice, the rhythm, which is mainly responsible for the
effect: the sustained clauses, the regular marked
stresses: 'Indeed, Diana is at her height, and in an
excess of hypnotic power she summons the yet remaining lords of the universe.' The emotive word is
occasionally used: 'entranced', 'ecstasy', 'ineluctable'
(also somewhat strangely applied): it is, however,
a delicate piece of work, and the effective additions
made to the main rhythmic structure are never harsh
or obvious.

In this chapter I have dealt with only one kind of
emotive prose: there are others, such as invective, or

the comic, both meant primarily to arouse your feelings, though invective may to some extent be expository, and the comic may be descriptive of action, of persons, or of things. Invective is rare today, not that people are kinder, far from it, but that they are indifferent; possibly also, being less robust than our ancestors, we do not take invective in good part, but go and see a lawyer about our prospects of winning a libel action. Also writers of personal invective would not wish to have their scathing words reprinted when their indignation has died down. I can, however, point to A. E. Housman's Preface to *Manilius* as an admirable example of invective prose aimed at (and hitting) bad editors of the classics. The comic is a little outside the range of this book; it does, it is true, depend to some extent on the tone of voice in which it is uttered—take, for instance, Max Beerbohm's *Zuleika Dobson*: but on the whole it depends more upon the images and ideas presented, on the words put into the mouths of comic characters, than on the writer's style. Think of W. W. Jacobs, or P. G. Wodehouse. So rather than swell this book with material which would not reveal very much, I feel it would be better to leave the reader to make his own researches into these styles, if he wishes to, to compare for instance the opposite comic styles of overstatement and understatement. It is time to see whether we can say anything general about modern prose.

PART IV

MODERN PROSE STYLE

§ 1

The New Way of Writing

CAN we say that there is, definitely, 'a new way of writing'? Is there such a thing as *modern* prose, with characteristics the older prose does not possess?[1] It may seem at first sight that the question cannot reasonably be put, for if we are agreed that style is the personal voice—which pierces through even the 'impersonal' manner—and that the voice is the man; and if we assume, as we plausibly can, that man does not alter except over very long periods, can we talk of a modern as opposed to an old-fashioned style?

One can make two answers to this. The first is, that though time may not change man physically, nor perhaps mentally, leaving his vocal chords and what he wants to do with them still the same, two things do change: the social being, and with him the method of speech he must use to be effective with other social beings. Man as a social animal alters in tune with what we call, since a better term is lacking, 'the spirit of the age', which we gauge by the different

---

[1] I may suggest, to begin with, that had I been writing thirty years ago, I should probably have felt constrained to write 'with characteristics *which* the older . . .'

approaches men make to the external universe, and, more important perhaps, to their own emotions. Man may be fundamentally unchanged, but in the social process of his time, different facets are polished, unfamiliar aspects emerge. To take a simple example: How would a fourteenth-century man react if he were asked to think of 'the wonders of the deep' compared with the way a twentieth-century man would react? Today we should at once let our minds turn to what we might roughly call 'scientific marvels', that is to various detailed manifestations of fish life, or of corals. The fourteenth-century man would shudder deliciously at a vision of leviathans, appallingly, even incredibly shaped, of mermaids, of ghostly inhabitants. Not only, then, will men of various ages wish to *ex*press different things, but they will wish to *im*press men differently. What would be the good, for instance, of a member of the House of Lords rising up and saying:

My Lords, this ruinous and ignominious situation, where we cannot act with success nor suffer with honour, calls upon us to remonstrate in the strongest and loudest language of truth, to rescue the ears of majesty from the delusions which surround it.

We can imagine a peer having similar feelings about, perhaps, the situation in Africa, but such language, used by Chatham in 1777, would have no result whatever now, though in its way it is splendid, and in its own age was no doubt very effective indeed. Our second answer arises out of the first: since the needs of the voice have changed, the instrument has been altered: we no longer use the same tool as our

ancestors did to move other people. And there is still
another consideration. If we use a different tool it is
that our emotions have changed, or at any rate, if our
emotions do not change, our attitude towards them
differs with the age in which we live. These things,
however, interact upon each other. We know, as once
we did not know, that our emotions vary with the language we use in describing them: the spirit of an age
may not only be reflected in its prose, it may be, indeed
it is, to some extent conditioned by it. This, however,
is an issue which would take us too far outside the
bounds of our subject; nor am I qualified to pursue it.

Let us now take two passages, dealing with much
the same range of ideas, written by men who were
each in their day stylists. We have already done something of the sort in the Introduction, but we can use
another example to reinforce the argument of the first.
This time one writer is Sir Thomas Browne, the other
William James, and I am taking Browne at his most
straightforward.

Let thy studies be free as thy thoughts and contemplations:
but fly not only upon the wings of imagination; join sense
unto reason, and experiment unto speculation, and so give life
unto embryon truths, and verities yet in their chaos. There
is nothing more acceptable unto the ingenious world, than
this noble eluctation of truth; wherein, against the tenacity of
prejudice and prescription, this century now prevaileth.

That is from *Christian Morals*: now let us take this
from *The Will to Believe*:

On the whole, then, we must conclude that no philosophy
of ethics is possible in the old-fashioned absolute sense of the

term. Everywhere the ethical philosopher must wait on facts. The thinkers who create the ideals come he knows not whence, their sensibilities are evolved he knows not how; and the question as to which of two conflicting ideals will give the best universe then and there, can be answered by him only through the aid of the experience of other men.

I take it that anybody, even neglecting Browne's obsolete forms, would at once recognize the first passage as belonging to the seventeenth century, and the second to our own time. Can we put our finger on where exactly the difference lies?

It is pretty obvious that the difference lies in the rhythm, but that is too easy a thing to say: and as a matter of fact, if we analyse these two passages into 'prose rhythms' in the way that Saintsbury did in his fascinating book, they are not, prosodically speaking at least, so different after all. Are not such cadences as

$$- \cup \cup \ - \ \cup \cup \ - \cup \cup \ - \cup \ \cup \ \ - \cup$$
embryon/truths, and/verities/yet in their/chaos

and

$$- \ \cup \ \cup \ - \cup \cup \ - \ \cup \cup \ -$$
old-fashioned/absolute/sense of the/term

of much the same order? Both are, in a sense, dactylic. What is different is the way the metres are used. In modern writing there is far less insistence on the rhythms; the unit into which the rhythms are woven, that is to say the phrase, is far more flexible, on the whole longer. The antithetical balance has gone. But what is more significant is that the written language today is much nearer the spoken language, with implications we shall follow up in a moment. But first

I must dispose of two possible objections. The first and lesser one is that for the seventeenth-century example we have a very conscious stylist. That is true, but Jeremy Taylor or Milton will give much the same result. Why do we remember, except for its insistence on rhythm, Milton's 'rousing herself like a strong man after sleep, and shaking her invincible locks'? But how do I know, it will be asked in the second place, that the older people did not speak as they wrote? The suggestion has often been made, most notably by Mr. Gordon Bottomley, that in the seventeenth century, especially in Shakespeare's time, the rhythms of everyday speech were more accentuated, approached even those of blank verse, or of obviously cadenced speech. Let us look at something from a contemporary of Sir Thomas Browne's:

Up, and by water, stopping at Michell's, and there saw Betty, but could have no discourse with her, but there drank. To White Hall, and there walked to St. James's, where I find the Court mighty full, it being the Duke of York's birthday; and he mighty fine, and all the musick, one after another, to my great content.

Pepys, you see at once, was not writing literary English: he was setting down his doings as he might have chatted about them to his wife—if, of course, he had been a brave enough man to do so.

It is fairly certain, I think, that the written language of the seventeenth century was farther from the spoken language than the written language of today is from our conversation, a division which probably began with Caxton. John Donne, one can be sure,

never spoke at home in the way that he thundered
from the pulpit. The proof is to be found in the
correspondence of the time, much of which has been
collected by Wyld in his *History of Modern Colloquial
English*, largely for this purpose; and what comes out
is that the language of the Elizabethans was not
essentially unlike our own. Here, for one example, is
Sir Philip Sidney writing to Edward Molyneux:

> Few words are best. My letters to my father have come to
> the eyes of some. Neither can I condemn any but you for it.
> If it be so you have played the very knave with me; and so
> I will make you know if I have good proof of it. But that
> for so much as is past. For that is to come, I assure you before
> God, that if ever I know you do so much as read any letter I
> write to my father, without his commandment, or my con-
> sent, I will thrust my dagger into you. And trust to it, for I
> speak it in earnest. In the mean time, farewell.

The sentiments of this prose (we trust) are not ours,
and the forms are not quite so, but the ring of it is. If
we were to say that sort of thing, we should say it in
that kind of way. Sidney's prose here, we see, is
altogether different from what he wrote for the press,
his 'Sidneyan showers of sweet discourse'. Here is
another example; and making allowance for stage
speech, does it sound very quaint or old-fashioned, or
very heavily rhythmed?

> Thou art so fat-witted, with drinking of old sack, and un-
> buttoning thee after supper, and sleeping upon benches after
> noon, that thou hast forgotten to demand that truly which
> thou wouldst truly know. What a devil hast thou to do with
> the time of day? . . .

Prince Hal probably spoke fairly current English; and the journalists of the time, Nashe, Greene, Dekker, wrote much in the way Prince Hal spoke, for they were not labouring after fine style, but trying to write as men talked. What appears to have happened is that in the seventeenth century a profound division developed between the spoken and the written language, a division bridged by the journalists and the comic writers. What seems to have occurred afterwards was, to cut a long story short, that the journalists, forgetting Dryden, deserted to the written side: one has only to think of Addison, and then of Dr. Johnson, who, far from trying to write as he naturally spoke, did his best to model his conversation on his writing. Everybody remembers how he let slip the remark about *The Rehearsal* not having wit enough to keep it sweet, and then amended the phrase to 'has not vitality enough to preserve it from corruption'. The stylists of the eighteenth century seem to have taken their writing farther and farther away from their speech—Gibbon, Burke, Smollett. This process went on through the nineteenth century; we have only to think of Carlyle or Pater, though it is true that some people all the while kept up the spoken tradition, Defoe, Sterne, and even Lamb, for though Lamb's style is artificial as regards words, his rhythms are those of his talk, or at any rate of his possible talk. What I think is going on at the present day is a return to speech rhythms: the conscious stylists are, so to speak, ridding themselves of 'style': not 'style', but *a* style is what they are aiming at, a style that will faithfully reflect their mind as it utters itself naturally.

What is curious is that now it is the leading authors who write naturally, style, so-called, being left to the journalists. I take the opening sentence of the first leading article of *The Times* of the day on which I happened to be taking notes for this chapter (19 August 1933): 'As soon as it was announced, on the morrow of Parliament's rising . . . .' One need not go on. Who would dream of *saying* 'on the morrow of Parliament's rising'? It is jargon. What we would probably say is, 'the day after Parliament rose'. Not that this *pompier* 'style' is confined to the august heights of journalism: it runs all through, and not long ago *The Daily Worker* printed with regard to certain prisons: 'No sound comes from out those walls.' Does the man who wrote those words habitually say 'from out'? Why does this happen? Why do people write forms which are dead, which they would never utter? In both the examples quoted one is tempted to diagnose insincerity of thought, or at least mental laziness.

Does it not seem, then, that the modern prose-writer, in returning to the rhythms of everyday speech, is trying to be more honest with himself than if he used, as is too wreckingly easy, the forms and terms already published as the expression of other people's minds? 'Style . . . is not an ornament; it is not an exercise, not a caper, nor complication of any sort. It is the sense of one's self, the knowledge of what one wants to say, and the saying of it in the most fitting words.'[1] And that is why it is extremely hard to achieve *a* style, for all these three things are very

[1] Introduction to *The London Book of English Prose*, by Herbert Read and Bonamy Dobrée, Eyre and Spottiswoode, 1931.

difficult to attain. Take only the last task, the saying of what one wants to say in the most fitting words. It seems almost impossible, for every time we speak we have virtually to re-create the instrument if we want to be faithful to our idea or feeling. Everywhere the words and phrasing of past generations interpose themselves between us and the reality. 'It is . . . a true and lamentable fact that, in ultimate analysis, one cannot speak about anything without altering it to some extent.'[1] It is the realization of this, a realization possibly new in our day, which impels authors to try to write as they speak in ordinary life on ordinary physical matters, for it is only in this way that one can achieve fidelity to one's self: otherwise the language and style of the literary tradition assert themselves. But the modern writer must not think of style: the man who thinks first of style is lost: the primary thing to do—this is an old observation— is to think clearly. As M. Jean Cocteau says, writing for modern authors: 'Style cannot be a starting-point: it happens. What is style? For a great many people it is a complicated way of saying very simple things. From our point of view it is a very simple way of saying complicated things.'[2] How does a modern writer tackle this problem? Here, I think, is a good example:

I had great ambitions. I have none now—and have not even the fear of failing. What matters to me and to many of the survivors of my generation is only that which is common to us all, our fear for our children. If it were not for that, I

[1] *The Theory of Speech and Language*, by A. H. Gardiner, Oxford, 1932.
[2] *A Call to Order*, Allen and Unwin, trs. 1933.

should know how to act in what remains of my life—that would be to withdraw as far as possible from the little world of writing and talking about books which is a microcosm of the whole, its values no finer than those accepted by the rest of the world, and only valid on the assumption that to a writer success means precisely what it means to a stockbroker or a multiple grocer. That is, material wealth, and the respect paid to it. This seems to me a denial of all the writer, the 'clerk', should stand for, but I can do nothing to alter it, and therefore I ought to run away for my life.

After all that turbulence of desire and ambitions it seems strange I should believe now that very little in me is real except the absolute need, intellectual and spiritual, for withdrawal, for resolving to satisfy in my life only the simple wants. It is as strange as that I am only just learning to write and don't care to.

There are days when I retract all this, and think how queer I shall grow if I live alone, and think too that what is needed is some effort to create cells inside the body social, groups of angry, last-minute saints. That would be no good. I should be weary in a week of the company of persons who thought and felt no differently from myself.[1]

That, as prose, is simple, easy, fluent, and flexible; what is important, however, is that it is written, apparently, in the *tones* of every day, though here and there we can detect traces of literary forms—'only that which' instead of 'only what': 'how to act' instead of 'what to do': it is extraordinarily difficult to rid one's self of terms of that kind. But to show how new the tone is, here is a passage from another autobiography written, one always thought, in a natural, confidential manner:

[1] From *No Time Like the Present*, by Storm Jameson, Cassell, 1933.

There were perhaps twenty boys in the school at most, and often fewer. I made the excursion between home and school four times a day; if I walked fast, the transit might take five minutes, and, as there were several objects of interest on the way, it might be spread over an hour. In fine weather the going to and from school was very delightful, and small as the scope was, it could be varied almost indefinitely.[1]

There are, we see immediately, one or two obvious 'literary' turns in that passage: 'I made the excursion between home and school', instead of 'I went to and from school': 'If I walked fast, the transit might take five minutes', instead of 'I could get there or back (or do the journey) in five minutes': 'objects of interest', with others of the same sort. And the general run, which is the important thing, though simple and easy, and we might perhaps admit fluent, is not flexible. Each sentence contains an idea and completes it. The mind comes to a full stop at the end of each phrase. But our minds in life do not work in that way; they are always ready to frame the next sentence, carried on by the impetus of the last. Gosse, in common with the older writers, was concerned, not to follow the movements of his mind, but to present something concrete.

To say, then, that the hall-mark of good modern prose style is an essential fidelity does not imply that writers of previous generations were charlatans and liars, only that they owed fidelity to other things. And it is here that the spirit of our age imposes itself upon our style. All the previous ages whose writers have been quoted or referred to here had something they could take for granted, and it never occurred to the

[1] From *Father and Son*, by Edmund Gosse, Heinemann, 1907.

older writers that they could not take themselves for granted. We can be sure of nothing; our civilization is threatened, even the simplest things we live by: we are on the verge of amazing changes. In our present confusion our only hope is to be scrupulously honest with ourselves, so honest as to doubt our own minds and the conclusions they arrive at. Most of us have ceased to believe, except provisionally, in truths, and we feel that what is important is not so much truth as the way our minds move towards truths. Therefore, to quote M. Cocteau again, 'Form must be the form of the mind. Not a way of saying things, but of thinking them.' Perhaps that is why we nowadays instinctively mistrust anyone who pontificates: and, as a matter of experience, if we examine the writings of the pontificators, people skilled in 'a way of saying things', we invariably find that their style is bad (see p. 11), that falsity has crept in somewhere. The writer is not being faithful to the movement of his mind; he is taking things for granted, and he fills us of today with uneasiness.

We have, then, to judge of the integrity of a modern writer by this sense of himself that we feel he has. If we are to respond, he must (we suppose) be aware of himself as something a little uncertain in this shifting universe: he also is part of the material which he has to treat with respect: he must listen to himself, so to speak, to hear what he has to say. He must not prejudge, or force an issue: we must be able to imagine that he is talking to himself. In no other way can he achieve *a* style, which is the sound of his voice, which is the man himself.

It is not so simple as it sounds for a man to watch his own mind; it is as difficult as writing in the way you ordinarily talk: literary habits continually get in the way. Nor must a man write as he might lazily talk, and it is more important than ever for him to reject the dead metaphor which can never be more than an approximation, to choose the exact, the expressive word, to rid his style of fat, to make it athletic. What he must really do, as the first essential, is to keep his awareness athletic, especially his awareness of himself. And he must not watch his mind idly; he must watch it as he might a delicate piece of machinery doing its work, and he must watch it, not flickering about in every direction, as an active mind does, but only in the direction he wants it to go. Otherwise the result may be disastrous. Even the following extremely clever attempt seems to me an object-lesson:

The problem from this time on became more definite.

It was all so nearly alike it must be different and it is different, it is natural that if everything is used and there is a continuous present and a beginning again and again if it is all so alike it must be simply different and everything simply different was the natural way of creating it then.

In this natural way of creating it then that it was simply different everything being alike it was simply different, this kept on leading one to lists. Lists naturally for a while and by lists I mean a series. More and more in going back over what was done at this time I find that I naturally kept simply different as an intention. Whether there was or whether there was not a continuous present did not then any longer trouble me there was or there was, and using everything no longer troubled me if everything is alike using everything could no longer trouble me and beginning again and again could no longer trouble me because if lists were inevitable if series were inevitable and the whole of it was inevitable beginning again and again could not trouble me so then with nothing to trouble me I very completely began naturally since everything is alike making it as simply different naturally as simply different as possible. I began doing natural phenomena what I call natural phenomena and natural phenomena naturally everything being alike natural phenomena are making things be naturally simply different. This found its culmination later, in the beginning it began in a center confused with lists with series with geography with returning portraits and with particularly often four and three and often with five and four. It is easy to see that in the beginning such a conception as everything being naturally different would be very inarticulate and very slowly it began to emerge and take the form of anything, and then naturally if anything that is simply different is simply different what follows will follow.[1]

One cannot say whether Miss Stein's mind really moved like that: possibly it did, and possibly most of our minds move more like that than we are aware of, or at any rate are prepared to admit. What is clear is that the mere following of the mind, its echoes and repetitions, does not really give its shape; and this makes us realize that to write naturally as the mind would wish to utter, is just as much an art—or an artifice—as to write in what we call an artificial style, say that of a Pater or a Meredith. What has happened is that the modern writer is faced with new material, and what he has to do is to discover the new form that this material requires.

But because this new form can only be an adaptation

[1] From *Composition as Explanation*, by Gertrude Stein, Hogarth Press, 1926.

of the old, it takes consummate art to prevent literature interposing itself between us and life. The problem, no doubt, has always existed, but if it has been
realized the solution has rarely, if ever, been hit on.
Yet there is Sterne, and what Mrs. Woolf had to say
about him is illuminating:

. . . With the first words—They order, said I, this matter
better in France—we are in the world of *Tristram Shandy*.
It is a world in which anything may happen. We hardly
know what jest, what jibe, what flash of poetry is not going
to glance suddenly through the gap which this astonishingly
agile pen has cut in the thick-set hedge of English prose. Is
Sterne himself responsible? Does he know what he is going
to say next for all his resolve to be on his best behaviour this
time? The jerky disconnected sentences are as rapid and it
would seem as little under control as the phrases that fall from
the lips of a brilliant talker. The very punctuation is that of
speech, not writing, and brings the sounds and associations of
the speaking voice in with it. The order of the ideas, their
suddenness and irrelevancy, is more true to life than to literature. . . . Under the influence of this extraordinary style the
book becomes semi-transparent. The usual ceremonies and
conventions which keep reader and writer at arm's length disappear. We are as close to life as we can be.[1]

That passage is not quoted as being characteristic of
Mrs. Woolf: to hear her real voice one must go to the
novels (see p. 52): it is quoted as an aid to my argument. And it serves it in two ways, because of what it
says and because of the way it says it, for if the prose
is not markedly Mrs. Woolf's, it is obviously modern:
the voice that is speaking is a voice of today: I shall not
be misunderstood, I hope, if I say that anyone might

[1] *The Common Reader*, 2nd series, Hogarth Press, 1932.

have written it. Now let us compare this with the way
Bagehot wrote about Sterne in the *National Review*
in 1864:

> But here the great excellence of Sterne ends as well as
> begins. In *Tristram Shandy* especially there are several
> defects which, while we are reading it, tease and disgust us
> so much that we are scarcely willing even to admire as we
> ought to admire the refined pictures of human emotion. The
> first of these, and perhaps the worst, is the fantastic disorder
> of the form. It is an imperative law of the writing art, that
> a book should go straight on. A great writer should be able
> to tell a great meaning as coherently as a small writer tells
> a small meaning . . .

and so it goes on. That is typical nineteenth-century
prose: we get something very like it in Matthew
Arnold, or Huxley, and in its way it is excellent. But
the rhythms and inflexions are quite different from
those of today: it consists, not of thoughts closely
followed, not of ideas suggested, but of utterances, of
pronouncements. Again, as with Gosse, we have the
end-stopped phrase: there is a door banged at the end
of each, and we feel as though we were on parade
receiving orders.

What seems to us to be lacking in the older prose
is the sense of the uninterrupted flow of the mind:
Bagehot, for example, appears to cut off this conti-
nuum, shall we call it, into arbitrary lengths, as we
slice chunks off a cucumber. This is to force on our
minds a logic that is not of their own making; and
though it may be true that, as T. E. Hulme said, 'All
styles are only means of subduing the reader', we must
not feel that our minds are being forced, and therefore

distorted. Perhaps it was George Moore's principal achievement to give this sense of flow: there is hardly an instant's pause in his mental processes. His style was very distinctive (see p. 30); all the time one hears a voice, a personal utterance, though pursued to the lengths to which he took it, or allowed it to carry him, it becomes in the end monotonous. The mind runs on too much; it has no form but that of a stream: no solid shape emerges. But the sort of flow we are talking about can, and sometimes does, take form. Here is an extract from Henry James, whose whole being was directed to following the movement of his mind, and who gave form to this movement, not indeed in a language natural to us, but one which seems to have been natural to him, a way which he could not have escaped from even if he had wanted to:

Momentary side-winds—things of no real authority—break in every now and then to put their inferior little questions to me; but I come back, I come back, as I say, I all throbbingly and yearningly and passionately, oh mon bon come back to this way that is clearly the only one in which I can do anything now, and that will open out to me more and more, and that has overwhelming reasons pleading all beautifully in its breast. What really happens is that the closer I get to the problem of the application of it in any particular case, the more I get *into* that application, so that the more doubts and torments fall away from me, the more I know where I am, the more everything spreads and shines and draws me on and I'm justified in my logic and my passion. . . . Causons, causons, mon bon—oh celestial, soothing, sanctifying process, with all the high sane forces of the sacred time fighting, through it, on my side! Let me fumble it gently and patiently out—with fever and fidget laid to rest—as in all the old enchanted months! It only looms, it only shines and shimmers, *too* beautiful and too interesting, it only hangs there too rich and too full and with too much to give and to pay; it only presents itself too admirably and too vividly, too straight and square and vivid, as a little organic and effective Action.[1]

We may think that artificial, but we do not feel, complicated as it is, that this is a literary language. It is the language of Henry James's speech; it reflects his mind accurately, a mind with a very definite form. James, if you like, had a tortuous way of thinking, but he had broken down the barriers between his mind and the expression of it.

What we look for, however, is a style which shall be as free and individual as in that passage, but which smacks less of idiosyncrasy, for something we might all use, though, no doubt, not so well as our model, for something which does not give us, as some recent prose does, the uneasy effect of submitting us to a laboratory experiment. Perhaps this is what we want:

The trouble with her ship was that it would *not* sail. It rode water-logged in the rotting port of home. All very well to have wild, reckless moods of irony and independence, if you have to pay for them by withering dustily on the shelf.

Alvina fell again into humility and fear: she began to show symptoms of her mother's heart trouble. For day followed day, month followed month, season after season went by, and she grubbed away like a housemaid in Manchester House, she hurried round doing the shopping, she sang in the choir on Sundays, she attended the various chapel events, she went out to visit friends, and laughed and talked and played games.

[1] *Letters*, Macmillan.

But all the time, what was there actually in her life? Not much. She was withering towards old-maiddom. Already in her twenty-eighth year, she spent her days grubbing in the house, whilst her father became an elderly, frail man still too lively in mind and spirit. Miss Pinnegar began to grow grey and elderly too, money became scarcer and scarcer, there was a black day ahead when her father would die and the home be broken up, and she would have to tackle life as a worker.

There lay the only alternative: in work. She might slave her days away teaching the piano, as Miss Frost had done: she might find a subordinate post as nurse: she might sit in the cash-desk of some shop. Some work of some sort would be found for her. And she would sink into the routine of her job, as did so many women, and grow old and die, chattering and fluttering. She would have what is called her independence. But, seriously faced with that treasure, and without the option of refusing it, strange how hideous she found it.

Work!—a job! More even than she rebelled against the Withams did she rebel against a job. . . .[1]

It is clear, I imagine, that that could not have been written in the last century; it speaks with the authentic voice of this. It has the ring of what we still hear around us every day: it has no air of 'style', yet it is extremely expressive. Certain liberties are taken, such as leaving out 'It is . . .' before 'all very well . . .' in the first paragraph. Here and there we feel just a touch of literary formulas, and we wish they were not there: 'as did so many women' instead of 'as so many women did', but these things are very rare in Lawrence. We feel that he was nearly always completely free of 'literature' and could be himself. We follow his mind working—and he spoke as it worked. Or, at least, that is

[1] From *The Lost Girl*, by D. H. Lawrence, Secker, 1920.

the impression we get. It is not true, of course: but at least he was using his material (part of which was his mind) with complete freedom, and finding a form which will make it tell.

Suppose that, before we go on to discuss experiments, we try to prophesy what direction our prose will take. We might perhaps say that it will be in that of greater flexibility and a more curious following of our mental processes, with, sometimes, violence offered to our old notions of syntax wherever we find them distorting or cumbrous. One would like to think that all of us will come to the stage of refusing to write what we would not, indeed could not, say, though that, of course, is not to limit our writing to what we actually do say. This is not to claim for a moment that by writing as we speak we shall achieve a style; before we do that we must go through at least three fundamental disciplines. First there is that of fidelity to thought, the extremely difficult task of complete honesty: we must not, as is so easy, allow language to condition our thought; then there is the labour of finding the exact words and the exact inflexion of phrase to carry the whole sense, the emotional colour, of the words; and thirdly, it is over and above these things that we have to model our prose to give it what seems to be the run and structure of our usual speaking. That is where the artifice comes in, and that is where we can achieve the art.

§ 2

Experiments

I n a sense, all good live prose is experimental—as all good poetry is—a desperate attempt to say what has never been said before in spite of having to use the same words to say it in. Any original writer is engaged in a continual struggle with words, to wrest out of them, to hammer into them, meanings they never had before: if he did not want to do this, he would not be an original writer. The problem would not be the same if it was a question of the mind alone, but it is a question of the whole sensibility. The plain unvarnished meaning, the scientific meaning we might call it, is there in every word, but how is the original writer to give the word that different colour, that strange feel, which makes it convey something new, or some old truth with aspects differently stressed? There are the usual poetic means, of course—analogy, new combinations, rhythmic effects, and others—but prose must not be allowed to become a museum of discarded poetic weapons. These at any rate have become part of tradition, and experimental prose is an attempt to break the barriers that traditional language imposes upon the personality which is trying to give its own vision or version of things. We have already come across prose of this kind, with Wyndham Lewis (p. 48), Hemingway (p. 58), Faulkner (p. 63), and Anderson (p. 196). What all these writers are doing is trying to revivify words, to strip

them of their old clogging associations, to give them
radiance as well as clarity, by making them correspond with what they see and feel.

There is more experimental prose being written in
America than in England, for which there are two
possible reasons. The first is that (for the moment at
least) social conditions in America are changing more
rapidly than in England, and with them the attitude
towards life of the individuals who compose the
society: this means that the latter have more things to
express that have never been expressed before. The
second is that English writers probably feel tradition
weigh more crampingly on them even when they have
something new to say. At the same time one feels that
a great deal of American experimentation begins at the
wrong end, simply with a desire to make something
new. Fresh material needs fresh forms, yes; but the
material should, so to speak, secrete its own forms;
otherwise you merely get another distortion of thought
and feeling no better than the old. To begin by saying
'Let us make a new instrument' before knowing what
you are going to ask the new instrument to do for
you, is sheer waste of wit. It is only when the old uses
of language will not let you do what you want to do,
when the material imperatively demands new forms,
that there is any point in harrying the language.

There is one thing the original prose writer has
always wanted to do—give objective reality to things,
translate sight into sound—and to do this he has
always had to coin new expressions, even new words,
because, as we have seen, the old words, expressions,
analogies, metaphors, become faded and dead: they

no longer convey what they used to. But the experimenter of today will want to do something besides this, which is, as suggested in the previous chapter, to follow all the curious transitions of the mind, its evolutions, its twists, so as to give a closer illusion of reality. Both old and new will work out the effect of various arrangements of sound, will try different successions, modulations, repetitions of vowel combinations and consonantal play. But the new will also try different arrangements of syntax, by which I do not mean trying to alter the grammar of the language, only the way in which it is applied. This was Miss Stein's method (see p. 223); she cared little about the word itself, or its sound, but gained her effects almost entirely by the arrangement of her sentences. Most writers work in the tradition they were brought up in; they hardly notice syntax except to get it 'right', that is to say, unnoticeable: but the experimentalist makes syntax a positive rather than a neutral element in his work. Here is a passage in which the feelings of a man in prison are described:

Or it is Sunday. You are locked in at midday. Till the next morning. It is hot, the men are supposed to be reading, and one of them has seen a servant girl leaning out of a window a long way off and shouts at her and calls her to him, entreats her to come to him and suddenly on that side of the prison all the men go mad suddenly and stand on stools at their windows, cat-calling and begging her to come to them, whistling and shouting and rattling the ventilating pane in front of them, and this goes on for a long time in rage, despair, madness, till you think the prison cannot stand it, that it will break apart, and you be free. The silence falls again.

You look out of the window, twilight is falling, agony;
you are shut in. The air is cool, smells sweet. You are shut
in. You are shut in and your heart is shut in and it tries to get
out and it stifles you and grows, it grows, and your being is
dissolved, it dissolves in longing, you do not know what is
happening to your life, you think of the others around you,
the man who walks to and fro in his cell from the time he is
shut in at night till the door is opened again in the morning,
whose silence you have never heard, who cannot bear it: of
the men in the trenches, and you want to be free with them,
for air, sweet air, and the sky overhead; you hear tapping in
the walls, it is the men who are talking to each other, who
have to talk to each other, to tell each other their names,
their age, who have learnt this complicated code to communicate nonsense to each other because the silence is unbearable
to them; then you think of the men on bread and water and
in darkness because somehow they are always in trouble, because they cannot help fighting, questioning every authority,
and suddenly your misery, your utter frustration fades, the
vibration ceases, you are calm.[1]

That passage recounts an especial emotional experience, a crisis: a certain tension runs through it. It
achieves its effect. What we have to ask ourselves is,
would the effect be the same if it were written in more
normal prose? Unfortunately that is a question we
cannot answer, because we have to say that at any rate
it might be. But I think everyone will agree that this
prose has certain qualities: it has the freshness of the
unusual: it keeps our minds alert: the punctuation,
which is what brings about the divergence from our
usual syntax, makes us concentrate: we cannot slide

[1] From *Memoirs of Other Fronts*, Anonymous (John Rodker), Putnam, 1932.

over anything, or take anything for granted. Let us look at the method in rather more detail.

There are the first two plain statements, as bare as they could be. Then, to reinforce them, the ungrammatical interpolation, 'Till the next morning'. Then a long sentence of no special up-and-down structure, no colons or semi-colons to make you halt anywhere; the continuous action is woven into the continuous feeling (an idea Miss Stein has called 'the continuous present'), the emotions or 'impulses' of the reader being brought into action by the repetition of 'to her' and the unexpected occurrence of the second 'suddenly', which is not tautological (see what happens if you leave it out). Then after the frenzy, indicated by the groups of threes, 'whistling and shouting and rattling the ventilating pane', and 'in rage, despair, madness'——the word 'mad' being repeated in this way ——there is the pulling up short, the abrupt cessation of movement given by the brief statement, 'The silence falls again'. The next paragraph takes you from the outside vision into the prisoner's mind. It is a normal mind; Rodker did not attempt to make it do anything extravagant or startling; we do not have to follow it into strange or unexpected regions. Yet all the time the mind is connected with the emotions, 'your heart is shut in', &c., and the two seem to go along together, in an even flow, sliding from one thing to another without effort or consciousness of sliding. Again it is the syntax which does this: the phrases, far from being chopped up into sentences or being end-stopped, do not stop at all. The sky overhead the men in the trenches is not separated from the tapping on the walls

as though these were quite different phenomena occurring in different places, because they are both happening in the consciousness of the prisoner, and nearly
at the same time: the one merges into the other.

But still, this prose is not utterly divorced from the
traditional: it has links such as 'then you think of'
which makes it more easily acceptable. The following
passage makes a more marked break, though indeed
there is 'and you thought' put in once to help you.
This is a more narrative style:

THE CAMERA EYE (18)

Mrs. Pinelli was a very fashionable lady and adored bullterriers and had a gentleman friend who was famous for his
resemblance to King Edward;

she was a very fashionable lady and there were white lilies
in the hall No my dear I can't bear the scent of them in the
room and the bullterriers bit the tradespeople and the little
newsy No my dear they never bit nice people and they're
quite topping with Billy and his friends.

They all went coaching in a four in hand and the man in
the back blew a long horn and that's where Dick Whittington stood with his cat and the bells. There were hampers full
of luncheon and Mrs. Pinelli had grey eyes and was very kind
to her friend's little boy though she loathed simply loathed
most children and her gentleman friend who was famous for
his resemblance to King Edward couldn't bear them or the
bullterriers and she kept asking Why do you call him that?

and you thought of Dick Whittington and the big bells of
Bow, three times Lord Mayor of London and looked into her
grey eyes and said Maybe because I called him that the first
time I saw him and I didn't like Mrs. Pinelli and I didn't like
the bullterriers and I didn't like the four in hand but I wished
Dick Whittington, three times lord mayor of London boomed

the big bells of Bow and I wished Dick Whittington I wished
I was home, but I hadn't any home and the man in the back
blew a long horn.[1]

For the most part that is the same method as Rodker's;
it is, however, more mixed: sometimes we are spectators, sometimes we are in the mind of the little boy,
but even so, when we are spectators we are little boy
spectators. And at the end of the passage a still further
departure from usual prose takes place. Rodker let us
follow the mind only when it has come to the state of
definition, of being able to separate ideas or concepts.
Language as we commonly use it helps to separate
ideas still further: it is a question of degrees of consciousness, and Dos Passos takes us a step deeper into
the semiconscious than Rodker did. We are given
a glimpse of how one idea emerges from another by
means of association in the way we occasionally trace
back how we come to think of something, a connexion
at some times due to association in fact or in feeling,
at others simply to a likeness in words: 'I wished
Dick Whittington three times lord mayor of London
boomed the big bells of Bow and I wished Dick
Whittington I wished I was home. . . .' And again we
have repetitions.

Much of this sort of writing derives from Miss
Stein; many writers who appear to us more or less
traditional have gained one part of their vividness
from her, such as Hemingway (see p. 58) and
Anderson (p. 196). She seems to have carried the
method to its ultimate end, as we saw in the last

[1] From *the forty second parallel*, by John Dos Passos, Constable,
Greenberg, N.Y., 1930.

chapter (p. 223), to an end indeed which for most of us defeats its own purpose. For language must do more than express the incoherence of the mind; it cannot stop short at recording the movements of the mind when it is not 'thinking': I say it *must*, not because I feel any moral necessity about it, but simply because words themselves are, by their very nature, the mind crystallized into 'thought'. However, in another manner, Miss Stein could be extremely effective:

Jeff Campbell never knew very well these days what it was that was going on inside him. All he knew was, he was uneasy now always to be with Melanctha. All he knew was, that he was always uneasy when he was with Melanctha, not the way he used to be from just not being very understanding, but now, because he never could be honest with her, because he was now always feeling her strong suffering, in her, because he knew now he was having a straight, good feeling with her, but she went so fast, and he was so slow to her: Jeff knew his right feeling never got a chance to show itself as strong, to her.

All this was always getting harder for Jeff Campbell. He was very proud to hold himself to be strong, was Jeff Campbell. He was very tender not to hurt Melanctha, when he knew she would be sure to feel it badly in her head a long time after, he hated that he could not now be honest with her, he wanted to stay away to work it out all alone, without her, he was afraid she would feel it to suffer, if he kept away now from her. He was uneasy always, with her, he was uneasy when he thought about her, he knew now he had a good, straight, strong feeling of right loving for her, and yet now he never could use it to be good and honest with her.

Jeff Campbell did not know, these days, anything he could do to make it better for her. He did not know anything he

could do, to set himself really right in his acting and his thinking toward her. She pulled him so fast with her, and he did
not dare to hurt her, and he could not come right, so fast, the
way she always needed he should be doing it now, for her. . . .

Sometimes now and again with them, and with all this
trouble for a little while forgotten by him, Jeff, and Melanctha,
with him, would be very happy in a strong, sweet loving.
Sometimes then, Jeff would find himself to be soaring very
high in his true loving. Sometimes Jeff would find then, in
his loving, his soul swelling out full inside him. Always Jeff
felt now in himself, deep feeling.

Always now Jeff had to go so much faster than was real
with his feeling. Yet always Jeff knew now he had a right,
strong feeling. Always now when Jeff was wondering, it was
Melanctha he was doubting, in the loving. Now he would
often ask her, was she real now to him, in her loving. He would
ask her often, feeling something queer about it all inside him,
though yet he was never really strong in his doubting, and
always Melanctha would answer to him, 'Yes, Jeff, sure, you
know it, always,' and always Jeff felt a doubt now in her loving.

Always now Jeff felt in himself, deep loving. Always now
he did not know really, if Melanctha was true in her loving.

All these days Jeff was uncertain in him, and he was uneasy
about which way he should act so as not to be wrong and put
them both into bad trouble. Always now he was, as if he must
feel deep into Melanctha to see if it was real loving he would find
she now had in her, and always he would stop himself, with
her, for always he was afraid now that he might badly hurt her.

Always now he liked it better when he was detained when
he had to go and see her. Always now he never liked to go
to be with her, although he never wanted really, not to be
always with her. Always now he never felt really at ease with
her, even when they were good friends together. Always
now he felt, with her, he could not be really honest to her.
And Jeff never could be happy with her when he could not

feel strong to tell all his feelings to her. Always now every day
he found it harder to make the time pass with her, and not
let his feeling come so that he would quarrel with her.[1]

A rather long extract has been necessary to give some
idea of the cumulative effect of this prose, its almost
hypnotic power. 'Miss Stein is a sort of Epstein in
words', Wyndham Lewis said: 'Her puissant, heavy,
churning temperament inspires respect.' But this
churning, after all, is what goes on in a good many
minds, and we feel as we follow in this book the stories
of her negroes, that we really are inside the minds of
her characters. The hypnotic effect is no doubt largely
due to the repetitions, almost the refrains, and perhaps
this hypnosis is Miss Stein's essential method of subduing her readers; yet the sense of being inside the
mind is due to her patient following of all the echoes
of a thought, the returns to a thought, that we recognize as going on inside our own minds. The language
is of the plainest, yet the final result is subtle, and I do
not think that this subtlety is added by ourselves as we
become more and more immersed in the story of Jeff
Campbell and Melanctha Herbert; at the same time
it is difficult to know how far the whole effect is due to
the suggestibility of words, to which the rhythm, quite
marked, and not very varied, adds considerably. Mr.
Wilson, we have seen, classes Miss Stein with the
Symbolists. But whatever we may think of the virtues
or vices of this style, we are forced to admit that we
follow with extraordinary closeness the workings of a
mind, though here not of the writer's. You may not

[1] From *Three Lives*, Rodker, 1927.

altogether like what it sets out to do, but you have to admit that it does it.

There is one thing common to the three passages I have quoted, and that is their plainness, almost, one might say, their starkness. There is not a metaphor in any of them: no tricks of allusion are played with us, except, in Dos Passos's more romantic piece, the allusions he makes as part of the small boy's mind. All of them try to reduce language to its simplest terms, so that neither they nor we shall be cheated by it; they are determined to make us feel or see only what they want us to feel or see: they are not going to rely on any chance associations in our minds. This is refreshing if we have previously been reading decorated prose: we feel that we are being given reality, not a toy. There is even an effort made to nullify the effects of rhythm. The musical phrase has given place to the drum-beat. It is an attempt to write prose untainted by poetry.

In the same book from which I have already quoted, Dos Passos has risked another sort of experiment, in which he tries to represent the general, the mass mind, instead of any particular one. He sees society as a congeries of people moved by suggestion, chiefly such suggestion as the press sees fitting it shall be submitted to. This mass mind is made up of newspaper headings, of 'pithy pars', of gobbets of information thrown to it in cinematograph theatres:

NEWSREEL XVII

an attack by a number of hostile airships developed before midnight. Bombs were dropped somewhat indiscriminately over localities possessing no military importance

Railroads Won't Yield An Inch

We shall have to make the passage under conditions not entirely advantageous to us, said Captain Koenig of the Deutschland ninety miles on his way passing Solomon's Island at 2.30. Every steamer passed blew his whistle in salute.

> *You made me what I am to-day*
> *I hope you're satisfied*
> *You dragged me down and down and down*
> *Till the soul within me died*

Sir Roger Casement was hanged in Pentonvill Gaol at nine o'clock this morning

U-BOAT PASSES CAPES UNHINDERED

Clad only in kimono girl bathers shock dairy lunch instead of first class cafe on amusement dock heavy losses shown in US crop report Italians cheered as Austrians leave hot rolls in haste to get away giant wall of water rushes down valley professor says Beethoven gives the impression of a juicy steak PRISON'S MAGIC TURNS CITY JUNK INTO GOLD MINE

Moon will Hide Planet Saturn From Sight Tonight

BROTHERS FIGHT IN DARK[1]

That, of course, is meant to be amusing and satirical, with a touch of bitterness, and perhaps it does not much advance the solution of the problem: but it is a question whether the headline style will not spread from the newspapers to other realms of literature. There are signs in America that it is doing so. The paragraph beginning 'Clad only in kimono' is in a

---

[1] From *the forty second parallel*, by John Dos Passos, Constable.

manner that lends itself to imitation and development. The real writer must resist journalism, but there is nothing to prevent his taking over some of its methods and moulding them to his purpose.

There is another kind of experimental prose which instead of trying to follow the convolutions of the mind, in the 'churning' manner developed by Miss Stein, adopts rather the method of poetry in leaping from one thing to another, leaving out the intermediate steps, using only such points as are useful to it in building up a special effect. It becomes in a way 'prose poetry', but in a sense different from that of the old-fashioned emotive prose:

The Hollies. Some blazers lounge beneath the calming tree; they talk in birds' hearing; girls come with roses, servants with a tray, skirting the sprinkler preaching madly to the grass, where mower worries in the afternoons; draw not your leagues away. Too-much-alone.

Between box-edges, past the weathering urns, walk, acquire their ruses. Visit enough till coat-stand in their hall seem arsenal stocked against a life-time's harm.

These also dogs follow, are loved by grooms; milder than hawks have conquered fear of ledges, sailed over fishes swaying with the sea; have looked in ponds but not for reassurance; bathing in front of inattentive weasels, a tan-armed gonsil or a first-of-May.

O turn your head this way, be faithful here. The working mouth, the flimsy flexing knee, the leap in summer in the rubber shoes, these signal in their only codes. There is no other rendezvous for you to keep before the simple night (at

night elopement is potty from the private drome. The little
train will halt to pick up flowers.) There are no other agents
if these were cads. You stand in time's nick now with all to
lose. The spies have gone to phone for their police—locked
behind mirrors in his study, his secret heroes ragging round
the fire, Death swots ungraceful, keen on his career; notes
in his journal 'I have never lived—left-handed and ironic, but
have loved'.

Again. Always the same weakness. No progress against
this terrible thing. What Would E say if she knew? Dare I
tell her? Does Derek suspect? He looked at me very
strangely at dinner. No; no one must ever know. If the
enemy ever got to hear of it, my whole work would be nulli-
fied. I must be careful to avoid sitting up with E alone to late
hours. The signed confession in my pocket shall remain
unread, always.

A cold bath every morning. Never to funk but to return
everything, no matter how distasteful the explanations. (The
Hollies this evening, mind.) Whenever temptation is felt go
at once to do mechanical drawing.

Hands, in the name of my Uncle, I command you, or....

Some of that passage becomes easily comprehensible
by reference to the earlier part of the book, but much
of it demands from the reader a surprising and stimulating agility in making mental transitions. You are
to imagine a man considering a household to which he
is invited, and which is filled with people hostile to
him in temperament and outlook. The sudden starts
of the mind are helped by the very marked, very short
rhythms. An extract of this sort, torn from its context, does not do the method justice, for it is in the end

1 From *The Orators*, by W. H. Auden, Faber and Faber, 1932.

evocative of a very distinct mood. It seems, perhaps, unsatisfactory and inconclusive, but at least to read prose of this sort is an adventure for the mind and the imagination. In some ways it adopts, and adapts, the headline method, with its omission of the article. It cuts away the inessential, and to follow it is at least an intellectual gymnastic.

The writer who took experimentation farthest of all was, of course, James Joyce. His early work is simple enough: there is no difficulty about *A Portrait of the Artist as a Young Man*: it is limpid in the traditional manner. This is not the place in which to discuss that brilliant masterpiece *Ulysses*, with its extremely complex and carefully woven texture of tale and allusion: it contains a number of experiments, all of them fascinating to anyone who cares in the least about the craft of writing. It will be more interesting here to go directly to some of the later writing, the *Work in Progress*, which used to appear in fragments. Before quoting a passage it is necessary to say that just as *Ulysses* was to contain all that passed through a man's mind during the day, so this book is to contain all the mental events of a night: what we are concerned with, therefore, is dream-consciousness. The level at which the words take form is below that of ordinary language: 'we are in the region whence all languages arise and where all the impulses to act have their origin.'[1] Each word, therefore, is charged with the sort of significance often associated with words in the half-waking state; it will carry two or three symbolic

[1] *Axel's Castle*. The chapter on James Joyce is illuminating. I am myself indebted to Mr. Wilson for much of what I say here.

meanings at one and the same time. Similarities of sound will be of extraordinary suggestiveness. In *Ulysses* Joyce took us into the minds of his characters when in a normal state of consciousness: here we are to be at one with their unconscious. When we realize this the work becomes more comprehensible. We can take one of the simpler passages from a fable by which the hero, a man named Earwicker, of Norwegian origin, tries to explain something. This is the beginning of 'The Mookse and the Gripes', an easy passage.

Eins within a space and a weary wide space it wast ere wohned a Mookse.

There is no difficulty about that, especially if we know a little German. 'Once within a space, and a weary wide space it was, there lived a Mookse.'

Eins within a space and a weary wide space it wast ere wohned a Mookse. The onesomeness wast alltolonely, archunsitslike, broady oval, and a Mookse he would a walking go (My hood! cries Antony Romeo) so one grandsumer evening, after a great morning and his good supper of gammon and spittish, having flabelled his eyes, pilleoled his nostrils, vacticanated his ears and palliumed his throats, he put on his impermeable, harped on his crown and stepped out of his immobile *De Rure Albo* (socolled becauld it was chalkful of masterplasters and had borgeously letout gardens strown with cascades, pintacostecas, horthoducts and currycombs) and set off from Ludstown *a spasso* to see how badness was badness in the weirdest of all pensible ways. As he set off with his father's sword, his *lancia spezzata*, he was girded on, and with that between his legs and his tarkeels, our once in only Bragspear, he clanked, to my clinking, from veetoes to threetop, every inch of an immortal. He had not walked over a pentiadpair of parsecs from his azylium when at the turning of the Shinshone Lanteran near Saint Bowery's-without-his-Walls he came (secunding to the one one oneth of the propecies, *Amnis Limina Permanent*) upon the most unconsciously boggylooking stream he ever locked his eyes with. Out of the colliens it took a rise by daubing itself Ninon. It looked little and it smelt of brown and it thought in narrows and it talked showshallow. And as it rinn it dribbled like any lively purliteasy: *My, my, my! Me and me! Little down dream don't I love thee!* And, I declare, what was there on the yonder bank of the stream that would be a river, parched on a limb of the olum, bolt downright, but the Gripes? And no doubt he was fit to be dried for why had he not been having the juice of his times?[1]

You may say that this sort of thing has been done before: ' 'Twas brillig, and the slithy toves . . .', but the point of Lewis Carroll's 'Jabberwocky' is not the same as Joyce's, or rather, it gives only a faint indication of what the point is. The Alice books, except for the Jabberwocky rhymes, are a child's dream co-ordinated and put together in rational language by a grown-up. Here we have the whole life-experience of a grown-up concentrated into this one night's dreaming, and the object is to represent human existence below the level of consciousness: it is the first attempt on anything like a large scale to make use of the new awareness of our being made possible by the psychology of this century. Sometimes it can become poetry, as can be seen from the end of the fragment published under the title *Anna Livia Plura-*

[1] From *Two Tales of Shem and Shaum*, Faber and Faber, 1932.

belle.[1] This consists of the conversation between two Dublin washerwomen as they scrub on the banks of the Liffey between a stone and an elm tree: darkness is falling at the end, the voices grow vague, and merge into the noise of the river.

> . . . Lord save us! And ho! Hey? What all men. Hot? His tittering daughters of. Whawk?
> Can't hear with the waters of. The chittering waters of. Flittering bats, fieldmice bawk talk. Ho! Are you not gone ahome? What T'om Malone? Can't hear with bawk of bats, all thim liffeying waters of. Ho, talk save us! My foos won't moos. I feel as old as yonder elm. A tale told of Shaun or Shem? All Livia's daughtersons. Dark hawks hear us. Night! Night! My ho head halls. I feel as heavy as yonder stone. Tell me of John or Shaun? Who were Shem and Shaun the living sons or daughters of? Night now! Tell me, tell me, tell me, elm! Night night! Telmetale of stem or stone. Beside the rivering waters of, hitherandthithering waters of. Night!

This is poetry not only because of its sound, its allusiveness, its concentration, but because of its use of words in the Symbolist manner. Joyce seems to have lived in words far more than in images, and we know this from many of the utterances of Stephen in *A Portrait of the Artist*. When, for instance, Stephen 'drew forth a phrase from his treasure and spoke it softly to himself—"A day of dappled seaborne clouds—"' he decided that what he liked about the phrase was not the colours, or the image at all, but 'the poise and balance of the period itself'. And then follows an amazingly revealing confession:

> Or was it that, being as weak of sight as he was shy of

---

[1] Faber and Faber, 1930.

mind, he drew less pleasure from the reflection of the glowing sensible world through the prism of a language many coloured and richly storied than from the contemplation of an inner world of individual emotions mirrored perfectly in a lucid supple periodic prose?

That is worth pages of analysis and explanation: Joyce was seeking a prism of language instead of a lucid supple periodic prose. It is, of course, a poetic method, and it is not merely jotting down what comes into the head, as can be seen from the difference between the three drafts of *Anna Livia Plurabelle*. The objection to it as reading-matter is that it demands the concentration which metaphysical poetry demands, and one simply cannot maintain this over a long stretch. Here is a more difficult passage:

Pepep. Pay bearer, sure and sorry, at foot of ohoho honest policist. On never again, by Phoenis, swore on him Lloyd's, not for beaten wheat, not after Sir Joe Meade's father, thanks! They know him, the covenanter, by rote at least for a chameleon at last in his true falseheaven colours from ultraviolent to subred tissues. That's his last tryon to march through the grand tryomphal arch. His reignbolt's shot. Never again! How you do that like, Mista Chimepiece? You got nice yum plemyums. Praypaid my promishles.

Agreed, Wu Welsher he was chogfulled to beacsate on earn as in hiving, of foxold conningnesses but who, hey honey, for all values of his latters, integer integerrimost was the formast of the firm? At folkmood hailed, at part farwailed accwmw- laded concloud, Nuah-Nuah, nebob of Nephilim! After all what followed for apprentice sake? Since the now nighs nearing as the yetst hies hin. Jeebies, ugh, kek, ptah, that was an ill man. Jawboose, puddigood, this is for treu a sweetish mand. But Jumbluffer, bagdad, sir, yond would be for once

over our all honoured christmastyde easteredman. Fourth
position of solution. How johnny! Finest view from horizon.
Tableau final. Two me see. Male and female unmask we hem.
Begum by gunne! Who now broothes oldbrawn. Dawn! the
nape of his nameshielder's scalp. Halp! After having drummed
all he dun. Hun! Worked out to an inch of his core. More!
Ring down. While the queenbee he staggerhorned blesses her
bliss for to feel her funnyman's functions Tag. Rumbling.[1]

Is this sort of writing, we ask, really suitable for
a novel? Some of Joyce's work is bewitching as
sound, especially when read aloud, and wonderfully
rhythmed, but another objection is that a great deal of
it depends so much upon Joyce's own experiences:
some of his allusions and references can have meaning
only for a pre-war Dubliner, and the phonetic render-
ings are sometimes purely local. Too much of it is
association of ideas through punning. But as method
the whole thing is extremely interesting, and has had
an influence on writing. It is perhaps an idle dream to
think that language can be broken up as a ray of light
is split up by a prism, to give us colours in which to
express new sensibilities; but a language lives by its
changes, by its capacity to adapt itself to new material:
and it is upon the power of our writers to make it do
this that the future of our language, and our literature,
will depend. That is why all experimentation should
be welcomed, not laughed at: and that is why I have
ventured to add this attempt at elucidation to this
book on modern prose.

There is one question, however, which ought to be
asked about Joyce's later work, and, in a less insistent

[1] From *Finnegans Wake*. End of Part III, Faber and Faber, 1939.

tone, that of Mr. Auden, a question which sounds
simple; namely, is it prose or poetry? Put in another
way, does it not depend too much on 'musical' effects,
does it not tend to make the unit of its fabric the
musical bar, so to speak, rather than the sentence, or
phrase, which can be definitely related to some external object, to some thought, or some feeling? It
even takes this method beyond the point where it
is normally used in poetry; it abstracts one of the
elements of poetry, and makes it all-important. One
cannot, of course, lay down the law about this sort
of thing; the line between poetry and prose is difficult
to draw. What we can ask ourselves, however, is
whether the effect made on us by this kind of writing
more resembles that made on us by the poetry we
know, or by the prose: and if by the poetry, whether
this will ultimately benefit that part of the craft of
writing which has natural laws of its own distinct
from poetry. If one art borrows means from another,
it is in danger of losing its effectiveness in its own
peculiar sphere.

PART V

ADDITIONS

A READER looking through the following extracts, which, generally speaking, lead from what we might call prose writing up to the thirties to that of 1961, will probably feel that there is a change of some sort, difficult to define. The syntax, one would say, is freer, more colloquial, a change if not set in motion by, at least first illustrated by, George Orwell. The words chosen are blunter, more ordinary, more earthy might perhaps be the right term. The prose is, in a way hard to define, more violent, corresponding with the violence of content which seems to imbrue so many works, as a kind of balance, one might think, to the balm of the Welfare State.

No extensive comment is made on the samples offered. For the general problems involved the reader may be referred to the appropriate sections in the earlier parts of this book. What I have tried to do, unnecessarily it may be thought, is to draw attention to the skill of the writers quoted, which might evade the careless reader simply because it is so skilful. Their prose does not draw attention to itself, but obeys its purpose. The more alert we as readers can be, the better, for without alertness there is little enjoyment, and enjoyment is the necessary condition of understanding. 'To please and instruct' was the old classical formula, and, as Dryden stressed, unless you please you do not instruct. Instruction, however, is a vague term: for us it must primarily mean a deeper understanding of our fellow human beings; to pursue this further would be to offer affront to the interested reader.

§ 1

Explanatory Prose

(i) CRITICISM

THERE is one type of criticism not illustrated earlier, in which the critic carefully examines a poem, say, arriving at its ultimate meaning by relating the work to the character of the poet and his experiences, together with drawing inferences from the time or times when it was written. Not only can this be illuminating, but it can help to make the poem part of one's own experience.

The 'Immortality' Ode

As with many poems, it is hard to understand any part of the Ode until we first understand the whole of it. I will therefore say at once what I think the poem is chiefly about. It is a poem about growing; some say it is a poem about growing old, but I believe it is about growing up. It is incidentally a poem about optics and then, inevitably, about epistemology: it is concerned with ways of seeing and then with ways of knowing. Ultimately it is concerned with ways of acting, for, as usual with Wordsworth, knowledge implies liberty and power. In only a limited sense is the Ode a poem about immortality.

Both formally and in the history of its composition the poem is divided into two main parts. The first part, consisting of four stanzas, states an optical phenomenon and asks a question about it. The second part, consisting of seven stanzas, answers that question and is itself divided into two parts, of which the first is despairing, the second hopeful. Some time separates the composition of the question from that of the answer; the evidence most recently adduced by Professor de Selincourt seems to indicate that the interval was two years.

The question which the first part asks is this:

> Whither is fled the visionary gleam?
> Where is it now, the glory and the dream?

And the first part leads to this question, but although it moves in only one direction it takes its way through more than one mood. There are at least three moods before the climax of the question is reached.

The first stanza makes a relatively simple statement. 'There was a time' when all common things seemed clothed in 'celestial light', when they had 'the glory and the freshness of a dream'. In a poem ostensibly about immortality we ought perhaps to pause over the word 'celestial', but the present elaborate title was not given to the poem until much later, and conceivably at the time of the writing of the first part the idea of immortality was not in Wordsworth's mind at all. Celestial light probably means only something different from ordinary, earthly, scientific light; it is a light of the mind, shining even in darkness—'by night or day'—and it is perhaps similar to the light which is praised in the invocation to the third book of *Paradise Lost*.

The second stanza goes on to develop this first mood, speaking of the ordinary, physical kind of vision and suggesting further the meaning of 'celestial'. We must remark that

in this stanza Wordsworth is so far from observing a diminution of his physical senses that he explicitly affirms their
strength. He is at pains to tell us how vividly he sees the rain-
bow, the rose, the moon, the stars, the water and the sunshine.
I emphasize this because some of those who find the Ode
a dirge over the poetic power maintain that the poetic
power failed with the failure of Wordsworth's senses. It is
true that Wordsworth, who lived to be eighty, was said in
middle life to look much older than his years. Still, thirty-
two, his age at the time of writing the first part of the Ode, is
an extravagantly early age for a dramatic failure of the senses.
We might observe here, as others have observed elsewhere,
that Wordsworth never did have the special and perhaps
modern sensibility of his sister or of Coleridge, who were so
aware of exquisite particularities. His finest passages are
moral, emotional, subjective; whatever visual intensity they
have, comes from his response to the object, not from his
close observation of it.[1]

The argument is convincingly arranged, opening
with a firm statement as to what Professor Trilling
thinks the poem to be about, phrased in a beautifully
succinct way: 'It is a poem about growing: some say
it is a poem about growing old, but I believe it is
about growing up.' This is developed in the first paragraph, or, rather, entered into with a little more detail.
We are then invited to look at the poem as a whole,
its logical as well as its emotional structure, this being
followed by a closer examination of mood and of word.
And as the process goes on the sentences become
longer, gradually shifting our receptivity from the
mind to the emotions. Beginning with 'understanding' what the poem is about, we go on to appreciate

[1] Lionel Trilling, *The Liberal Imagination*, Secker and Warburg, 1951.

sympathetically what was happening to Wordsworth. The tone is easy, impersonal, the phrasing almost colloquial—'Still, thirty-two . . .'—but never slack, always making its point firmly, with here and there a slight emphasis. Nor is there anything combative in the manner, as there so often is in the criticism of today, as though the outraged critic were refuting some colleague or rival, or forcing you to agree with his doctrine, a refusal implying crass stupidity on your part, or a failure in your moral nature.

To turn now to purely explanatory prose, two examples by writers who had not achieved their present distinction in 1934 offer themselves as differing from what has been so far illustrated. They may be placed here since both are in a sense critical, explaining what the authors are after, the first by giving reasons, the second by stating a point of view.

A writer approaching a controversial and lively subject on which much has been written owes it to the reader to make his own position at least as clear as it is to himself. The causes of the Civil Wars have been analysed, the rights of the combatants have been judged and weighed by Churchman and Dissenter, Whig and Tory, Liberal and Marxist, utilitarian and romantic. The religion, the political morality and the philosophies of his own time colour the outlook of every writer, however conscientious, although, wise in his generation, each may add something to our understanding of the past. No historian has ever been, or ever will be, omniscient in his knowledge or infallible in his deductions. None can see the whole and undivided truth.

The contemporary could not do so either. Puzzled by the variety of events which came so confusingly upon him from

day to day, and ignorant of much that time alone would bring
to light, he steered his way through his own world—as we
do now—by the imperfect judgment of an ill-informed mind.
But the contemporary knew one thing that the historian
can only imagine: he knew what it felt like to be alive at that
time, to experience those religious doubts, political fears, and
economic pressures as a part of his life. He may not have
known or suspected influences which have been later revealed;
but he knew what he experienced in his mind or suffered in
his flesh, and he knew what beliefs and what interests he admitted to be the motives of his action. 'Here we are subject to
error and misjudging one another,' said Strafford on the scaf-
fold. The day-to-day events of history arise at least in part
from error and misjudgment. On this level falsehood itself
is a part of truth.

Before history can be put into a coherent perspective it is
often necessary to clear away the misinterpretations and the
half-knowledge by which contemporaries lived. But the application of modern methods of research, together with modern
knowledge and prejudice, can make the past merely the subject of our own analytical ingenuity or our own illusions.
With scholarly precision we can build up theories as to why
and how things happened which are convincing to us, which
may even be true, but which those who lived through the
epoch would neither recognise nor accept. It is legitimate for
the historian to pierce the surface and bring to light motives
and influences not known at the time; but it is equally legitimate to accept the motives and explanations which satisfied
contemporaries. The two methods produce different results,
but each result may be a fair answer to the particular question
that has been asked. They become misleading only if either
is accepted as the whole truth.

I have not attempted in this book to examine underlying causes, but rather to give full importance and value
to the admitted motives and the illusions of the men of the

seventeenth century. I have sought to restore their immediacy of experience.[1]

That is a beautifully lucid explanation of the historian's position, and it is musical prose, varied in the run of the sentences, and convincing largely because of the form: such prose could never fatigue the mind since it never wearies the ear. Take the beginnings of the paragraphs, with their different attacks, the first and third opening with long sentences, the second, picking up the first paragraph, with a short one. There is no monotony either in the weight of the stress on verbs, or in the vowel sounds, as can be well exemplified by the second sentence of the second paragraph. There is a heavy stress, as the attacking word, on 'puzzled', less weight on 'ignorant', and still less on 'steered'. Yet where Dr. Wedgwood wants an equal stress she uses words of a very different sound: 'omniscient in his knowledge or infallible in his deductions'. Again, the long sentences give point to the short ones, or the short phrases, while the end-words of clauses vary in vowel-sound: 'the imperfect judgment of an ill-informed mind'.

Moreover Dr. Wedgwood hazards something very dangerous in concluding three successive paragraphs with the same word, the centre, of course, of the matter she is concerned with, bringing to a close short emphatic sentences: 'None can see the whole and undivided truth', '. . . a part of truth', '. . . the whole truth.' It puts the argument beyond question; it rams home the state of the case with perfect urbanity.

[1] C. V. Wedgwood, *The King's Peace, 1637–1641*, Collins, 1955.

It is not so easy to be urbane when you are, besides stating your own position, at the same time attacking a different one. Yet it is perfectly possible to be level-headed and even-tempered.

I take the somewhat naïve view that the literature of the past began somewhere a few minutes ago and that the literature of the present begins, say, with Homer. While there is no doubt that we need as much knowledge of all kinds, from all sources, as we can get if we are to see the slightest lyric in all its richness of meaning, we have nevertheless an obligation, that we perilously evade, to form a judgment of the literature of our own time. It is more than an obligation; we must do it if we would keep on living. When the scholar assumes that he is judging a work of the past from a high and disinterested position, he is actually judging it from no position at all but is only abstracting from the work those qualities that his semi-scientific method will permit him to see; and this is the Great Refusal.

We must judge the past and keep it alive by being alive ourselves; and that is to say that we must judge the past not with a method or an abstract hierarchy but with the present, or with as much of the present as our poets have succeeded in elevating to the objectivity of form. For it is through the formed, objective experience of our own time that we must approach the past; and then by means of a critical mastery of our own formed experience we may test the presence and value of form in works of the past. The critical activity is reciprocal and simultaneous. The scholar who tells us that he understands Dryden but makes nothing of Hopkins or Yeats is telling us that he does not understand Dryden.

Perhaps the same scholar acknowledges the greatness of Dryden and the even more formidable greatness of Milton and Shakespeare; and if you ask him how they became great he will reply, that History did it and that we have got to wait until History does it, or declines to do it, to writers of our own time. Who is this mysterious person named History? We are back again with our old friend, the Great Refusal, who thrives upon the naturalistic repudiation of the moral obligation to judge. If we wait for history to judge there will be no judgment; for if we are not history then history is nobody. He is nobody when he has become the historical method.

One last feature of this illusion of the fixed hierarchy I confess I cannot understand. It is the belief that the chief function of criticism is the ranking of authors rather than their use. It is the assumption that the great writers of the past occupy a fixed position. If we alter the figure slightly, admitting that History has frozen their reputations, we must assume also that the position from which we look at them is likewise fixed; for if it were not we should see them in constantly changing relations and perspectives, and we should think their positions were changing too. If you will now see this same figure as a landscape of hills, trees, plains, you will quickly become fearful for the man who from a fixed point surveys the unchanging scene; for the man, the only man, who cannot change his position is a dead man: the only man for whom the greatness of the poets is fixed is also dead. And so, if we look at this Homeric simile with the eyes of Bishop Berkeley, we must conclude that the great authors are dead too, because there is nobody to look at them. I have adapted this figure from one of the Prefaces of Henry James because it seems to me to be a good way of saying that the literature of the past can be kept alive only by seeing it as the literature of the present. Or perhaps we ought to say that the literature of the past lives in the literature of the present and nowhere else; that it is all present literature.[1]

Mr. Tate is stating his belief in the living quality of old literature. Just as Dr. Wedgwood says at the

[1] Allen Tate, *Collected Essays*, 1959, Scribner.

end of what has been quoted from her Introduction that she has sought to restore the immediacy of the experience of the men of the seventeenth century, so does Mr. Tate insist upon our sharing the immediacy of the poetic experience of past times. He begins with what may seem an outrageous paradox, and goes on to make a direct statement as to a certain type of scholar. Then the explanation follows, the formulation of his own position. The prose depends for its effect upon such direct statements, on the force of the statements themselves, and not at all upon the music of the words. The only divagation is the telling metaphor of the dead man being the only man whose position is fixed, with its extension into the Berkeleyan point of view.

But there is no attempt to write musical prose, with the effect that a play of vowel-sounds can have; the prose gives pleasure from the firmness of each sentence, a buoyancy which carries us on to the next. There is never a word too much. Of course a certain play in the vowel-sounds is audible, enough to avoid monotony: '. . . he will reply that History did it, and that we have got to wait until History does it, or declines to do it, . . .' Mr. Tate's repetition of a word does not make for the deadening of that word, but for its reinforcement. 'If we wait for history to judge, there will be no judgment; for if we are not history then history is nobody. He is nobody when he has become the historical method.'

Neither of these two writers introduces anything new, but they illustrate the varieties of tone, the differences in voice, of two people writing in what is clearly the tradition of this century.

(ii) PHILOSOPHY

The kind of prose last quoted may seem uncompromising enough: but it makes concessions to human emotions. By its main metaphor it invites the collaboration of the imagination, and moreover the phrasing at the least suggests an underlying music. The following passage offers nothing to the senses, either in itself or by metaphor; all through it attacks the reasoning faculties, and those alone.

The fact is, however, that while the causal theory of perception may be represented as a theory about the meaning of a certain class of propositions, it is not from considerations of meaning that philosophers have actually come to adopt it. They have assumed rather that the argument from illusion proves that it is false, as a matter of fact, that anyone ever directly observes a material thing; and they have then had recourse to a causal theory as the only means of accounting for the knowledge of the existence and behaviour of material things, which they did not doubt that they possessed. The important feature of this procedure is that it rests upon the assumption that the character of our sense-data, or whatever objects it is held that we do directly observe, gives us good reason to believe that they are dependent upon external causes. And it is in this assumption, whether it takes the form of discovering these causes in material things, as they are conceived by common sense, or, what is now more fashionable, in scientific objects, such as atoms and electrons, or, as in Berkeley's philosophy, in the activities of a God, that the main interest of the causal theory lies. It is possible indeed both to deny this assumption and still to adhere to a causal analysis of propositions asserting the presence of material things, if one is prepared, as Hume apparently was, to draw the conclusion that one's beliefs in the existence of material things are altogether unjustifiable. But such a procedure would be reasonable only if there were good grounds, independently of any argument that involved this assumption, for supposing that the meaning of such propositions was correctly rendered by some form of the causal theory. And this does not appear to be the case.

The argument that is supposed to justify this postulation of external causes proceeds by the following stages. It is maintained, first, that every event has a cause; secondly, that sense-data are events; thirdly, that one's sense-data are not, for the most part, caused by one's own volitions or by any other of one's own conscious mental activities or states; and fourthly, that they are not caused by one another. From these premises it is deduced that they must, for the most part, have causes that one cannot directly observe; and that an attempt may be made to show how the specific character and behaviour of these external causes may be inferred from the character of one's sense-data. Up to this final step, the argument is substantially the same for all versions of the theory. The differences between them relate only to the nature of these external causes and the degree to which they can be known. The most common assumption has been that one is justified in ascribing to them at any rate the primary qualities of extension, figure, solidity, number and motion; and ingenious methods have been devised by means of which one is supposed to be able to discover by what determinate forms of these qualities they are characterized on particular occasions. But there is no point in my discussing the validity of these methods before I have settled the question whether there is any reason to believe in the existence of such external causes at all. For if it turns out that there is no reason to believe in their existence, the question of the means by which one is to ascertain their specific character will not arise.[1]

[1] Alfred J. Ayer, *The Foundations of Empirical Knowledge*, Macmillan & Co., 1940.

Philosophy today no longer seems to be concerned with how men ought to live, but has largely become, so it seems to the layman, a matter of semantics, though this particular extract might be allowed to come under the heading of criticism, since it is directed towards correcting common assumptions. We need not bend our interest so much to the argument itself, convincing though it may be, but, rather, to the prose in which it is couched, which differs radically from that of passages quoted earlier in this book under the heading of Philosophy. It makes no attempt to persuade, and if it does not exactly bludgeon you into acquiescence, it orders you into obedience. There is no grace in this prose, but a continual piston-like power. Most sentences begin with a noun: 'The fact is . . .', 'The argument that is . . .', 'The differences between . . .', sometimes reinforced by an adjective: 'The important feature of . . .'. The reader can hardly avoid putting some weight on the beginning of a sentence, and he must, willy-nilly, bear down firmly, if not heavily, at its end: . . . 'come to adopt it . . .' or, '. . . the causal theory lies'. Or, again, '. . . versions of the theory'. A good clinching end to a paragraph is: 'And this does not appear to be the case.'

Though there may be differences in tone where philosophers are concerned, this would not seem to be true of scientific writing, which ideally is impersonal, 'the meaning of the voice' being subdued. Sir Cyril Hinshelwood, for example, in his lucidly written *The Kinetics of Chemical Change* (1940) humanizes the inhuman in much the same way as Bragg did (see p. 92), and can write: 'When two or more molecules must interact, their encounter is obviously facilitated by a more or less prolonged sojourn of one of them on the surface', 'sojourn' being the word that makes us see what is going on, and establishes a kind of imaginative relation. Yet the scientific description of things extends readily, as stated earlier, into that of field naturalists: which leads us, as before, to

§ 2

Descriptive Prose

(i) DESCRIPTION OF THINGS

WHERE animals are the material, some sense of personal relation creeps in, some quality of living communication. To describe even a dead lion—really describe, not imagine about it—requires not only a different attitude, but the different prose such an attitude demands. Where live animals are the subject, a sense of their being related to the human not only should be there, but insidiously creeps in.

The Orange Armadillos

. . . I glanced at my bed, and, to my horror, saw that the armadillo had disappeared.

I dug down among the bed-clothes and felt the armadillo scrabbling frantically in a tangle of sheets. I hauled him out, and he immediately rolled into a tight ball again. Sitting down on the bed, I examined him. Rolled up, he was about the size and shape of a small melon; on one side of the ball were the three bands from which he got his name, horny stripes which were separated from each other by a thin line of pinkish-grey skin that acted as a hinge; on the other side of the ball you could see how his head and tail fitted into the general scheme of armour-plating. Both these extremities were guarded on top by a section of armour-plate, very gnarled and carunculated, shaped like an acute isosceles triangle. When the head and tail were folded into the ball, these two pieces of armour lay side by side, base to point, together forming a broad triangle which effectively blocked the vulnerable entrance that led to the armadillo's soft undersides. Seen in the light, this armour-plating was a pale amber colour, and appeared as though it had been constructed from a delicate mosaic work. When I had pointed out to my audience the marvels of the creature's external anatomy, I put him on the floor, and we sat in silence, waiting for him to unroll. For some minutes the ball lay immobile; then it started to twitch and jerk slightly. I saw a crack appear between the triangle of head and tail and, as it widened, a small pig-like snout was pushed out. Then, with speed and vigour, the armadillo proceeded to unroll himself. He just split open like some weird bud unfolding, and we had a quick glimpse of a pink, wrinkled tummy covered with dirty white hair, small pink legs, and a sad little face like a miniature pig's, with circular protuberant black eyes. Then he rolled over and righted himself, and all that was visible beneath the shell were the tips of his feet and a few wisps of hair. From the back of his humped shell his tail protruded like one of those ancient war-clubs, covered with spikes and lumps. At the other end his head stuck out, decorated with its triangular cap of knobbed plating, on either side of which had blossomed two tiny, mule-like ears. Beneath this cap of horn I could see the bare cheeks, pink nose, and the small suspicious eyes gleaming like drops of tar. His hind feet were circular, with short blunt nails, and looked rather like the feet of a miniature rhinoceros. His fore-feet were so completely different that they might have belonged to another species of animal: they were armed with three curved nails, the centre one of which was the largest, and resembled the curved talon of some bird of prey. The weight of his hind-quarters rested on his flat hind-feet, but that of his fore-quarters rested on this large nail, so the sole of the foot was raised off the ground, making it seem as though he were standing on tip-toe.[1]

[1] Gerald Durrell, *The Drunken Forest*, Rupert Hart-Davis, 1956.

That is a brilliantly visual piece of writing; our eyes are kept on the object all the time, and there is no excuse for our not knowing exactly what an orange armadillo looks like, either rolled up or 'unfolded', or getting into motion. The imagery is the striking thing, all perfectly simple and homely, except for the word 'carunculated'——a caruncle being 'a small fleshy excrescence' (*O.E.D.*); things that one can see—— armour plating, triangle, mosaic work, 'small suspicious eyes gleaming like drops of tar'. The words are always beautifully chosen: 'scrabbling frantically in a tangle of sheets', the repetition of the short 'a' sounds giving the sound of what is going on. There is a curious sense of organic things happening to the creature, rather than his willing himself to do them. Just as he 'split open like some weird bud unfolding', so two tiny mule-like ears 'blossomed' on either side of his head. Ever and again the unfamiliar is compared with something that one knows, as when the armadillo's nails are described. The sentences vary in length, neither too short nor too complicated, and end firmly, usually on a noun, the whole passage giving an acute sense of visual alertness.

Yet the description of things need not always be rigorously visual; some things can be seen through an imaginative haze, and the sense given of having seen rather than of seeing. Here is a picture of old Cathay, not in actuality, but as seen, supposedly, through the eyes of generations of Western Europeans, though it is ostensibly, and essentially, a description of Chinese porcelain ware.

The Vision of Cathay

Cathay is, or rather was, a continent of immeasurable extent lying just beyond the eastern confines of the known world. Of this mysterious and charming land, poets are the only historians and porcelain painters the most reliable topographers. They alone can give an adequate impression of the beauty of the landscape with its craggy snow-capped mountain ranges and its verdant plains sprinkled with cities of dreaming pagodas and intersected by meandering rivers whose limpid waters bear whole fleets of delicately wrought junks, all a-flutter with bedragonned pennants and laden with precious cargoes of jade, porcelain, samite, silk, green ginger, and delicately scented teas. Beside their banks the palm and the weeping willow flourish amidst phoenix-tail bamboos and a proliferation of exotic flora. Giant flowers abound here: chrysanthemums which tower above the men who tend them, paeonies which dwarf the birds nesting in their branches, and convolvulus whose blossoms serve as hats, as parasols, and even, on occasion, as the roofs of huts. Indeed, the natural landscape is so beautiful that when laying out their gardens the Cathaians could desire no more than to reproduce it on a miniature scale, with paths serpentining round hillocks of artificial rock-work, sinuous rills, and forests of tiny gnarled trees. The fauna is no less extraordinary. Huge and fiery dragons lurk in every mountain cave; gaudy birds with rainbow-hued plumage swoop over the plains; butterflies the size of puffins hover round the pendent blossoms of *Wisteria sinensis*, and diaphanous-tailed goldfish play amidst the water-lilies and chrysolite rocks of stream and pond.

The inhabitants of Cathay are small and neat. Hats, shoes, and cheekbones are worn high, while moustaches, pigtails and finger-nails are encouraged to grow to inordinate length. Their similarity of appearance—like so much else about them —is proverbial, but they try to disguise it by the prodigiously rich variety of their clothes. Flowing robes of silk, elaborately embroidered with gold, are much in favour since they hide their diminutive stature while emphasizing the nobility of their bearing and the studied grace of their movements. A peace-loving and, perhaps, an effete race, they avoid martial combat save when ancestral voices are heard prophesying war and Tartar warriors clad in clinking armour swoop down on them from beyond the mountains. Their true talent is for a serene contemplative life. *Belles-lettres* are honoured in Cathay as nowhere else; the emperor himself is a philosopher and poet while the officials of his far-reaching despotism are chosen and promoted according to the excellence of their verses.

Save for the rustics who joyfully tend their flocks or drowse on the backs of water-buffaloes, and for the maidens who so elegantly carry their *famille rose* pitchers to the fountains, work seems ever at a standstill in this lotus land of everlasting afternoon, where the employment of leisure is commonly regarded as the serious business of life. Occasionally the courtiers may go a-hunting after strange beasts, mounted on fleet and magnificently accoutred ponies. But most of the inhabitants of Cathay pass their time less strenuously, gently wafting themselves to and fro in swings, or reclining in willow cabins to watch their cormorants retrieving goldfish from a near-by stream. For hours they will sit in their gardens, drinking tea out of tiny cups, rising only to dance a stately rigadoon to the faint twanging and high-pitched tinkling of their unearthly orchestras, while their children play complicated games, juggling dextrously with filigree balls of porcelain or ivory and flying fantastic kites.

This luxurious people has created a style of architecture to suit its leisured life. In a country of perpetual spring, where the prunus is always in blossom, no very substantial buildings are needed, and the climate permits a long duration to the flimsiest construction. The fancy of their architects has therefore been unbridled in the creation of delicate, brightly painted latticed garden houses, jade pavilions, pleasure domes open to the sky, little huts in trees which might be mistaken for the nests of exotic birds, tall pagoda towers built of porcelain, and spindly bridges spanning rivers which never have the discourtesy to run in flood. On the eaves of every building—absurdly wide and turned up at the corners—hang carillons of tiny bells, set a-jingling by the reverberations of great gongs booming from near-by temples.

Such is the vision of Cathay which shone in many a westerner's eye. . . .[1]

The problem in craftsmanship presented here is to make the quality of the prose correspond with the fanciful vision evoked by the objects. Mr. Honour achieves this partly by the clarity of the images presented (relying naturally a good deal on the common knowledge of Chinese porcelain), such as that of the cormorants retrieving goldfish from near-by streams, and partly by the choice of words and the flow of the sentences. As regards the former, take the word 'retrieving' rather than 'catching'; the brutality of actual life is avoided. The inhabitants 'gently waft' themselves in swings. The words demand an alertness of imaginative vision rather than of immediate actuality: a slight distance is interposed between you and the object. As to the flow of the sentences, one, for example, in which occurs the set of threes, the kind of waltz-like movement so favoured by English prose writers: 'Giant flowers abound here: chrysanthemums which tower above the men who tend them, paeonies which dwarf the birds nesting in their branches, and convolvulus whose blossoms serve as

[1] Hugh Honour, *Chinoiserie. The Vision of Cathay*, John Murray, 1961.

hats, as parasols, and even, on occasion, as the roofs of huts.' The verbs and the adjectives are skilfully, and sensitively chosen, and the fantasy of the picture is reinforced by the progressive lengthening of the clauses, and the play of vowel-sounds, which, never too marked, is continually varied. So too is the opening impact of each paragraph: 'Cathay . . .'; 'The inhabitants of Cathay . . .'; 'Save for the rustics . . .'; 'This luxurious people . . .'. The passage asks to be tasted.

(ii) DESCRIPTION OF EVENTS

I am calling this section 'description of events' rather than of action, since the examples offered deal with happenings to people rather than with people doing things. This necessarily involves the visual to a great degree, but also the aural, and the imaginative seizing of the emotions of the people involved. The last is the least important in this description of the eruption which destroyed the island of Saint-Jacques in 1902.

A deep rumbling groan accompanied this journey of destruction. Now and again the dark mass would kindle from inside, and the black sails of smoke glowed crimson and scarlet and then changed to soft pink without the seething interior flames once breaking through the containing folds, which momentarily appeared as thin and transparent as the surface of a balloon. At last the entire cloud was growing from the island's side in a great unfolding rose. It slowly faded again into fire-rimmed blackness and all was opaque and impenetrable. Gently it settled over the town and enfolded the houses and the spires.

The streets had fallen silent. The citizens had been halted in their flight and then laid low in swathes, as though one invisible sweep of a sickle had reaped them all, by the descending gas which had invaded the capital the moment the mountain-side opened. The flaming Serindan house was the first to disappear and then the black tide flowed wreathing and eddying over the roofs and down the alleyways. Long before it reached the waterfront, Berthe could see the slender dolphin lamp-posts drooping like dying flowers before they finally melted away. The ships caught fire and the burning masts and hulls glowed redly for a moment through the cloud as it rolled out over the bay. The flames deepened to scarlet and purple, then they too were hidden in darkness.

Soon the whole island was obscured in the black and all-enveloping volume which, now fed ceaselessly from behind by the widening rent in the side of Saint-Jacques, rose high in the air in a dark flickering wall. Hot black ash as fine as soot had begun to rain over the schooner and an over-powering smell of sulphur filled the variable twilight. The Captain and the sailors and Berthe had fallen to their knees long ago and, against the crackling and groaning of the hidden conflagration, she could hear their deep voiced wavering prayers. As the cloud spread over the water and the furnace-like heat advanced, the speed of the prayers grew and the pitch of the Captain's voice rose. Sometimes, for a few seconds, the world was in darkness except for the burning sparks that flew from Plessis and the forests. The whole sky was now afloat with them. The bank of cloud would flicker from inside with an upheaval of the burning gases it contained. Then lightning began to shower to and fro. Sometimes it was held captive within the cloud-bank, illuminating its incandescent concavity with a shuddering electric glare, and sometimes it burst forth helter-skelter into the night in branching prongs and zigzags that fissured the sky's surface and lighted for a wild second or two the great quaking pile and the empty sea and the faces of the sailors shining under rivers of sweat. Close over their heads they could hear the disordered wingbeats and the alarmed cries of birds. Some of them collided with the masts and the rigging and perched in the stays, or, overcome by the gaseous fumes loosed all round Saint-Jacques, fell lifeless to the deck and over the surrounding water. A brief outburst of light from the shifting cloud-stack revealed a ragged troop of flamingoes among the floating motes, flown there from the high pools of the forest. Soon they too were hidden in the universal gloom.[1]

The first two paragraphs open with short sentences, the third with one not too long. All end with a brief statement, bringing to a pause the quickening speed, the increasing tension, of the middle of the paragraphs. In the main we are asked to take in the whole vast scene, but sometimes to concentrate on a detail, such as 'the slender dolphin lamp-posts drooping like dying flowers before they finally melted away'. Complex as the sentences sometimes are, with a play of varied vowel-sound, they end on a firm note, often with a fairly striking but not too insistent rhythm. One may take as an extremely skilful example the sentence:

Sometimes it was held captive within the cloud-bank, illuminating its incandescent concavity with a shuddering electric glare, and sometimes it burst forth helter-skelter into the night in branching prongs and zigzags that fissured the sky's surface and lighted for a wild second or two the great quaking pile and the empty sea and the faces of the sailors shining under rivers of sweat.

[1] Patrick Leigh Fermor, *The Violins of Saint-Jacques*, John Murray, Derek Verschoyle, 1953.

There we get a modulated play of vowels, such as 'shuddering electric glare', a broader effect in 'the night in branching prongs and zigzags', though perhaps the repetition of the long 'i' sounds—night, wild, pile, shining—is a little dangerous. The rapid rhythm is held up at the end: 'the wild pile and the empty sea,' concluding firmly with

$$- \cup \quad \cup \cup \quad - \cup \cup \quad -$$

and the faces of the sailors shining under rivers of sweat.

How far the urgency, the terrible immediacy of the scene is conveyed by the rhythms may be assessed by comparison with the following passage, where an almost dream-like state of consciousness is being conveyed to the reader.

The punt which now carried him, thrust by slow thrust across the turbid water, was turning slowly eastward to take up its position in the great semicircle of boats which was being gradually closed in upon a target-area marked out by the black reed spines of fish-pans. And as they closed in, stroke by stroke, the Egyptian night fell—the sudden reduction of all objects to bas-reliefs upon a screen of gold and violet. The land had become dense as tapestry in the lilac afterglow, quivering here and there with water-mirages from the rising damps, expanding and contracting horizons, until one thought of the world as being mirrored in a soap-bubble trembling on the edge of disappearance. Voices too across the water sounded now loud, now soft and clear. His own cough fled across the lake in sudden wing-beats. Dusk, yet it was still hot, his shirt stuck to his back. The spokes of darkness which reached out to them only outlined the shapes of the reed-fringed islands, which punctuated the water like great pin-cushions, like paws, like hassocks.

Slowly, at the pace of prayer or meditation, the great arc of boats was forming and closing in, but with the land and the water liquefying at this rate he kept having the illusion that they were travelling across the sky rather than across the alluvial waters of Mareotis. And out of sight he could hear the splatter of geese, and in one corner water and sky split apart as a flight rose, trailing its webs across the estuary like seaplanes, honking crassly. Mountolive sighed and stared down into the brown water, chin on his hands. He was unused to feeling so happy. Youth is the age of despairs.

Behind him he could hear the hare-lipped younger brother Narouz grunting at every thrust of the pole while the lurch of the boat echoed in his loins. The mud, thick as molasses, dripped back into the water with a slow *flob*, *flob*, and the pole sucked lusciously. It was very beautiful, but it all stank so: yet to his surprise he found he rather enjoyed the rotting smells of the estuary. Draughts of wind from the far sea-line ebbed around them from time to time, refreshing his mind. Choirs of gnats whizzed up there like silver rain in the eye of the dying sun. The cobweb of changing light fired his mind. 'Narouz,' he said, 'I am so happy,' as he listened to his own unhurried heart-beats. The youth gave his shy hissing laugh and said: 'Good, good,' ducking his head. 'But this is nothing. Wait. We are closing in.' Mountolive smiled. 'Egypt,' he said to himself as one might repeat the name of a woman. 'Egypt.'[1]

An effect of languor is given from the start: such phrases as 'thrust by slow thrust' which cannot be said fast, slowed down still further by

$$- \quad - \quad -$$

the black reed spines of fish-pans

seem to set the pace. This is reinforced by the repetition of long vowel-sounds—slow, slowly, boats,

[1] Lawrence Durrell, *Mountolive*, Faber and Faber, 1958.

closed—followed in the next sentence by 'closed' once more, and 'stroke by stroke', then, with a happy variation, 'a screen of gold and violet'. Sound, and the sense of gentle motion, are as important as the visual effect; only once is there a feeling of speed: 'His own cough fled across the lake in sudden wing-beats.' And where in the previous passage no metaphor is employed, or even imagery, here we have such invitations as to see the gnats as they murmur whizzing up to look like silver rain, or to visualize a cobweb of changing light. It is a passage evocative of one's own memories of similar moments, giving a sense of thought-free laziness. You are asked to share a vague emotion, lulled by the smooth phrasing, the sense of gentle movement, the idea of soft sounds hardly disturbed by, even enhanced by, the distant 'splatter of geese'.

It is, however, to the aural imagination that the following extract largely appeals, a passage that opens briskly to lead in its central portions to a sense of meditation.

The temple was a building of massive red sandstone blocks. They could see it through the trees after they had walked for a few minutes. Miss Bullen could hear music and she stopped. She could hear the low notes of a flute, the urgent yet un-hurried melancholy of the melody so moving that it caught at her heart.

'Do you know what that is?' she asked the boys almost in a whisper. Impressed by the mysterious quality of the music, they shook their heads as they listened.

'That's *bhairavi*,' she said. '*Raga bhairavi*, and it's being played at the wrong time of day too. But it doesn't matter.

It's my favourite and I could listen to it at any hour.' She had never heard the *raga* played with such feeling and skill, for this *raga* produced a sensation of unfathomable mystery, always giving her an impression of the load of eternity which man could never shift from himself, and at the same time it was full of a tenderness and sadness which stopped the tread of the mind. It was for the early morning, when man woke up out of his dreaming withdrawal from daytime, out of his sleep in which he had slipped the chain of his conscious living, and that was *bhairavi* time, dawn, sad but sweet, painful but glad, the re-entry into the world of struggle and appetite. It was a kind of sad gladness in the waking up for another day, instead of sleeping on, dead, gone. That was the *raga bhairavi*, which she had remained attracted to since she had first heard it played by a Muslim *Ustad* in Delhi forty years ago.

The flute notes, liquid and dark, fluttered in the hot air and went echoing in the trees about them, the player shedding long cascades of his own design, and then building up slowly to the theme again, which was like a question, full of un-answerable dolour, rueful and languorous. It was the music of estrangement and forsakenness made tender with hope and wonder. Its magic had never been so powerful for her as now while she stood in the midst of the flute notes so knowingly woven, inducing a desire to shed tears, neither of sorrow nor pleasure, but for the feeling of mystery it always awoke, mystery and spiritual unrest. It was as though that cherished anguish which haunts the human being was given shape in sound, the ghost of time and living awakened in the body by the magic of these peculiar and special sounds which someone, centuries ago, had devised as the feeling of the tropical morn-ing, those moments of languor between darkness and the first fire of the sun against the palm fronds.

They went quietly towards the sound of the flute and Narendra Nath said quietly, 'It's Uncle Prem.' She recog-nised Prem, whom she had met for five minutes the night before. He was sitting cross-legged, slightly hunched, with his black hair hanging down like the wings of a shot raven in the sunlight. He was playing a short bamboo flute and three of the temple priests were sitting opposite him, absolutely still, dressed in blood-red gowns of cotton, small turbans of the same violent colour on their heads. Two were grave and handsome, while the other one had an animal expression on his face, feral and aware and roused, his black eyes full of unguessable dreams, excited by the music. Prem swayed with the music, bending his head as if the better to coax out the marvellous weave of sound he had stored up in the flute. He finished with a long, low quivering note, holding it and then letting it slowly diminish in the hot silence.

'More,' one of the priests said seriously, as if he had to hear more immediately.

'Yes, more,' the other two said.

'You said it was the wrong time,' Prem accused them, smiling.

'Even though it is the wrong time, more,' one of them urged, smiling back at Prem. 'You are a master.'

'No more to-day,' Prem said, and got up, brushing dust from his white cotton pyjamas. He turned and waved to Miss Bullen and the twins. 'You can come now,' he called, smiling at them.[1]

That is, if you like to call it so, a sentimental passage, with such phrases as 'sad but sweet, painful but glad', but it is so of set purpose, bringing to us the division in the heart of Miss Bullen, the elderly missionary in a distant Indian village, where the inhabitants will not accept her religion, though loving and respecting her for herself. We are meant to *hear* the flute notes, liquid and dark, the cascades building

[1] Gerald Hanley, *The Journey Homeward*, Collins, 1961.

up to the theme again, while at the same time we get a vivid impression of the scene, with Uncle Prem, 'his black hair hanging down like the wings of a shot raven in the sunlight'. The quick movement of the day accentuates rather than lightens the weight of melancholy dragging at Miss Bullen's heart, inducing in her only a kind of sad gladness at the re-entry from sleep 'into the world of struggle and appetite'. The words never overstress: they themselves form a kind of music, 'the music of estrangement made tender with hope and wonder'. It is, of course, Miss Bullen's emotions that are being described rather than the scene itself, and the prose is never obtrusive, though it avoids the dull and commonplace, as when we read of the sadness 'that stops the tread of the mind', or of the languor, not between darkness and dawn, but between darkness and 'the first fire of the sun against the palm fronds'. Nothing startles, but nothing lulls, though the whole soothes you into that kind of contemplation, or melancholy musing, to which most of us are at times subject. The sentiment is enclosed between the brisk beginning and the commonplace end with Uncle Prem in his white cotton pyjamas. It can perhaps be described as a piece of wonderfully tactful prose, musical in rhythm and sound, yet never obtruding itself.

In the extracts from Mr. Leigh Fermor and Mr. Hanley the reader is distanced to the position of an observer; he is not involved. In that from Mr. Durrell he is gently invited, as suggested earlier, to share the quiet feeling. But if the happening is made immediate enough, the emotion urgent enough, the reader is almost forced to participate, almost to be the person about whom the description is written. This would seem to depend upon how far the author identifies himself with that person. The following passage seems to be as close as we can get, the author's imagination compelling the reader to partake of the experience.

He began to swim again, feeling suddenly the desperate exhaustion of his body. The fierce, first excitement of sighting had burned up the fuel and the fire was low again. He swam grimly, forcing his arms through the water, reaching forward under his arches with sight as though he could pull himself into safety with it. The shape moved. It grew larger and not clearer. Every now and then there was something like a bow-wave at the forefoot. He ceased to look at her but swam and screamed alternately with the last strength of his body. There was a green force round him, growing in strength to rob, there was mist and glitter over him; there was a redness pulsing in front of his eyes—his body gave up and he lay slack in the waves and the shape rose over him. He heard through the rasp and thump of his works the sound of waves breaking. He lifted his head and there was rock stuck up in the sky with a sea-gull poised before it. He heaved over in the sea and saw how each swell dipped for a moment, flung up a white hand of foam and then disappeared as if the rock had swallowed it. He began to think swimming motions but knew now that his body was no longer obedient. The top of the next swell between him and the rock was blunted, smoothed curiously, then jerked up spray. He sank down, saw without comprehension that the green water was no longer empty. There was yellow and brown. He heard not the formless mad talking of uncontrolled water but a sudden roar. Then he went under into a singing world and there were hairy shapes that flitted and twisted past his face, there were sudden notable details close to of intricate rock and weed. Brown tendrils slashed across his face, then with a destroying shock he hit solidity. It was utter difference, it was under his body, against his knees and face, he could close fingers on it, for an instant he could even hold on. His mouth was needlessly open and his eyes so that he had a moment of close and intent communion with three limpets, two small and one large, that were only an inch or two from his face. Yet this solidity was terrible and apocalyptic after the world of inconstant wetness. It was not vibrant as a ship's hull might be but merciless and mother of panic. It had no business to interrupt the thousands of miles of water going about their purposeless affairs and therefore the world sprang here into sudden war. He felt himself picked up and away from the limpets, reversed, tugged, thrust down into weed and darkness. Ropes held him, slipped, and let him go. He saw light, got a mouthful of air and foam. He glimpsed a riven rock face with trees of spray growing up it and the sight of this rock floating in mid Atlantic was so dreadful that he wasted his air by screaming as if it had been a wild beast. He went under into a green calm, then up and was thrust sideways. The sea no longer played with him. It stayed its wild movement and held him gently, carried him with delicate and careful motion like a retriever with a bird. Hard things touched him about the feet and knees. The sea laid him down gently and retreated. There were hard things touching his face and chest, the side of his forehead. The sea came back and fawned round his face, licked him. He thought movements that did not happen. The sea came back and he thought the movements again and this time they happened because the sea took most of his weight. They moved him forward over the hard things. Each wave and each movement moved him forward. He felt the sea run down to smell at his feet then come back and nuzzle under his arm. It no longer licked his face. There was a pattern in front of him

that occupied all the space under the arches. It meant nothing.
The sea nuzzled under his arm again.

He lay still.[1]

As we read this example, we are at first outside of
what is happening, but if we have read the book so
far we are already inside. And as we read the extract
we are drawn within. We come gradually to *feel* what
is going on: 'there was a green force around him . . .',
'there was a redness pulsing in front of his eyes', and
so on. We begin to see with 'his' eyes, by virtue
almost of the generality of the terms. All the time
there is a clash of moods, of the apprehension of what
is occurring both outside and inside 'him'. 'Brown
tendrils slashed across his face, then with a destroying
shock he hit solidity', as compared with: 'It had no
business to interrupt the thousands of miles of water
going about their purposeless affairs. . . .' Our visual
imagination is also called upon: 'He . . . saw how each
swell dipped for a moment, flung up a white hand of
foam. . . .' Then the 'pathetic fallacy' element intrudes,
with what the sea was doing, as when, finally, it
'nuzzled under his arm again'. It is an extraordinarily
effective passage. There is a sharpness in the consonantal effects to balance the music of the vowels:
'He felt himself picked up and away from the limpets,
reversed, tugged, thrust down into weeds and darkness.' The temptation, too seductively offered by
Mr. Golding, is to read the passage too fast. It should
be done so once, possibly, but then, certainly, more
slowly.

[1] William Golding, *Pincher Martin*, Faber and Faber, 1960. Penguin,
1962.

(iii) DESCRIPTION OF PEOPLE

It is not very often today that we are given a straight, rounded description of character, even in biography. The person grows during the course of the tale, by hints, by observations on him here and there, and, naturally, through his actions. But sometimes large aspects of a character are given, not enough to make him or her into a 'humour', but enough to act as a solid basis for future observations.

. . . They had married when he was a young don, and she his pupil. That relation, which can always so easily fill itself with emotion, had never died. He wanted people to recognize her quality, how gifted she was, how much held back by her crippling sensitiveness. He wanted us to see that she was gallant, and misjudged; he was burning to explain that she went through acuter pain than anyone, when the temperament she could not control drove his friends away. His love remained love, and added pity: and sight of her in a mood which others dismissed as grotesque still had the power to take and rend his heart.

He suffered for her, and for himself. He loathed having to make apologies for his wife. He loathed all his imagination could invent of the words that were spoken behind his back— 'poor Jago . . .'. But even those wounds to his pride he could have endured, if she had been happier. He would still, after twenty-five years, have humbled himself for her as for no one else—just to see her content. As he told me on the night when we first knew the Master was dying, 'one is dreadfully vulnerable through those one loves'.

*   *   *   *   *

Jago enjoyed the dramatic impact of power, like Chrystal: but he was seeking for other things besides. He was an ambitious man, as neither Brown nor Chrystal were. In any society he would have longed to be first; and he would have longed for it because of everything that marked him out as different from the rest. He longed for all the trappings, titles, ornaments, and show of power. He would love to hear himself called Master; he would love to begin a formal act at a college meeting 'I, Paul Jago, Master of the college . . .' He wanted the grandeur of the Lodge, he wanted to be styled among the heads of houses. He enjoyed the prospect of an entry in the college history—'Dr. P. Jago, 41st Master'. For him, in every word that separated the Master from his fellows, in every ornament of the Lodge, in every act of formal duty, there was a gleam of magic.

There was something else. He had just said to Chrystal 'we can make it a great college'. Like most ambitious men, he believed that there were things that only he could do. Money did not move him in the slightest; the joys of office moved him a great deal; but there was a quality pure, almost naïve, in his ambition. He had dreams of what he could do with his power. These dreams left him sometimes, he became crudely avid for the job, but they returned. With all his fervent imagination, he thought of a college peaceful, harmonious, gifted, creative, throbbing with joy and luminous with grace. In his dreams he did not altogether know how to attain it. He had nothing of the certainty with which, in humility, accepting their limitations, Chrystal and Brown went about their aims, securing a benefaction from Sir Horace, arranging an extra tutorship, making sure that Luke got a grant for his research. He had nothing of their certainty, nor their humility: he was more extravagant than they, and loved display far more; in his ambition he could be cruder and more predatory; but perhaps he had intimations which they could not begin to hear.[1]

[1] C. P. Snow, *The Masters*, Macmillan, 1951.

Built up in enough detail, this kind of description can become subtle and yielding, and Sir Charles pursues this method throughout the book, picking up the developed character again in a later phase of his life story, in the volume *The Affair*. The style we might call austere, the reverse of the 'fine writing' just illustrated. It is plain, straightforward, in the simplest of ordinary language such as we all use in everyday converse. There is no metaphor, no emotive use of words; our attention is never for a moment distracted, our minds being kept on the object itself. The phrases may seem to be clichés: 'he was *burning* to explain'; 'he *loathed* having to make apologies for his wife'; 'he *longed* for all the trappings . . . .' Yet they are not dull phrases, and say exactly what is meant. It might be complained that all the work is done for you, that you are not asked to partake of the creative process: and that is perhaps a weakness, since in making you take too much for granted the actuality never becomes immediate. The only point where the imagination is called upon to work is in the last clause quoted: 'but perhaps he had intimations which they could not begin to hear'. The method, however, is extremely effective, especially where questions of conscience are involved. And since Sir Charles's novels turn largely on such, the style is seen to be happily appropriate.

The method opposite to this is to describe the character mainly by implication, rather after the manner of Faulkner:

Miss Hare was observing the progress of a beetle across the mouth of a silted urn. She would have much preferred not to be disturbed.

'It was a letter from Mrs Apps,' Mrs Jolley pursued. 'That is Merle, the eldest. Merle has a particular weakness for her mum, perhaps because she was delicate as a kiddy. But struck lucky later on. With a hubby who denys her nothing—within reason, of course, and the demands of his career. Mr Apps—his long service will soon be due—is an executive official at the Customs. I will not say well-thought-of. Indispensable is nearer the mark. So it is not uncommon for Merle to hobnob with the high-ups of the Service, and entertain them to a buffy at her home. *Croaky de poison.* Chipperlarters. All that. With perhaps a substantial dish of, say, *Chicken à la King.* I never believe in blowing my own horn, but Merle does things that lovely. Yes. Her buffy has been written up, not once, but several times.'

Miss Hare observed her beetle.

'Now Merle writes,' the housekeeper continued, 'and does not, well, exactly *say,* because Merle is never one to *say,* but lets it be understood she is not at all satisfied with the steps her mum has taken to lead an independent life since their father passed on, like that, so tragically.'

Mrs Jolley watched Miss Hare.

'Of course I did not tell her half. Because Merle would have created. But you will realize the position it has put me in. Seeing as I am a person that always sympathises with the misfortunes of others.'

Mrs Jolley watched Miss Hare. The wind had started up and the housekeeper did not like it in the open. She was one who would walk very quickly along a road and hope to reach the shops.

'Everybody is unfortunate if you can recognize it,' said Miss Hare, helping her beetle. 'But there are usually compensations for misfortune.'

Mrs Jolley drew in her breath. She hated it on the horrid terrace, the wind tweaking her hair-net, and the smell of night threatening her.

'At a nominal wage,' she protested, 'it is hard lines if a lady has to look for compensations.'

'How people can talk!' Miss Hare exclaimed, not without admiration. 'My parents would be at it by the hour. But one could sit quite comfortably inside their words. In a kind of tent. Do you know? When it rains.'

'Your parents, poor souls!' Mrs Jolley could not resist.

So that Miss Hare was cut. She removed her finger from the beetle, which ultimately she could not assist.

'Why must you keep harping on my parents?'

The marbled sky was heartrending, if also adamant, its layers of mauve and rose veined now with black and indigo. The moon was the pale fossil of a moth.[1]

There we get, at a bound, the garrulous vulgarian and the reserved woman who approaches to the state of being of, to use a rather loose phrase, a mystic, a rider in the chariot to heaven. Mr. White is the most notable example of a writer who, without attempting to burst the bounds of the old traditional forms and usages, nevertheless gives them new life, partly by his metaphor, such as that of sitting quite comfortably inside other people's words 'in a kind of tent', and partly by the *mot juste*, as in the last short paragraph quoted. Everywhere in his writing there is that kind of freshness, nothing outraging or purposively startling, but always new and arresting, not by its wildness but by its rightness. He makes one see with an eye cleared of the veil of custom, at once held by the word that brings the image vividly to the faculty called upon. The characters even in that short passage are beautifully depicted. Mrs. Jolley 'was one who would

[1] *Riders in the Chariot*, by Patrick White, Eyre & Spottiswoode, 1961.

walk very quickly along a road and hope to reach the shops'. Miss Hare's attention is on the beetle. Such a passage is, of course, only a tiny portion of the portraits that are ultimately built up, but that portion is in itself directive. The sentences are simple, as the words are, but the juxtaposition of the latter is striking: 'The marbled sky was heartrending.' The word makes one pause: it gives an added dimension to the character of Miss Hare, while the last phrase actively demands the alert collaboration of the reader's imagination.

Something between the two methods can be employed, with a good deal of direct description intricately allied with action.

Teddy was standing on the broad side of a new-looking cowhide Gladstone, the better to see out of his parents' open porthole. He was wearing extremely dirty, white ankle-sneakers, no socks, seersucker shorts that were both too long for him and at least a size too large in the seat, an overly laundered T shirt that had a hole the size of a dime in the right shoulder, and an incongruously handsome, black alligator belt. He needed a haircut—especially at the nape of the neck—the worst way, as only a small boy with an almost full-grown head and a reed-like neck can need one.

'Teddy, did you hear me?'

Teddy was not leaning out of the porthole quite so far or so precariously as small boys are apt to lean out of open portholes—both his feet, in fact, were flat on the surface of the Gladstone—but neither was he just conservatively well tipped; his face was considerably more outside than inside the cabin. Nonetheless, he was well within hearing of his father's voice—his father's voice, that is, most singularly. Mr. McArdle played leading roles on no fewer than three daytime

radio serials when he was in New York, and he had what
might be called a third-class leading man's speaking voice:
narcissistically deep and resonant, functionally prepared at
a moment's notice to out-male anyone in the same room with
it, if necessary even a small boy. When it was on vacation
from its professional chores, it fell, as a rule, alternately in
love with sheer volume and a theatrical brand of quietness-
steadiness. Right now, volume was in order.

'*Teddy*. God damn it—did you hear me?'

Teddy turned around at the waist, without changing the
vigilant position of his feet on the Gladstone, and gave his
father a look of inquiry, whole and pure. His eyes, which were
pale brown in colour, and not at all large, were slightly
crossed—the left eye more than the right. They were not
crossed enough to be disfiguring, or even to be necessarily
noticeable at first glance. They were crossed just enough to be
mentioned, and only in context with the fact that one might
have thought long and seriously before wishing them straigh-
ter, or deeper, or browner, or wider set. His face, just as it was,
carried the impact, however oblique and slow-travelling, of
real beauty.[1]

As the story, which is named 'Teddy', goes on, it
reveals itself as a description of the boy's personality
by what he says and does, but as a setting we are made
to know something of what his parents were like—
the mother intrudes a little later. We are told earlier
what Mr. McArdle's inflamed-pink right arm looks
like, and how he rests his debilitated-looking body
against the headboard almost as though he wanted to
hurt himself. We are now told of his voice, 'narcissistically deep and resonant, functionally prepared at a
moment's notice to out-male anyone in the same room

[1] J. D. Salinger, *For Esmé—with Love and Squalor*, Penguin 1954.

with it'. What is ingenious here is the use of adverbs. By both seeing Mr. McArdle and hearing his voice we know a good deal about him, and much in the same way we learn a good deal about the boy, and his relation with his parents. The 'vigilant' position of his feet gives one an indication, and we gather some more from 'the look of inquiry, whole and pure' that he gives his father. We gain further insight from the oblique and slow-travelling impact of his face. Here it is the choice of words, arresting but never startling, unexpected but not too much so, that gives the passage its effect—not rhythm, nor any kind of music, but the words, exact enough, but not just plain, with a certain aura around them.

§ 3

New Methods

WHETHER there is any new way in writing may well
be queried, as was done by G. M. Young. Yet there
is appearing at the moment a good deal of prose
written by various authors all working in much the
same manner, which would seem to be an attempt to
follow, not so much what goes on in the mind, as
what flits across it. This is not quite the same as the
Shandean attempt to write 'the history of what passes
in a man's own mind', since there we always meet some
sort of logical process. This is, rather, an endeavour
to eliminate the structure of thought, and not at all a
return to the anti-literary manner. It does, certainly,
avoid 'fine writing' in the old sense, but it seems consciously to be working out a pattern, a different way
of writing, vaguely related to the 'stream of consciousness' method. Yet though not anti-literary, it would
seem to be a 'calculated carelessness', a term applied
to Mr. Salinger's style in *The Catcher in the Rye* and
later work. As a stepping-stone to this manner the
reader may be referred back to the passage from
Mr. Golding, where we read that 'He began to think
swimming motions . . .', or 'he thought movements
that did not happen'. The defect of this method would
seem to be that it is of service only when describing
the minds of neurotic adolescents, as with Mr. Salinger, or of people with no trained intelligence, as
in the following.

I recognize in the guide of the first dream an ancient figure, temporarily disguised only to make my dread greater when he revealed himself.

Our first encounter was in a muddy back lane. By day it was a wagon thoroughfare, but at this evening hour only a goat wandered over the cold ruts that had become as hard as the steel rims that made them. Suddenly I heard another set of footsteps added to mine, heavier and grittier, and my premonitions leaped into one fear even before I felt a touch on my back and turned. Then that swollen face that came rapidly towards mine until I felt its bristles and the cold pressure of its nose; the lips kissed me on the temple with a laugh and a groan. Blindly I ran, hearing again the gritting boots. The roused dogs behind the snaggled boards of the fences abandoned themselves to the wildest rage of barking. I ran, stumbling through drifts of ashes, into the street.

Could the fallen man of last week have seen, had he chanced to open his eyes, his death in the face of that policeman who bent over him? We know we are sought and expect to be found. How many forms he takes, the murderer. Frank, or simple, or a man of depth and cultivation, or perhaps prosaic, without distinction. Yet he is *the* murderer, the stranger who, one day, will drop the smile of courtesy or custom to show you the weapon in his hand, the means of your death. Who does not know him, the man who takes your measure in the street or on the stairs, he whose presence you must ignore in the darkened room if you are to close your eyes and fall asleep, the agent who takes you, in the last unforgiving act, into inexistence? Who does not expect him with the opening of the door; and who, after childhood, thinks of flight or resistance or of laying any but ironic, yes, even welcoming hands on his shoulders when he comes? The moment is for him to choose. He may come at a climax of satisfaction or of evil; he may come as one to repair a radio or a faucet; mutely, or to pass the time of day, play a game of cards; or, with no preliminary, colored with horrible anger, reaching out a muffling hand; or, in a mask of calm, hurry you to your last breath, drawn with a stuttering sigh out of his shadow.

How will it be? How? Falling a mile into the wrinkled sea? Or, as I have dreamed, cutting a wire? Or strafed in a river among chopped reeds and turning water, blood leaking through the cloth of the sleeves and shoulders?

I can safely think of such things on a bright afternoon such as this. When they come at night, the heart, like a toad, exudes its fear with a repulsive puff. But toward morning I have a way, also, of holding court on myself, and that is even more intolerable. Half-conscious, I call in a variety of testimony on my case and am confronted by the wrongs, errors, lies, disgraces, and fears of a lifetime. I am forced to pass judgment on myself and to ask questions I would far rather not ask: 'What is this for?' and 'What am I for?' and 'Am I made for this?' My beliefs are inadequate, they do not guard me. I think invariably of the awning of the store on the corner. It gives as much protection against rain and wind as my beliefs give against the chaos I am forced to face. 'God does not love those who are unable to sleep soundly,' runs an old saying. In the morning I dress and go about my 'business.' I pass one more day no different from the others. Night comes, and I have to face another session of sleep—that 'sinister adventure' Baudelaire calls it—and be brought to wakefulness by degrees through a nightmare of reckoning or inventory, my mind flapping like a rag on a clothesline in cold wind.[1]

This is not 'fine writing'; it does not move by its music and its rhythm, but the imagery is undeniably 'literary': 'the heart, like a toad, exudes its fear with a repulsive puff'. All the time we get, as described in another striking image, the sense of a 'mind flapping like a rag on a clothesline in a cold wind'. It is, we

[1] Saul Bellow, *Dangling Man*, Weidenfeld and Nicolson, 1946.

feel, a terrible vision, or, rather, a terrible apprehension expressing itself as a vision, or a series of glimpses that flit across the perturbed consciousness. Take the number of images that occur in the paragraph beginning 'Could the fallen man of last week . . .' who was, in fact, murdered in the street. The narrator is not exactly thinking; things are happening in his mind. And that is not quite the same.

This method, to call it so, though the manner might be considered instinctive rather than considered, is well illustrated in the work of Miss Janet Frame. The difficulty in discussing her work, as with that of Mr. Salinger, is that its full effect is to be registered rather from the novels than from the stories, since to take extracts from the former would be meaningless to the reader here who possibly has not read what precedes the passage. It would in some ways have been more satisfactory to quote from Miss Frame's *Owls do Cry*, for example, as it would have been to offer a passage from *The Catcher in the Rye* Mr. Salinger. But perhaps the following may give some flavour of what Miss Frame gives us to taste.

It should not have rained. The clothes should have been slapped warm and dry with wind and sun and the day not have been a leafless cloudy secret hard to understand. It is always nice to understand the coming and going of a day. Tell her, blackbird that pirrup-pirruped and rainwater that trickled down the kitchen window-pane and dirty backyard that oozed mud and housed puddles, tell her though the language be something she cannot construe having no grammar of journeys.

Why is the backyard so small and suffocating and untidy? On the rope clothes-line the washing hangs limp and wet,

Tom's underpants and the sheets and my best tablecloth.
We'll go away from here, Tom and me, we'll go some other
place, the country perhaps, he likes the country but he's going
on and on to a prize in Tatts and a new home, flat-roofed with
blinds down in the front room and a piano with curved legs,
though Tom's in the Dye Works just now, bringing home
handkerchiefs at the end of each week, from the coats with
no names on.

—Isn't it stealing Tom?

—Stealing my foot, I tell you I've worked two years without a holiday. You see? Tom striving for his rights and getting
them even if they turn out to be only a small anonymous pile
of men's handkerchiefs, but life is funny and people are funny,
laugh and the world laughs with you.

She opens the wash-house door to let the blue water out of
the tubs, she forgot all about the blue water, and then of all the
surprises in the world there's a sheep in the wash-house, a poor
sheep not knowing which way to turn, fat and blundering
with the shy anxious look sheep have.

—Shoo Shoo.

Sheep are silly animals they're so scared and stupid, they
either stand still and do nothing or else go round and round
getting nowhere, when they're in they want out and when
they're out they sneak in, they don't stay in places, they get
lost in bogs and creeks and down cliffs, if only they stayed
where they're put.

—Shoo Shoo.

Scared muddy and heavy the sheep lumbers from the wash-
house and then bolts up the path, out the half-open gate on to
the street and then round the corner out of sight, with the
people stopping to stare and say well I declare for you never
see sheep in the street, only people.

It should not have rained, the washing should have been
dry and why did the sheep come and where did it come from to
here in the middle of the city?

A long time ago there were sheep (she remembers, pulling out the plug so the dirty blue water can gurgle away, what slime I must wash more often why is everything always dirty) sheep, and I walked behind them with bare feet on a hot dusty road, with the warm steamy nobbles of sheep dirt getting crushed between my toes and my father close by me powerful and careless, and the dogs padding along, the spit dribbling from the loose corners of their mouths, Mac and Jock and Rover waiting for my father to cry Way Back Out, Way Back Out. Tom and me will go some other place I think. Tom and me will get out of here.

She dries her hands on the corner of her sack apron. That's that. A flat-roofed house and beds with shiny covers, and polished fire-tongs, and a picture of moonlight on a lake.

She crosses the backyard, brushing aside the wet clothes to pass. My best tablecloth. If visitors come tonight I am sunk.[1]

There we have the thoughts (not the 'mind') jumping from one thing to another as various things strike the eye and lead to associations. It is in its way extremely effective, because that, we feel, is just the way external things set off cogitations—understanding the coming and going of a day, the journeys of birds who have no grammar of journeys, Tom's underpants, a new house, Tom's pilferings; then the sheep, musings about sheep, and so on, till, finally, 'If visitors come tonight, I am sunk.' The words too, perfectly ordinary, except perhaps for the anonymous pile of men's handkerchiefs, are always apt: the dirty blue water can gurgle away, sheep dirt is in warm steamy nobbles. The inconsequence is gathered together by the repetition of 'It should not have rained',

[1] Janet Frame, *The Lagoon & Other Stories*, The Caxton Press, Christchurch; 1951.

and going back to the flat-roofed house. Such prose would seem to take as far as it is possible the description of that particular aspect of living.

There are, as will be evident to any 'general reader', other ways of writing, not met with in the earlier work of this century, yet using what might be thought the old methods in such a way as to contribute something new. It may be of some interest to conclude with examples in contradistinction from those just quoted. The first comes under 'description of character'.

Taxis were drawing up in the late sunshine before several of the houses in the square, and young men in tails and girls in evening dress, looking rather self-conscious in the bright daylight, were paying fares or ringing front-door bells. It was that stagnant London weather without a breath of air. One might almost have been in the tropics. Even Archie Gilbert, who had immediately preceded me in the hall—he had never been known to be late for dinner—looked that night as though he might have been feeling the heat a little. His almost invisibly fair moustache suggested the same piqué material as the surface of his stiff shirt; and, as usual, he shed about him an effect of such unnatural cleanliness that some secret chemical process seemed to have been applied, in preparation for the party, both to himself and his clothes: making the body and its dazzling integument, sable and argent rather than merely black and white, proof against smuts and dust. Shirt, collar, tie, waistcoat, handkerchief and gloves were like snow: all these trappings, as always, apparently assumed for the first time: even though he himself looked a shade pinker than usual in the face owing to the oppressive climatic conditions.

His whole life seemed so irrevocably concentrated on 'débutante dances' that it was impossible to imagine Archie Gilbert finding any tolerable existence outside a tail-coat.

I could never remember attending any London dance that could possibly be considered to fall within the category named, at which he had not also been present for at least a few minutes; and if two or three balls were held on the same evening, it always turned out that he managed to look in at each one of them. During the day he was said to 'do something in the City'—the phrase 'non-ferrous metals' had once been mentioned in my presence as applicable, in some probably remote manner to his daily employment. He himself never referred to any such subordination, and I used sometimes to wonder whether this putative job was not, in reality, a polite fiction, invented on his own part out of genuine modesty, of which I am sure he possessed a great deal, in order to make himself appear a less remarkable person than in truth he was: even a kind of superhuman ordinariness being undesirable, perhaps, for true perfection in this rôle of absolute normality which he had chosen to play with such *éclat*. He was unthinkable in everyday clothes; and he must, in any case, have required that rest and sleep during the hours of light which his nocturnal duties could rarely, if ever, have allowed him. He seemed to prefer no one woman—débutante or chaperone—to another; and, though not indulging in much conversation, as such, he always gave the impression of being at ease with, or without, words; and of having danced at least once with every one of the three or four hundred girls who constituted, in the last resort, the final cause, and only possible justification, of that social organism. He appeared also to be known by name, and approved, by the mother of each of these girls: in a general way, as I have said, getting on equally well with mothers and daughters.[1]

What, we may ask, is the purpose of this stately manner, 'mandarin' style if you will, which must be

[1] Anthony Powell, *A Buyer's Market*, Heinemann, 1952.

supposed to be deliberately assumed, to judge from
Mr. Powell's earlier writing, and which characterizes
the whole 'Music of Time' series. It is not only such
turns of phrase as 'oppressive climatic conditions' for
the hot, damp weather, and 'that social organism' for
what one believes to be a dance. Mr. Powell, one
cannot but think, enjoys such convoluted turns of
speech, though it must be recognized that he is speaking through the mouth of his narrator, Nicholas
Jenkins. In the same book where most would write,
say, 'Later I became rather muddled as to the order
in which things happened at that stage of the party',
Mr. Powell (or Mr. Jenkins) prefers: 'Chronological
sequence of events pertaining to that interlude of the
party became afterwards somewhat confused in my
head.' Or where we might say, 'I didn't know how
long the affair had been going on, nor how serious it
might be', Mr. Powell (or Mr. Jenkins) constructs:
'I did not know how long in duration of time the
affair had already extended; nor how seriously it was
to be regarded.'

This is not exactly a pompous style, but it has a cere-
monious, even a ceremonial movement, gently enli-
vened by a sense of humour. Indeed the ceremony is
part of the humour, and here the elaborate façade of
the style serves to point the equally elaborate façade
that Archie Gilbert chooses to present to the world;
and it is also, we can see, a part of the delineation of
the 'character' of Jenkins, just as the language used
by Lewis Eliot in Sir Charles Snow's series indicates
the latter's character. But the main effect of this
measured and modulated prose is to give a curious

sense of distance, of detachment, inviting leisurely reading, even contemplation with a slightly satirical
flavour. Mr. Powell does not rush and hurry us, as
Mr. Salinger does: he makes us taste rather than
swallow. The style is positive, but you must be careful
not to miss the undertones.

The writing of the next passage, which might come
under the heading of 'description of action', depends
for its effect almost entirely on the rhythms. The language is extremely simple, the sentences short, but
never jagged.

'I cannot live with your family without giving them an
account of the strangeness that is in me. I cannot let them see
the self I show them, as the self I might have been. It may be
thinking too much about myself, but I can only see it in that
way. I must feel that my distance and sadness are assigned to
their source. I shall be distant, Edmund; I shall be sad. I know
you will not, though you have the reason. I almost wish you
would, that we might be nearer. But I must be myself; I can
be no other person; and the burden we both carry is heavier
for me. I know my weakness bears you down, but I would
not fetter you or bind you to me. Order your life as you will;
give your feeling where you can. We need not say again what
cannot be given to me.'

'You are taking more on yourself than you have ever
taken.'

'I feel it will lift the burden. That will lighten it. And I
dread it too much to delay. More than I thought anything
could be dreaded. But it can only be what it is. And your
mother will learn that I can do no more than I have done,
that my life takes all I have to give. That I cannot lend her
an ear about the children. I cannot harass and harm them.
They are mine; they have my sadness in them, my burden in

wait for them, the curse that is mine, upon them. I know I am using tragic words, but they are the words that fit the truth. We do not imagine anything. The tragedy is there. What light words are there to use?'

'We cannot use light words, but we could use none. But you have overborne me. When you say that your weakness bears me down, you say the truth. You are too weak to face your weakness, and there is no truer strength. You will say what you must, shed your own light, bring your own darkness. And I shall stand by you, making your will mine, I have no will of my own.'

'We are fluent, Edmund. We have said it before. We seem to be acting a scene. And that is what we are doing. But it will not help us when the time comes. The scene will rise out of the moment, as scenes do. I can feel your mother's eyes on me, my own eyes falling before them. These rehearsals will not stand us in any stead.'

'Yes, that is the sadness in our sorrow, that it takes the guise of shame. That is what I would spare you, if you would be spared. Shame is no less, that it is helpless, and pity may carry much that destroys itself. And we shall face it in its hardest form, the form that carries self-pity. We shall have to give pity ourselves.'

'That may be a good thing,' said Bridget, in her other tone. 'We shall be revenged on people for our troubles. You suggest they will be revenged on us. And it does seem we ought to do something about this one.'[1]

This is extraordinarily intense and poignant; the speakers seem to be breathing their profound emotion and this may be because of what Mr. Robert Liddell has called 'a tendency to verse . . . perhaps given more attention than it should be by an ear accustomed to

[1] Ivy Compton-Burnett, *Darkness and Day*, Gollancz, 1951.

Mr. Eliot's later rhythms'.[1] And he puts passages into free verse form, as, for one instance:

BRIDGET. We are fluent, Edmund. We have said it before.
We seem to be acting a scene. And that is what we are doing.
But it will not help us when the time comes.
The scene will rise out of the moment, as scenes do.
I can feel your mother's eyes on me, my own eyes falling before them.
These rehearsals will not stand us in any stead.

Yet it is not the rhythms alone that produce the effect, for these carry on into the last remark quoted above which Bridget spoke 'in her other tone', that more usual with Miss Compton-Burnett, so that here the heavily loaded effect of the earlier part becomes the delightfully barbed epigrammatic manner of most of her writing. But though the rhythm is weighty, it is never burdensome, since the words are of the utmost simplicity, the phrases often terse, though varied in vowel-sound: 'Order your life as you will; give your feeling where you can.' Or, a little later: 'I cannot harass and harm them. They are mine; they have my sadness in them, my burden in wait for them, the curse that is mine, upon them.' And here again we are not hurried, but it is the rhythm that slows us down, not the elaboration of the language.

The temptation to quote a passage from De Quincey as a peroration to this discourse is irresistible.

[1] *The Novels of I. Compton-Burnett*, Gollancz, 1955.

He is talking about the dubbing of Herodotus 'The Father of Prose', in his essay on 'The Philosophy of Herodotus':

> . . . If prose were simply the negation of verse, were it the fact that prose had no separate laws of its own, but that, to be a composer in prose meant only his privilege of being in-artificial—his dispensation from the restraints of metre—then, indeed, it would be a slight nominal honour to have been the Father of Prose. But this is ignorance, though a pretty common ignorance. To walk well it is not enough that a man abstain from dancing. Walking has rules of its own the more difficult to perceive or to practise as they are less broadly *prononcés*. To forbear singing is not therefore to speak well or to read well: each of which offices rests upon a separate art of its own. . . . Each mode of composition is a great art: well executed, is the highest and most difficult of arts.

It is one of the fascinations of any art, that the rules, that is, the formulations of what has proved to be most effective, most moving, are continually being modified.

ALPHABETICAL LIST OF MODERN WRITERS QUOTED IN THE TEXT